BABOK 3.0 REVISION GUIDE

Amit Lingarchani / Abhishek Srivastava

@Techcanvass 2019 All rights reserved. This book is under the Intellectual property Rights of Techcanvass. Copying, editing or using any part of the book is not permitted.

Table of Contents

Business Analysis Key Concepts 11
   Business Analysis Core concepts model (BACCM) 11
   Key Terms 15
   Requirements Classification 16

Chapter 1 : Business Analysis Planning and Monitoring 19
   1.1   Business Analysis Planning and Monitoring Tasks 19
      1.1.1   Task 1: Plan Business Analysis Approach 19
      1.1.2   Task 2: Plan Stakeholder Engagement 24
      1.1.3   Task 3: Plan Business Analysis Governance 28
      1.1.4   Task 4: Plan Business Analysis Information Management 32
      1.1.5   Task 5: Identify Business Analysis Performance Improvements .. 36
   1.2 Glossary 39
   1.3 Exercises and Drills 41

Chapter 2: Elicitation and Collaboration 47
   2.1 Elicitation and Collaboration Tasks 48
      2.1.1 Task 1: Prepare for Elicitation 48
      2.1.2 Task 2: Conduct Elicitation 51
      2.1.3 Task 3: Confirm Elicitation Results 53
      2.1.4 Task 4: Communicate Business Analysis Information 55
      2.1.5 Task 5: Manage Stakeholder Collaboration 57
   2.2 Glossary 60
   2.3 Exercises and Drills 61

Chapter 3: Requirements Life Cycle Management 67
   3.1 Requirements Life Cycle Management Tasks 68
      3.1.1 Task 1: Trace Requirements 68

3.1.2 Task 2: Maintain Requirements 70
3.1.3 Task 3: Prioritize Requirements 72
3.1.4 Task 4: Assess Requirements Changes 74
3.1.5 Task 5: Approve Requirements 77
3.2 Glossary 79
3.3 Exercises and Drills 80

Chapter 4: Strategy Analysis 85
4.1 Strategy Analysis Tasks 86
4.1.1 Task 1: Analyse Current State 86
4.1.2 Task 2: Define Future State 91
4.1.3 Task 3: Assess Risks 97
4.1.4 Task 4: Define Change Strategy 101
4.2 Glossary 106
4.3 Exercises and Drills 107

Chapter 5: Requirements Analysis and Design Definition 111
5.1 Requirements Analysis and Design Definition Tasks 112
5.1.1 Task 1: Specify and Model Requirements 112
5.1.2 Task 2: Verify Requirements 116
5.1.3 Task 3: Validate Requirements 118
5.1.4 Task 4: Define Requirements Architecture 121
5.1.5 Task 5: Define Design Options 124
5.1.6 Task 6: Analyze Potential Value and Recommend Solution 127
5.2 Glossary 131
5.3 Exercises and Drills 132

Chapter 6: Solution Evaluation 137
6.1 Solution Evaluation Tasks 138
6.1.1 Task 1: Measure Solution Performance 138
6.1.2 Task 2: Analyze Performance Measures 140

    6.1.3 Task 3: Assess Solution Limitations 142

    6.1.4 Task 4: Assess Enterprise Limitations 145

    6.1.5 Task 5: Recommend Actions to Increase Solution Value 149

  6.2 Glossary 152

  6.3 Exercises and Drills 154

Chapter 7 - Techniques 157

  7.1 Acceptance and Evaluation Criteria 157

  7.2 Backlog Management 159

  7.3 Balanced Scorecard 161

  7.4 Benchmarking and Market Analysis 164

  7.5 Brainstorming 166

  7.6 Business Capability Analysis 168

  7.7 Business Cases 170

  7.8 Business Model Canvas 172

  7.9 Business Rules Analysis 175

  7.10 Collaborative Games 178

  7.11 Concept Modelling 180

  7.12 Data Dictionary 182

  7.13 Data Flow Diagrams 184

  7.14 Data Mining 185

  7.15 Data Modelling 188

  7.16 Decision Analysis 190

  7.17 Decision Modelling 192

  7.18 Document Analysis 194

  7.19 Estimation 195

  7.20 Financial Analysis 198

  7.21 Focus Groups 201

  7.22 Functional Decomposition 203

  7.23 Glossary 204

- 7.24 Interface Analysis 206
- 7.25 Interviews 207
- 7.26 Item Tracking 209
- 7.27 Lessons Learned 211
- 7.28 Metrics and Key Performance Indicators (KPIs) 212
- 7.29 Mind Mapping 214
- 7.30 Non-Functional Requirements Analysis 216
- 7.31 Observation 218
- 7.32 Organizational Modelling 220
- 7.33 Prioritization 222
- 7.34 Process Analysis 223
- 7.35 Process Modelling 225
- 7.36 Prototyping 227
- 7.37 Reviews 229
- 7.38 Risk Analysis and Management 231
- 7.39 Roles and Permissions Matrix 233
- 7.40 Root Cause Analysis 234
- 7.41 Scope Modelling 235
- 7.42 Sequence Diagrams 237
- 7.43 Stakeholder List, Map or Personas 238
- 7.44 State Modelling 240
- 7.45 Survey or Questionnaire 241
- 7.46 SWOT Analysis 243
- 7.47 Use Cases and Scenarios 245
- 7.48 User Stories 247
- 7.49 Vendor Assessment 248
- 7.50 Workshops 250
- 7.51 Glossary 252
- 7.52 Exercises and Drills 254

Chapter 9: Perspectives 273

   8.1 Agile Perspective 273

   8.2 Business Intelligence Perspective 277

   8.3 Information Technology Perspective 281

   8.4 Business Architecture Perspective 285

   8.5 Business Process Management Perspective 290

   8.6 Glossary 295

   8.7 Exercises and Drills 296

PREFACE

This book is authored with the intention of creating a concise revision guide for IIBA Business Analysis body of knowledge (BABOK) guide v3.0.

We have not written this guide as an alternative to BABOK v3.0. Instead it is written as a concise and summarized version of BABOK to help you in quick revision of BABOK. What's more, we have added revision exercises at the end of every knowledge area too.

The guide is meant for professionals who are planning to undertake ECBA, CCBA or CBAP certification examination.

This revision guide captures the key concepts, definitions, business analysis practices as mentioned in the BABOK guide. To really understand the thought process behind this revision guide, consider your university exam and the notes you used to create for every exam. This is essentially a guide comprising of important notes.

For best results, this revision guide must be picked up after you have gone through the BABOK guide once.

If you are planning for ECBA certification, please read it keeping in mind the knowledge areas weightages applicable for ECBA.

Business Analysis Key Concepts

This chapter lays down the foundation for the business analysis body of knowledge guide by explaining and discussing fundamental concepts used throughout the book. The chapter covers core concepts model and explains key terms used throughout the book.

Business Analysis Core concepts model (BACCM)

The Business Analysis Core Concept Model (BACCM) describes the relationships amongst six core concepts. It's a conceptual framework encompassing two important aspects:

- What is business analysis?
- What does it mean for business analysts irrespective of perspective, industry, methodology or level in the organization?

None of the core concepts in the model holds good in isolation. Each core concept is defined by the other five core concepts and cannot be fully understood until all the concepts are understood. None of the core concepts is more important than the other.

Let's understand the concepts, which form the core concepts model

Need

A problem or opportunity or a constraint with potential value to a stakeholder.

- A need is the reason for undertaking an initiative or a project, in simple terms.
- A need causes changes in the enterprise.

Example

A car agency wants to improve the processing time and efficiency of loan sanction so that it can close the sale of a car faster. This is an example of a need.

Change

The act of transformation in response to a need. A controlled transformation of an organization facilitated by a business analyst. This is the most fundamental aspect of business analysis activity. This change is not about individual change, but a change initiated to address a need.

- Business Analyst is responsible for facilitating the change in an enterprise in a controlled and deliberate manner to improve performance.
- The change is a result of implementing a solution to address the needs of the enterprise.

Example

Continuing the previous example, the project/change would be the implementation of a loan processing and approval system.

Solution

A specific way of satisfying one or more needs in a context. The specific way is chosen based on analysis and fact finding. It can also be referred to as a specific way of delivering value to a stakeholder.

Example

Multiple solutions are available for fulfilling the needs of the car agency:

- Creating a customized solution
- Using an existing product and get it customized

Business analyst has to determine and find & recommend the most apt solution based on the context.

Stakeholder

A group or individual with a relationship to the change (or for whom the change is relevant), the need, or the solution

- A group or an individual who has an impact on the change initiative or can influence the outcome of this initiative.
- Stakeholders can be internal or external
- Business Analysts perform stakeholder analysis to identify the stakeholders for the project (change)

Example

Considering the loan processing system for the car agency, who are the stakeholders? For whom this solution is relevant or who are going to influence the change/project? Some stakeholders are:

- The sales Manager or front office staff dealing with customer
- The load approving officer
- Director of Car agency (as sponsor or sign off authority)

Value

The worth, importance, or the usefulness of something to a stakeholder within a context

- A value is the reason, why enterprise invests in a solution as an exercise to address the need.
- An enterprise can target tangible or intangible value.
- Increasing the revenue by 10% every year is an example of tangible value
- Improving the customer experience (by enhancing the user interface) is an example of intangible value

Example

The value for the stakeholders is the ability to close the sale deal faster & having a happier customer.

Context

The circumstances that influence, are influenced by, and provide understanding of the change.

- A context defines everything that is relevant to a change but not the change itself.

- A context comprises of enterprise background, demographics, culture, products, projects etc.

Context and change initiative together present a unique situation to a business analyst.

Example

The loan processing system will be different if the car agency is not a single location agency but having presence in multiple cities. The situation in this case demands an internet enabled solution. It also demands approval and reporting facilities based on locations. That's the impact of a context in a solution.

Key Terms

Business Analysis

The BABOK® Guide describes and defines business analysis as the practice of enabling change in an enterprise by defining needs and recommending solutions that deliver value to stakeholders.

(We have not changed the definition used by BABOK guide)

Please note the use of core concepts in the definition. We have discussed these in the previous section.

Business Analysis Information

The use of term 'information' is significant as opposed to earlier use of word 'requirements'. It widens the scope of business analysis work.

Business analysis information is gathered as a result of business analysis activities and it can be:

- Requirements
- Elicitation results
- Designs
- Solution Options
- Solution scope
- Change Strategy

Requirements and Design

It's important to understand the meaning of these two terms in BABOK context.

A requirement is a usable representation of a need.

A design is a usable representation of a solution.

A design is used in a different context in this guide. In software parlance, design is referred to as the solution design representing technical design like table structures, code components, library design, interface design etc.

Enterprise and Organization

A differentiation has been made in the guide between an Enterprise and an organization.

An enterprise is a system of one or more organizations and the solutions they use to pursue a shared set of common goals.

An autonomous group of people under the management of a single individual or board, that works towards common goals and objectives.

As per BABOK guide, an organization refers to a company which is created to run on a continuous basis.

An enterprise is a more heterogeneous grouping of organizations, legal entities, government bodies etc. A change may span an enterprise going beyond just an organization. But an enterprise is a temporary phenomenon considered for the purpose of a change initiative, once the change is completed, it's disbanded.

Example of an Enterprise and Change

In India, Goods and Services tax has been implemented by replacing the old multi-tax system. This change is not just for the tax body of the government but for all the partners as well as tax payers. The government is not only upgrading the software, they have also launched massive training and awareness campaigns. This change spans an enterprise comprising of:

- Tax bodies of government
- Partners
- Tax payers

Risk: Risk is a possibility of occurrence of an event, which is likely to have an impact on the change, solution or the enterprise. Managing risks involves identification, assessment, prioritization or ranking by business analysts and the stakeholders.

Requirements Classification

BABOK guide has the following classification of requirements:

Business Requirements: The requirements stating the primary reason (s) for change. This can include – Statements describing the goal, objectives and expected outcomes.

Example

We would like to automate our account opening process to eliminate duplicate data entries and reduce the time frame to open the account from 3 days to a single day.

This is an example of business requirement for a bank. It is a high level yet objective statement of purpose.

Stakeholder Requirements: Stakeholders requirements are specific needs of stakeholders. They must be addressed by the solution in order to achieve business requirements.

Essentially BABOK establishes that stakeholders collectively and exhaustively represent the business requirements.

Example

Continuing the account opening system, a stakeholder may ask for a specific function as that concerns him/her. For example, we must ask for the account holder's spouse details as the stakeholder is part of customer relationship team. Knowing more about the customer will help in making the communications more personalized.

Solution Requirements: describe the capabilities and qualities of a solution that meets the stakeholder requirements. It is supposed to be detailed and carry information that will help the technology team in implementing it.

Solution requirements are of two types:

Functional Requirements: describe the capabilities that a solution must have in terms of the behaviour and information. In other words, this represents the way a user is going to interact with the system or view the information.

Example

The account holder's demographic data capturing is a feature that represents functional requirement.

Non-Functional Requirements: Does not describe the behaviour of the system but concerns the conditions under which the system is expected to work effective.

Example

Considering the banking environment, the account opening system should be a secured site.

Transition Requirements: Are temporary requirements, which arise because of the change becoming implemented. Once completed, they are not needed and are expired. All other types of requirements are managed throughout the change/project.

Example

In the account opening system, data for the existing account holders needs to be captured into the new system. This is called data migration and is an example of transition requirements. Once the migration is finished, it's no longer needed.

Chapter 1 : Business Analysis Planning and Monitoring

This knowledge area describes the activities associated with planning the business analysis activities as well as measuring and finding ways to improve the performance of business analysis activities.

1.1 Business Analysis Planning and Monitoring Tasks

- Task 1: Plan Business Analysis Approach
- Task 2: Plan Stakeholder Engagement
- Task 3: Plan Business Analysis Governance
- Task 4: Plan Business Analysis Information Management
- Task 5: Identify Business Analysis Performance Improvements

1.1.1 Task 1: Plan Business Analysis Approach

This task describes the following:

- Method or process to conduct the business analysis activities
- The schedule of activities
- What will be the output of the business analysis activities?

1	Purpose	Define an appropriate method to conduct business analysis activities

2	Description	➢ Business analysis approaches describe an **overall method** that will be followed
		    ○ when **performing business analysis work** on a given initiative
		    ○ how and when **tasks** will be performed
		    ○ **deliverables** that will be produced
		➢ Business analyst may also identify an initial set of **techniques** to use.
		➢ Business analysis approach may be defined by a **methodology** or by **organizational standards** which could be formalized into a repeatable business analysis process which can be leveraged for each effort.

		➤ Business analysis approach should highlight 　○ align to overall goals of the change, 　○ coordinate the business analysis tasks with the **activities** and **deliverables** of the overall change, 　○ include tasks to manage any **risks** that could reflect the quality of the business analysis deliverables, 　○ leverage upon **approaches** and select **techniques** and **tools** that have historically worked well
3	Inputs	➤ **Needs** – Business analysis approach is shaped by the problem or opportunity faced by the organization. This is required at the time of the planning which evolves throughout the business analysis approach.
4	Elements	➤ **Planning Approach** – Planning methods fit between predictive and adaptive approaches. Planning is an essential task to ensure value is delivered to an enterprise. It happens more than once on a given initiative as the plans are updated to address **changing business conditions**. 　○ **Predictive Approach** – Focus on minimizing upfront uncertainty and ensuring that the solution is defined before implementation begins in order to maximize control and minimize risk. Best applied for the projects where requirements can effectively be defined ahead of implementation, the risk of incorrect implementation is unacceptably high, or when engaging stakeholders presents significant challenges. Very good approach for **traditional waterfall** methodology. 　○ **Adaptive** Approach – Focus on rapid delivery of business value in short iterations in return for acceptance of a higher degree of uncertainty regarding the overall delivery of the solution. It is best applied when taking an exploratory approach to find best solution or for incremental improvement of an existing solution. Very good approach for **agile** methodology. ➤ **Formality and Level of Detail of Business Analysis deliverables** – Business analyst need to consider the level of formality that is appropriate for the approach 　○ **Predictive** approach – Calls for a significant amount of formality and details. 　　▪ Information is captured at various level of detail and following standardized templates such as **Business Requirement Document (BRDs)**

and Functional Requirement Document (FRDs).
- Activities required to complete deliverables are identified first and then divided into tasks. This is initiated and mostly done in **Analysis** and **Design** phase of traditional SDLC
- Tasks are performed in specific phases.

o **Adaptive** approach – Mandatory requirements documentation is often limited to a prioritized requirements list.
- Favour defining requirements and designs through **team interaction** and through gathering **feedback** on a working solution in an informal format. This feedback is incorporated into **Product Backlog** for initiative.
- Activities are divided into iterations with deliverables first and then the associated tasks are identified. This is conducted during **Backlog Refinement sessions** as well as **Sprint planning** sessions as part of various frameworks such as Scrum within Agile methodology
- Tasks are performed iteratively.

o Other considerations that may affect the approach include:
- very complex and risky changes
- the organization operates in heavily regulated industries
- contracts or agreements necessitate formality
- stakeholders are geographically distributed
- resources are outsourced
- staff turnover is high and / or team members may be inexperienced
- requirements must be formally signed off
- business analysis information must be maintained long term or handed over for use on future initiatives

➢ **Business Analysis Activities** – Incorporating business analysis activities within business analysis approach includes:
o identifying **activities** required to complete each deliverable and then breaking them into tasks

		o dividing the **work** into **iterations** o Identifying the **deliverables** for each iteration and then identifying associated activities and tasks or using a previous similar initiative as an outline and apply detailed tasks and activities unique to the current initiative. ➢ **Timing of Business Analysis Work** – Planning includes determining whether the business analysis tasks will be performed primarily in specific phases or iteratively. Timing of business analysis activities can also be affected by: o availability of the resources o priority / urgency of the initiative o other concurrent initiative o constraints such as contract terms or regulatory deadlines ➢ **Complexity and Risk** – Complexity, size of change and overall risk of the effort is to be considered while determining approach. o Factors affecting **complexity** are – size of the change, number of business areas or systems affected, geographic and cultural considerations, technological complexities and any other risks o Factors impacting **risk** level are – experience level of business analyst, extent of domain knowledge held by the business analyst, level of experience stakeholders have in communicating their needs, stakeholder attitude about the change, amount of time allocated by stakeholder to activities and any pre-selected framework, tool or technique imposed by organizational policies and cultural norms of organization. o Complexity and risk can be **better** handled in adaptive approach as compared to predictive approach. ➢ **Acceptance** – Business analysis approach is reviewed and agreed upon by key stakeholders. Business analysis process must be tailored to a structure where key stakeholders ensures that all business analysis activities are identified, realistic view of estimates is created and proposed roles/responsibilities are correct. Stakeholders also play a vital role in **reviewing** and **accepting** changes to the approach.
5	Guidelines & Tools	➢ Business Analysis Performance Assessment – Provides results of previous assessments that should be reviewed and incorporated

		➤ Business Policies – Define the limits within which decisions must be made. ➤ Expert Judgement – Expertise may be provided from a wide range of sources including stakeholders on initiative, organizational centres of excellence, consultants, associations or industry groups and prior experiences of business analyst and other stakeholders. ➤ Methodologies and Framework – Methods, techniques, procedures, working concepts and rules shape up the approach ➤ Stakeholder Engagement Approach – Understanding stakeholders concerns and interest may influence decisions within business analysis approach
6	Techniques	➤ **Brainstorming** – Identify possible business analysis activities, techniques, risks and other relevant items to build approach ➤ **Business Cases** – Used to understand time-sensitivity of the problem or opportunity or to find out particular uncertainty around elements of possible need or solution ➤ **Document Analysis** – Review existing organizational assets that might assist in planning the approach ➤ **Estimation** – Determine the time component to perform business analysis activities ➤ **Financial Analysis** – Used to assess how different approaches affect the value delivered ➤ **Functional Decomposition** – Used to break down complex business analysis processes into more feasible components ➤ **Interviews** – Used to help build the plan with an individual ➤ **Item Tracking** – Used to track any issues raised during planning activities with stakeholders ➤ **Lessons Learned** – Used to identify an enterprise's previous experience with planning business analysis approach ➤ **Process Modelling** – Used to define and document business analysis approach ➤ **Reviews** – Used to validate selected approach with stakeholders ➤ **Risk Analysis and Management** – Used to assess risks in order to select proper business analysis approach ➤ **Scope Modelling** – Used to determine boundaries of solution as an input to planning and to estimating ➤ **Survey or Questionnaire** – Used to identify possible business analysis activities, techniques, risks and other relevant items to build the approach

		➤ **Workshops** – Used to help build the plan in a team structure
7	Stakeholders	➤ Domain Subject Matter Expert ➤ Project Manager – Determines that the approach is **realistic** for the overall schedule and timelines. ➤ Regulator ➤ Sponsor – Provides **needs** and **objectives** for the approach and makes sure that organizational objectives are followed.

8	Output	➤ **Business Analysis Approach** – Identifies the approach and activities that will be performed including
		  ○ who will perform the activities
		  ○ timing and sequencing of the work
		  ○ deliverables that will be produced
		  ○ business analysis techniques that may be utilized

1.1.2 Task 2: Plan Stakeholder Engagement

This task describes the following:

- Approach to having an effective collaboration with the stakeholders to achieve the business objective, as planned
- How to conduct stakeholder analysis
- Develop a stakeholder collaboration/management plan

Imp: It's not a one-time activity but rather an ongoing activity as the project goes on.

1	Purpose	Plan an approach for establishing and maintaining effective working relationships with the stakeholders.
2	Description	➤ Planning stakeholder engagement involves conducting a thorough **stakeholder analysis** to identify all the involved stakeholders which help to plan for stakeholder risks. ➤ As number of stakeholder's increases, degree of complexity also increases. Therefore new techniques need to be used to manage stakeholder engagement.
3	Inputs	➤ **Needs** – Understanding the business need helps in identification of stakeholders. It may evolve as stakeholder analysis is performed.

		➤ **Business Analysis Approach** – Incorporating overall business analysis approach into stakeholder analysis, collaboration and communication approaches is required to ensure consistency.

4	Elements	➤ **Perform Stakeholder Analysis** – Stakeholder analysis involves **identifying the stakeholders** who will be directly or indirectly impacted by the change and their **characteristics** as well as analysing the information once collected. It is a **repetitive** action as business analysis activities continue.
		○ Business Analyst may miss uncovering critical needs if stakeholders are not identified. Stakeholders needs uncovered late will often require a revision to the tasks which are in progress or have been completed which in turn can **increase costs** and **decreased stakeholder satisfaction**.
		○ A company's organizational chart and business processes, sponsors as well as any existing contacts outside organization can serve as an **initial source** for identifying internal and external stakeholders. In addition, any regulatory or governing bodies, shareholders, customers and suppliers can also influence the work and assist in searching for external stakeholders.
		○ **Roles** – This is identified by business analyst to understand where and how the stakeholders will contribute to the initiative. For e.g. business owners and product owners.
		○ **Attitudes** – Stakeholders with positive attitudes may be strong champions and great contributors, but it may require collaboration approaches that increase their cooperation when change is viewed negatively. Business analyst analyse stakeholder attitudes about:
		    ▪ business goals, objectives of initiative and any proposed solutions
		    ▪ business analysis in general
		    ▪ the level of interest in change
		    ▪ the sponsor, team members and other stakeholders as well as
		    ▪ collaboration and a team-based approach
		○ **Decision Making Authority** – Identify the authority level a stakeholder possesses over business analysis activities, deliverables and changes to business

analysis work. For example in agile methodology, product owner giving authority to proxy product owner (business analyst) to take decisions.
- **Level of Power or Influence** – Understanding of influence and attitude each stakeholder may have can help develop strategies for obtaining **buy-in** and **collaboration**.
- **Define Stakeholder Collaboration** – Collaboration can be a **spontaneous event** but most of the times, it is **considered** and **planned**, with specific activities and outcomes determined ahead of time in form of **stakeholder collaboration plan**. The objective is to select the approaches that work best to **meet the needs of each stakeholder group** and ensure their **interest and involvement is maintained**. Some considerations while planning collaboration include:
  - timing and frequency of collaboration
  - location
  - available tools such as wikis
  - delivery method such as in-person or virtual
  - preferences of the stakeholders
- **Stakeholder Communication Needs** – Documented in form of stakeholder communication plan. Evaluation of communication needs by business analyst includes:
  - **what** needs to be communicated
  - what is the appropriate **delivery method** (written or verbal)
  - who the appropriate **audience** is
  - **when** communication should occur
  - **frequency** of communication
  - **geographic location** of stakeholders who will receive communications
  - **level of detail** appropriate for the communication and stakeholder and
  - **level of formality** of communications

5	Guidelines & Tools	<ul><li>Business Analysis Performance Assessment – Provides results of previous assessments that should be reviewed and incorporated</li><li>Change Strategy – Helps in assessment of stakeholder impact and development of more effective stakeholder engagement strategies.</li></ul>

		➢ **Current State Description** – Provides the context in which the work needs to be completed.
6	Techniques	➢ **Brainstorming** – Used to identify stakeholder list and their roles and responsibilities ➢ **Business Rules Analysis** – Used to identify stakeholders who were the **source** of business rules ➢ **Document Analysis** – Used to review existing organizational assets for effective stakeholder engagement ➢ **Interviews** – Interact with specific stakeholders to gain more information or knowledge ➢ **Lessons Learned** – Used to identify an enterprise's previous successes and challenges while planning stakeholder engagement ➢ **Mind Mapping** – Identify potential stakeholders and help understand relationships between them ➢ **Organizational Modelling** – Used to determine if the organizational units or people listed have any unique needs and interests that should be considered. ➢ **Process Modelling** – Used to categorize stakeholders by the systems that support their business processes ➢ **Risk Analysis and Management** – Used to identify the risks to the initiative resulting from stakeholder attitudes. ➢ **Scope Modelling** – Used to develop scope models to show stakeholders that fall outside the scope of solution but still interact with it ➢ **Stakeholders List, Map or Personas** – Used to depict the relationship of stakeholders to the solution and to one another ➢ **Survey or Questionnaire** – Used to identify shared characteristics of stakeholder group ➢ **Workshops** - Used to interact with groups of stakeholders to gain more information
7	Stakeholders	➢ Customers – source of **external** stakeholders ➢ Domain Subject Matter Expert ➢ End User – source of **internal** stakeholders ➢ Project Manager ➢ Regulator – may require certain stakeholders to participate ➢ Sponsor - may request to involve specific stakeholders ➢ Supplier – source of **external** stakeholders.
8	Output	➢ **Stakeholder Engagement Approach** – Contains a list of stakeholders, their characteristics which were analysed and a listing of roles and responsibilities for the change.

1.1.3 Task 3: Plan Business Analysis Governance

Governance process defines how decisions and approvals take place in a change initiative.

This task describes the following:

- How a change request will be initiated and communicated (Responsible person and the process)
- How the change will be analyzed and impact analysis will be conducted (Impact Analysis)
- Who will approve the changes?
- The process of recording the changes (Change request log for example)

A representative change control process could be as shown below:

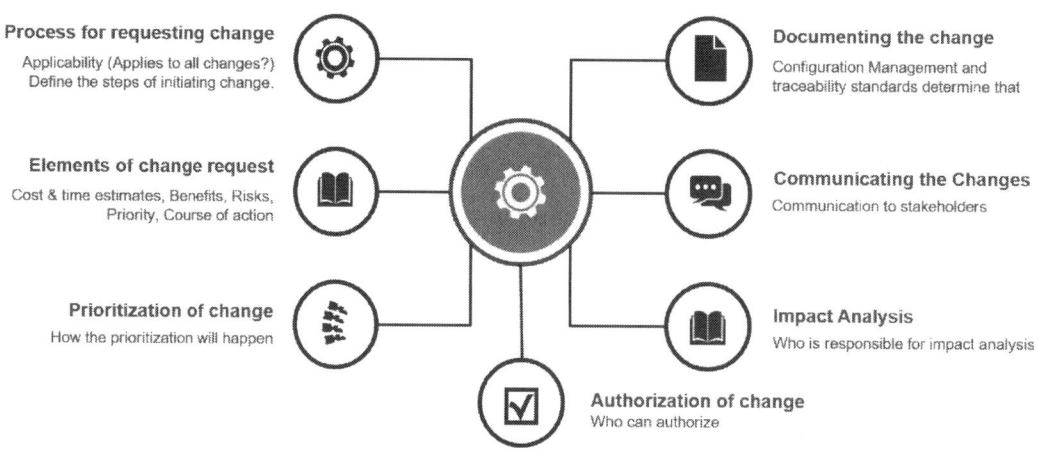

1	Purpose	Define how decisions are made about requirements and designs, including reviews, change control, approvals and prioritization.
2	Description	➤ Business analysts ensure that a **governance process** is in place that identifies decision makers, process information and give a view on approach for approvals and prioritization decisions. ➤ Business analysts identify following things when planning the governance approach:

		<ul><li>**how** business analysis work will be approached and prioritized</li><li>**what** the process for proposing a change to business analysis information is</li><li>**who** has the **authority** and responsibility to **propose** changes and who should be **involved** in the change discussions?</li><li>who has the responsibility for **analysing** change requests?</li><li>who has the authority to **approve** changes?</li><li>how changes will be **documented** and **communicated**</li></ul>
3	Inputs	<ul><li>**Business Analysis Approach** – Incorporating overall business analysis approach into governance approach is required to ensure consistency</li><li>**Stakeholder Engagement Approach** – Identifying stakeholder and understanding their communication and collaboration needs is useful to determine their participation in governance approach</li></ul>
4	Elements	<ul><li>**Decision Making** – The decision-making process defines what happens when teams cannot reach consensus by identifying escalation paths and key stakeholders holding final decision making authority. A stakeholder may serve in various roles in decision making process such as **participant** in decision making discussions or **subject matter expert** lending experience and knowledge or a **reviewer** of information or an **approver** of decisions. The reviewer of information and/or approver of decisions might be different in predictive approach (e.g. Waterfall SDLC) as compared to adaptive approach (e.g. only one entity - Product owner in Agile methodology)</li><li>**Change Control Process** – When business analyst develop a change control process, they:<ul><li>Determine the **process** for requesting changes – defining change control process to handle changes</li><li>Determine the **elements** of change request<ul><li>Cost and time estimates</li><li>Benefits</li><li>Risks</li><li>Priority</li><li>Course of action</li></ul></li><li>Determine how changes will be **prioritized** – priority is based on competing interests within initiative</li></ul></li></ul>

- o Determine how changes will be **documented** – configuration management and traceability standards
- o Determine how changes will be **communicated** – communication plan for communicating changes
- o Determine who will perform the **impact analysis** – identifying responsible parties to conduct analysis
- o Determine who will **authorize** changes – include a designation of approvers with authority level

➤ **Plan Prioritization Approach** – Timelines, expected value, dependencies, resource constraints, adopted methodologies and other factors influence prioritization. Following factors are considered in prioritization process:
- o **formality** and **rigour** of the prioritization process
- o **participants** who will be involved in prioritization
- o **process** for deciding how prioritization will occur including which techniques will be used
- o **criteria** to be used for prioritization

➤ **Plan for Approvals** – An approval formalizes the agreement between all stakeholders that the **content** and **presentation** of the requirements and designs are **accurate**, **adequate** and contain **sufficient detail** to allow for continued progress to be made.
- o **Timing** and **frequency** of approvals are dependent on the size and complexity of the change and associated risks of foregoing or delaying an approval.
- o Business analyst must determine the **type** of requirements and design to be approved, **timing** for the approvals, **process** to be followed to gain approval and **who** will approve the requirements and designs.
- o Business analysts consider the **organizational culture** and **type of information** being approved. New systems or processes in highly regulated industries will require **frequent** and **rigorous** review and **approval** of very detailed specifications. This is conducted by change control board in traditional methodology whereas it is performed by product owner in agile.
- o **Schedule of events** for approvals and their **tracking mechanism** is included in planning for approvals.
- o **Stakeholder availability, attitude and willingness to engage** determine the efficiency of approval process.

5	Guidelines & Tools	<ul><li>Business Analysis Performance Assessment – Provides results of previous assessments that should be reviewed and incorporated</li><li>Business Policies – Define the limits within which decisions must be made.</li><li>Current State Description – Provides the context within which the work needs to be completed which can help drive how to make better decisions</li><li>Legal /Regulatory Information – Describes legislative rules or regulations that must be followed to develop a framework for sound decision making</li></ul>
6	Techniques	<ul><li>**Brainstorming** – Used to generate an initial list of potential stakeholders' names who may need to be approvers in defined governance process</li><li>**Document Analysis** – Evaluate existing governance processes or templates</li><li>**Interviews** – Used to identify possible decision making, change control, approval or prioritization approaches and participants with an individual or group</li><li>**Item Tracking** – Used to track any issues that arise when planning a governance approach</li><li>**Lessons Learned** – Used to find if past initiatives have identified valuable experiences with governance that can be leveraged on current or future initiatives</li><li>**Organizational Modelling** – Used to understand roles /responsibilities within the organization in an effort to define a governance approach</li><li>**Process Modelling** – Used to document the process or method for governing business analysis</li><li>**Reviews** – Used to review the proposed governance plan with key stakeholders</li><li>**Survey or Questionnaire** – Used to identify possible decision making, change control, approval or prioritization approaches</li><li>**Workshops** - Used to identify possible decision making, change control, approval or prioritization approaches</li></ul>
7	Stakeholders	<ul><li>Domain Subject Matter Expert – May be possible **source** of a requested change or may be identified as needing to be involved in changing decisions</li><li>Project Manager</li></ul>

		➢ Regulator – May **impose** rules or regulations that need to be considered in determining the business analysis governance plan and can be a possible source of a requested change ➢ Sponsor – **Participates** in change discussions and **approves** proposed changes.
8	Output	➢ **Governance Approach** – Identifies the stakeholders who will have the responsibility and authority to make decisions, setting priorities and approving changes to business analysis information. It also lays down the process to manage requirement and design changes across the initiative.

1.1.4 Task 4: Plan Business Analysis Information Management

This task deals with the management (storage and access) of business analysis information. Business analysis information includes elicitation results, requirements, designs, solution options, solution scope, and change strategy.

Business analysis information:

- Comprises of all the information captured by a business analyst during elicitation, modelling, compilation and in any of the business analysis activities
- Examples include functioning prototypes, Requirements specifications document, User stories, use cases etc.
- Planning of business analysis information includes detailing and formality of the information, the access to information, requirement architecture, identifying re-usability across the enterprise.

1	Purpose	Develop an approach for how business analysis information will be stored and accessed.
2	Description	➢ Business analysis information is comprised of formal requirement documents, user stories and functioning prototypes, solution designs as well as solution options. ➢ Information management helps ensure that business analysis information is organized in a **functional and useful manner, is easily accessible to appropriate personnel and is stored for the necessary length of time.** ➢ Information management entails identifying: o how information should be **organized**

		<ul><li>the **level of detail** at which information should be captured</li><li>any **relationships** between the information</li><li>how information may be **used across multiple initiatives**</li><li>how information should be **accessed and stored**</li><li>**characteristics** about the information that must be maintained</li></ul>
3	Inputs	<ul><li>**Business Analysis Approach** – Incorporating overall business analysis approach into governance approach is required to ensure consistency</li><li>**Stakeholder Engagement Approach** – Identifying stakeholder and understanding their communication and collaboration needs is useful to determine their participation in governance approach</li><li>**Governance Approach** – Defines how changes are managed to requirements and designs, how decisions and approvals for business analysis deliverables will be made and how priorities will be set</li></ul>
4	Elements	<ul><li>**Organization of Business Analysis Information** – Business analysis information must be organized in a manner that allows for **efficient access and use**, must be structured to be easily **located**, must not **conflict** with other information and must not be **duplicated**.</li><li>**Level of Abstraction** – Level of abstraction describes the breadth and depth of the information being provided. **Needs of stakeholders, complexity of what is being explained and the importance of the change** is considered in determining the level of the detail provided to each stakeholder.</li><li>**Plan Traceability Approach** – Traceability approach is based on:<ul><li>the **complexity of the domain**</li><li>the **number of views of requirements** that will be produced</li><li>any requirement related **risks, organizational standards, applicable regulatory requirements**</li><li>an understanding of the **costs** and **benefits** involved with tracing</li></ul></li><li>**Plan for Requirements Reuse** – Business analyst identifies how best to **structure, store and access** requirements so they are usable and accessible for future. Requirements must be</li></ul>

clearly **named, defined and stored in a repository** that is available to other business analysts. Requirements that are potential candidates for long term use are of following types:
- regulatory requirements
- contractual obligations
- quality standards
- service level agreements
- business rules
- business processes
- requirements describing products the enterprise produces

➤ **Storage and Access** – Storage decisions depend on many factors such as **who** must access the information, **how often** they need to access it, and what **conditions** must be present for access.
- **Organizational standards** and **tool availability** will also influence storage and access decisions.
- Tools may shape the selection of business analysis **techniques, notations** to be used and the **way that information is organized**.
- The repository must be able to indicate the **status** of any stored information, and **allow for modification** of that information over time.

➤ **Requirements Attributes** – Requirements attributes provide **information** about requirements, and aid in the **ongoing management** of the requirements throughout the change. Better trade-offs between requirements and identification of stakeholders affected by potential changes can be achieved via requirements attributes. Commonly used requirements attributes include:
- **Absolute Reference** – Provides a unique identifier
- **Author** – Name of the person to be consulted in case of ambiguous or unclear requirements found later
- **Complexity** – Indicates how difficult the requirement will be to implement
- **Ownership** – Individual or group that needs the requirement
- **Priority** – Relative importance of requirements. Refers to the relative value of a requirement or sequence of implementation

		o **Risks** – Identifies uncertain events impacting requirements
		o **Source** – Identifies origin of requirement
		o **Stability** – Indicates the maturity of requirements
		o **Status** – Indicates the state of requirement
		o **Urgency** – Indicates how soon the requirement is needed
5	Guidelines & Tools	➢ Business Analysis Performance Assessment – Provides results of previous assessments that should be reviewed and incorporated ➢ Business Policies – Define the limits within which decisions must be made. ➢ Information Management Tools – This refers to the tool that is used to store, retrieve and share business analysis information. Examples – simple whiteboard, complex global wiki, requirements management tool ➢ Legal/Regulatory Information – Legislative rules or regulations to be followed for managing business analysis information.
6	Techniques	➢ **Brainstorming** – Used to help stakeholders uncover their business analysis information management needs ➢ **Interviews** – Used to help specific stakeholders uncover their business analysis information management needs ➢ **Item Tracking** – Used to track issues with current information management processes ➢ **Lessons Learned** – Used to create a source of information for analyzing approaches for efficiently managing business analysis information ➢ **Mind Mapping** – Used to identify and categorize the kinds of information that need to be managed ➢ **Process Modelling** – Used to document process or method for managing business analysis information ➢ **Survey or Questionnaire** – Used to ask stakeholders to provide input into defining business analysis information management ➢ **Workshops** – Used to uncover business analysis information management needs in a group setting
7	Stakeholders	➢ Domain Subject Matter Expert ➢ Regulator – Defines rules and processes related to information management ➢ Sponsor – Reviews, comments and approves business analysis information

| 8 | Output | ➢ **Information Management Approach** – Includes the defined approach for how business analysis information will be storied, accessed and utilized during the change and after the change is complete. |

1.1.5 Task 5: Identify Business Analysis Performance Improvements

This is an iterative task and happens throughput the software development lifecycle. Business analysis activities and processes are evaluated to identify improvement areas and incorporate them.

Organizational metrics can be used for measuring the performance of the business analysis activities.

Examples of metrics for measuring Business Analysis performance

Review Efficiency Index
How efficient was the review during requirements phase? Based on number of defects detected during post-coding phase, with origin of defect as "Requirements phase"

Missing Requirements
Number of requirements added or modified after the baseline approval

Stakeholder satisfaction Index
An interview/survey based metric, where a set of calibrated yet not-leading questions targeted to understand the satisfaction levels

Schedule variance
The delay in completing the business analysis activities vs the planned schedule.

1	Purpose	Assess business analysis work and to plan to improve processes when required.
2	Description	➢ Performance analysis is an ongoing task throughout an initiative. The improvements identified as part of this process will become guidelines for future task execution. To monitor and improve performance, it is necessary to ○ **establish** the performance measures ○ **conduct** the performance analysis ○ **report** on the results of the analysis

		o **identify** any necessary preventive and corrective actions
3	Inputs	➤ **Business Analysis Approach** – Identifies business analysis deliverables that will be produced, activities that need to be performed (including who and when) and techniques that will be used ➤ **Performances Objectives (external)** – Describes the desired performance outcomes that an enterprise is hoping to achieve

4	Elements	➤ **Performance Analysis** – Reports on business analysis performance can be **informal** and **verbal**, or they may include **formal** documentation and are **designed** and **tailored** to meet the needs of the various types of reviewers.
		➤ **Assessment Measures** – Business analyst may leverage measures if they are existing or may also elicit from stakeholders.
		   o Performance measures may be based on
		      ▪ **deliverables due dates** as specified in the business analysis plan
		      ▪ **metrics** such as frequency of changes to work products, number of review cycles required, task efficiency or
		      ▪ **qualitative feedback** from stakeholders and peers regarding business analyst's deliverables
		   o Measures may be both **qualitative** and **quantitative**
		   o **Qualitative** measures are **subjective** and can be heavily influenced by the **stakeholder's attitudes, perceptions and other subjective criteria**.
		   o Some possible measures are:
		      ▪ Accuracy and Completeness
		      ▪ Knowledge
		      ▪ Effectiveness
		      ▪ Organizational Support
		      ▪ Significance
		      ▪ Strategic
		      ▪ Timeliness

		➢ **Analyze Results** – The analysis may be performed on the **business analysis process, resources involved and deliverables**. Certain bodies like line managers, Centre of Excellence may provide assessments and come up with those who have authority to set the targets for measuring performance.
		➢ **Recommend Actions for Improvement** – Business Analyst engages appropriate stakeholders to identify the actions. These actions are likely to result in changes to business analysis approach, repeatable processes and tools. Actions could be as follows:
		    ○ **Preventive** – reduces the probability of an event with a negative impact
		    ○ **Corrective** – establishes ways to reduce the negative impact of an event
		    ○ **Improvement**

5	Guidelines & Tools	➢ Organizational Performance Standards – Include performance metrics or expectations for business analysis work mandated by the organization.
6	Techniques	➢ **Brainstorming** – Used to generate ideas for improvement opportunities ➢ **Interviews** – Used to gather assessments of business analysis performance ➢ **Item Tracking** – Used to track issues occurring during performance of business analysis ➢ **Lessons Learned** – Used to identify recommended changes to organizational process assets that can be incorporated into current and future work ➢ **Metrics and Key Performance Indicators (KPIs)** – Identify metrics appropriate for assessing business analysis performance and how they may be tracked ➢ **Observation** – Used to witness business analysis performance ➢ **Process Analysis** – Used to analyse existing business analysis processes and identify opportunities for improvement ➢ **Process Modelling** – Used to define business analysis processes and understand how to improve those processes to reduce problems from hand-offs and improve cycle times

		➤ **Reviews** – Used to identify changes to business analysis processes and deliverables that can be incorporated into future work ➤ **Risk Analysis and Management** – Used to identify and manage potential conditions and events that may impact business analysis performance ➤ **Root Cause Analysis** – Used to help identify the underlying cause of failures or difficulties in accomplishing business analysis work ➤ **Survey or Questionnaire** – Used to gather feedback from stakeholders about their satisfaction with business analysis activities and deliverables ➤ **Workshops** – Used to gather assessments of business analysis performance and generate ideas for improvement opportunities
7	Stakeholders	➤ Domain Subject Matter Expert ➤ Project Manager ➤ Sponsor – May require **reports** on business analysis performance to address the problems identified. Business analyst manager could be a sponsor too.
8	Output	➤ **Business Analysis Performance Assessment** – Includes a 　o comparison of planned versus actual performance 　o identifying root cause of **variances** from the expected performance 　o proposed approaches to address issues 　o other findings to help understand the performance of business analysis performance

1.2 Glossary

- **Predictive** – Predictive refers to an approach which we can predict and act accordingly. This is mostly applied for traditional/Waterfall SDLC where there is a linear and structured plan to product a decided outcome within a decided timeframe. As part of this approach, time and scope component remains static and pre-decided.
- **Adaptive** – Adaptive refers to an approach where the project keeps on evolving and changing conditions are encountered as part of the process. This is mostly applied for Agile SDLC where there is an unstructured plan and undetermined timelines to allow

ultimate flexibility in directing the course of project. Time and scope component remain flexible and allowed to be customized based on need.

- **Governance** – It is an action of governing and monitoring by creating policies, rules as well as regulations and properly managing them.
- **Current State** – This is "as-is" state on which analysis is conducted and may need a change from business perspective
- **Future State** – This is "to-be" state in which business foresees itself in upcoming future. This is the state which is an outcome of carrying out business analysis activities.
- **Agile** – A methodology which is characterized by division of work into short phases and frequently deliver the work in form of short iterations.
- **Scrum** – Iterative and incremental agile development framework for managing product development.
- **Product Backlog** – A list of ideas from stakeholders, business sponsors and owners as part of agile methodology towards an initiative.
- **Backlog Refinement Sessions** – A session in which agile team discusses product backlog with product owner and try to refine it to make it suitable for commencing work on the same.
- **Sprint Planning** – A scrum ceremony where team discusses and plans the work for the short iteration (so called sprint).
- **Stakeholder** - A group or person who has interests that may be affected by an initiative or influence over it
- **Stakeholder List** – An exhaustive list of stakeholders appropriately categorized and structured.
- **Stakeholder matrix** - Maps the level of stakeholder influence against the level of stakeholder interest
- **Requirements attributes** - Provide information about the requirements e.g. Author, Owner, Complexity, Priority, Absolute reference, status, etc.
- **Risk** - Risk refers to future uncertainty about deviation from expected outcome. The impact could be positive or negative
- **Tailoring** - Tailoring means taking a deviation (change) from the standardized process or documentation. Tailoring a process means asking for a change in the process for a customer.
- **Approach** - It refers to a way of completing a task or achieving a goal.
- **Deliverable** - Any unique and verifiable work product/ service that a party has agreed to deliver

1.3 Exercises and Drills

Q1. Match the terms in the first column with the descriptions in the second column

1. Adaptive	A. Uncertainty
2. Predictive	B. Formal approach to capturing information
3. Risk	C. Rapid delivery of business value
4. Approach	D. A detailed proposal or Step-by-step method to complete a task
5. Plan	E. Informal approach to capturing information
	F. A way to complete a task

Q2. Match the following requirements attributes with their meaning:

1. Urgency	A. unique numbering of the requirements
2. Absolute reference	B. Postponed, verified, accepted, cancelled
3. Status	C. Maturity of the requirement
4. Stability	D. timeframe for delivery
5. Priority	A. Relative importance of requirements

Q3: Solve this crossword puzzle

Down
1. The value added by a change, a synonym (8)
3. Level of importance of change relative to the other factors (8)
5. A way of completing a task or achieving a goal (8)

Across
2. _____ Analysis of change requests (5)
4. I am not detailed though I still represent what the customer wants (5)

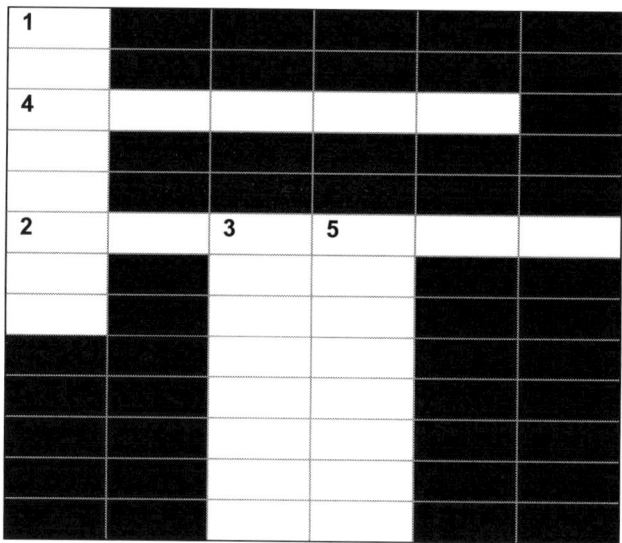

Q4. Match the terms in the first column with the descriptions in the second column

1. Components to consider on a change request are	A. Timelines, expected value, dependencies, resource constraints, adopted methodologies
2. Elements of Plan Business Analysis governance task are	B. Requirements and designs, reviews, change control, approvals and prioritization
3. Factors influencing requirements and design prioritization are	C. Cost estimates, time estimates, benefits, risks, priority, course of action
4. Purpose of Plan business analysis governance is to define how decisions are made about	D. Decision making, Change control process, Plan prioritization approach, and Plan for approvals

Q5. Complete the crossword puzzle

Across

1. Deliverables are broken down into activities and each activity is broken into _____ (5).

3. Planning approach that calls for formal documentation and representations (10)

5. The process of changing the organizational template or process to suit a project (9)

Down

2. Approach that focuses on rapid delivery of business value in short iterations (8)

4. Input to the task 'Plan Business Analysis Approach' (5)

6. Used to manage associated risks (11)

Answers to Exercises & Drills

Answer 1: 1 – E, 2 – B, 3 – A, 4 – F, 5 – D

Answer 2: 1 – D, 2 – A, 3 – B, 4 – C, 5 – E

Answer 3:

1 B					
E					
4 N	E	E	D	S	
E					
F					
2 I	M	3 P	5 A	C	T
T		R	P		
S		I	P		
		O	R		
		R	O		
		I	A		
		T	C		
		Y	H		

Answer 4: 1 – C, 2 – D, 3 – A, 4 - B

Answer 5:

Chapter 2: Elicitation and Collaboration

The Elicitation and Collaboration knowledge area describes the tasks that business analysts perform to obtain and gather information from stakeholders and confirm the results.

Elicitation is the **drawing forth** or **receiving** of the information from stakeholders or other sources which might involve interacting with stakeholders directly, performing research activities, conducting experiments or using existing information to discover requirements and design information.

Collaboration is the act of two or more people working together towards a **common goal**. Elicitation and collaboration work is never a phase rather it is an ongoing activity as long as business analysis work is occurring.

Elicitation activities can be **planned**, **unplanned** or **both**. Planned activities are organized in advance where unplanned activities are 'just in time' collaboration or conversations. Information derived from unplanned activity may require deeper exploration through a planned activity.

Eliciting business analysis information is not an isolated activity and may trigger additional analysis for details to fill in gaps or increase understanding.

The usage and application of each of the core concepts within the context of Elicitation and Collaboration is as follows:

- **Change** – Use a variety of elicitation techniques to fully identify the characteristics of the change including concerns that stakeholders have about the change.
- **Need** – Elicit, confirm and communicate needs and supporting business analysis information.
- **Solution** – Elicit, confirm and communicate necessary or desired characteristics of proposed solutions.
- **Stakeholder** – Manage the collaboration with the stakeholders who participate in the business analysis work.
- **Value** – Collaborate with stakeholders to assess the relative value of information provided through elicitation and apply a variety of techniques to confirm and communicate that value.
- **Context** – Apply a variety of elicitation techniques to identify the information about the context that may affect the change.

2.1 Elicitation and Collaboration Tasks

- Task 1: Prepare for Elicitation
- Task 2: Conduct Elicitation
- Task 3: Confirm Elicitation Results
- Task 4: Communicate Business Analysis Information
- Task 5: Manage Stakeholder Collaboration

2.1.1 Task 1: Prepare for Elicitation

1	Purpose	To understand the scope of the elicitation activity, select appropriate techniques and plan for appropriate supporting materials and resources.

2	Description	➢ The preparation for elicitation is done by defining the **desired outcomes** of the activity, considering the **stakeholders** involved and the **goals** of the initiative. This includes deciding on:
		    o **work products** that will be produced using results,
		    o **techniques** that are best suited to product results,
		    o establishing the elicitation **logistics**,
		    o identifying any supporting **materials** needed,
		    o understanding circumstances to foster **collaboration** during an elicitation activity

3	Inputs	➢ **Needs** – Provides guidance for preparation in terms of scope and purpose of elicitation activities. ➢ **Stakeholder Engagement Approach** – Understanding stakeholder's communication and collaboration needs to help plan and prepare for elicitation events.
4	Elements	➢ **Understand the Scope of Elicitation** – Business analysts considers business domain, overall corporate culture, stakeholder and their locations, expected outputs the elicitation activities will feed, skills of the business analysis practitioner, strategy, solution approach, scope of future solution and possible sources of the business analysis information to determine the type of the business analysis information and techniques that may be used. o Understanding the scope of elicitation activity helps to keep the activity within intended **scope** and to

recognize if **people** and **material** are available as well as when the activity is **complete**.
- **Select Elicitation Techniques** – Choosing the right techniques and ensuring each technique is performed correctly is extremely important to success of elicitation activity. When selecting elicitation techniques, business analysts consider techniques which are **common** to similar initiatives, or those which are specifically **suited** to the situation and **tasks** needed to prepare, execute and complete each technique. Multiple techniques are used during an elicitation activity which depend on:
  - **cost** and **time** constraints,
  - **type** of business analysis information sources and their access,
  - **culture** of organization and desired **outcomes**,
  - **needs** of stakeholders, their availability and their location
- **Set Up Logistics** – Logistics are planned prior to an elicitation activity. This include identifying activity goals, participants and their roles, scheduled resources, locations, communication channels, techniques, languages used by stakeholders and may sometimes involve creating an agenda if other stakeholders are involved.
- **Secure Supporting Material** – Business analysts identify **sources** of information which include people, systems, historical data, materials and **documents** such as existing system documents, relevant business rules, regulations, contracts as well as **supporting materials** in form of outputs of analysis work to conduct the elicitation activity.
- **Prepare Stakeholders** – Business analysts may need to explain a particular elicitation technique to stakeholders who are not involved in this activity if they feel that it is not aligned to their individual objectives or are not able to understand process or are confused about it. There is a need to have **buy-in** from all stakeholders in order to conduct elicitation. In order to avoid issues,
  - Business analysts may ask stakeholders to **review** required supporting material upfront so that elicitation activity can be conducted effectively.
  - An **agenda** may be published in advance so that stakeholders come prepared to the activity

			o In case of elicitation that is conducted via research or exploration, business analyst is a solo participant for it.
5	Guidelines & Tools		➢ Business Analysis Approach – Sets the general strategy to be used to guide the business analysis work which involves methodology, types of stakeholders and their involvement, timing of work and expected format as well as level of detail of results. ➢ Business Objectives – Describe the desired direction needed to achieve the future state. ➢ Existing Business Analysis Information – Helps in preparing for elicitation by providing a better understanding of goals ➢ Potential Value – Describes the value to be realized by implementing the proposed future state.
6	Techniques		➢ **Brainstorming** – Used to collaboratively identify and reach consensus about sources that need to be consulted and techniques that might be most effective. ➢ **Data Mining** – Used to identify information or patterns which require further investigation. ➢ **Document Analysis** – Used to identify and assess candidate sources of supporting materials. ➢ **Estimation** – Used to estimate the time and effort required for elicitation and associated cost. ➢ **Interviews** – Used to identify concerns about the planned elicitation and can be used to seek authority to proceed. ➢ **Mind Mapping** – Used to collaboratively identify and reach consensus about sources that need to be consulted and techniques that might be most effective. ➢ **Risk Analysis and Management** – Used to identify, assess and manage conditions that could disrupt the elicitation or affect the quality and validity of elicitation results. ➢ **Stakeholder List, Map or Personas** – Used to determine who should be consulted while preparing for elicitation and who should participate in the event.
7	Stakeholders		➢ Domain Subject Matter Expert ➢ Project Manager ➢ Sponsor – Has the **authority** to approve or deny a planned elicitation event and to authorize and require **participation** of certain stakeholders.
8	Output		➢ **Elicitation Activity Plan** – Used for each elicitation activity to include logistics, scope, selected techniques and supporting materials.

2.1.2 Task 2: Conduct Elicitation

1	Purpose	To draw out, explore and identify information relevant to the change.
2	Description	➤ Stakeholders may collaborate in elicitation by participating and interacting as part of activity or by researching, studying and providing feedback on documents, models and interfaces. ➤ There are 3 common types of elicitation: 　o **Collaborative** – Direct interaction with stakeholders and relies on their experiences, expertise and judgement. 　o **Research** – Involves systematically discovering and studying information from materials or sources that are not directly known by stakeholders involved in the change. 　o **Experiments** – Involves identifying information that via controlled test such as observational studies, proofs of concept and prototypes.
3	Inputs	➤ **Elicitation Activity Plan** – Includes the planned elicitation activities and techniques, activity logistic, scope and available sources for background information.
4	Elements	➤ **Guide Elicitation Activity** – The format of business analysis information defined in planning helps ensure that the elicitation activities are producing intended information at the desired level of detail. 　o In order to help guide an facilitate towards the expected outcomes, business analysts consider: 　　▪ elicitation activity goals and agenda, 　　▪ scope of the change 　　▪ the forms of output generated, 　　▪ other representations that activity results will support, 　　▪ integration of output into what is already known, 　　▪ source provider of information, consumer of information and the process by which that information will be used. ➤ **Capture Elicitation Outcomes** – On basis of the scope, elicitation is conducted iteratively and in multiple parallel or in sequence sessions. Capturing the elicitation outcomes helps

			to ensure that the information produced during elicitation is recorded for later reference and use. These outcomes are documented in requirements management tools. By using a tool, we can make sure that requirements will be available for future use too.
5	Guidelines & Tools		➤ Business Analysis Approach – Influences how each elicitation activity is performed, as it identifies the types of outputs that will be needed based on the approach. ➤ Existing Business Analysis Information – May guide the questions posed during elicitation and the approach to draw out information from various stakeholders. ➤ Stakeholder Engagement Approach – Provides collaboration and communication approaches that might be effective during elicitation. ➤ Supporting Materials – Includes any materials to prepare for elicitation as well as any information, tools or equipment to be used during elicitation.
6	Techniques		➤ **Benchmarking and Market Analysis** – Used as a source of business analysis information by comparing it with some external baseline such as a standard created by industry association. Market analysis is used to determine what customers want and what competitors provide. ➤ **Brainstorming** – Used to generate, organize and prioritize number of ideas from a group of stakeholders in short period. ➤ **Business Rules Analysis** – Used to identify the rules that govern decisions in an organization. ➤ **Collaborative Games** – Used to develop a better understanding of a problem or to stimulate creative solutions. ➤ **Concept Modelling** – Used to identify key terms and idea of importance and define relationships between them. ➤ **Data Mining** – Used to identify relevant information and patterns. ➤ **Data Modelling** – Used to understand entity relationships during elicitation. ➤ **Document Analysis** – Used to review existing systems, policies and standards. ➤ **Focus Groups** – Used to identify and understand ideas and attitudes from a group. ➤ **Interface Analysis** – Used to understand the interaction between two entities such as two systems, people or roles.

		➤ **Interviews** – Used to ask questions to uncover needs, identify problems or discover opportunities. ➤ **Mind Mapping** – Used to generate, organize and prioritize many ideas in short time. ➤ **Observation** – Used to gain insight about how the work is currently done. ➤ **Process Analysis** – Used to understand current processes and to identify opportunities for improvement in those processes. ➤ **Process Modelling** – Used to elicit processes with stakeholders during elicitation activities. ➤ **Prototyping** – Used to elicit and validate stakeholder's needs though an iterative process that creates a requirements model. ➤ **Survey or Questionnaire** – Used to elicit business analysis information from a group of people in a structured way and in short period of time. ➤ **Workshops** – Used to elicit business analysis information from a group of people in a collaborative, facilitated way.
7	Stakeholders	➤ Customer – Will **provide** valuable business analysis information during elicitation. ➤ Domain Subject Matter Expert ➤ End User ➤ Implementation Subject Matter Expert ➤ Sponsor – Authorizes and ensures that the stakeholders necessary to participate in elicitation are involved. ➤ Any stakeholders
8	Output	➤ **Elicitation Results (unconfirmed)** – Captured information in a format that is specific to the elicitation activity.

2.1.3 Task 3: Confirm Elicitation Results

1	Purpose	To check the information gathered during an elicitation session for accuracy and consistency with any other information.
2	Description	➤ Elicited information is **compared** against their **source** and other **elicitation results** and **confirmed** to identify any **problems** and **resolve** them before resources are committed to using the information. Committing resources to business

		analysis activities based on unconfirmed elicitation results may mean stakeholder expectations are not met. ➤ Confirming the elicitation results is a much **less rigorous** and formal review than it occurs during analysis.
3	Inputs	➤ **Elicitation Results (unconfirmed)** – Capture information in a format specific to the elicitation activity.

4	Elements	➤ **Compare Elicitation Results Against Source Information** – Follow up meetings can be arranged by business analyst to correct and verify elicitation results. On other hand, it can be done independently too by stakeholders.
		➤ **Compare Elicitation Results Against Other Elicitation Results** – Results collected through multiple elicitation activities are compared to find out if the information gathered is consistent and accurately represented. Variations in results are identified and resolved in collaboration with stakeholders.
		   o In some cases, historical data is also compared to confirm recently collected elicitation results.
		   o Inconsistencies are uncovered when business specifications and models are created which can be removed by improving collaboration with stakeholders.

5	Guidelines & Tools	➤ Elicitation Activity Plan – Used to guide which alternative sources and which elicitation results are to be compared. ➤ Existing Business Analysis Information – Can be used to confirm the results and draw out more detailed information.
6	Techniques	➤ **Document Analysis** – Used to confirm elicitation results against existing documents. ➤ **Interviews** – Used to confirm the business analysis information that is collected is correct. ➤ **Reviews** – Informal or formal reviews to confirm on the set of elicitation results. ➤ **Workshops** – Used to conduct reviews of the drafted elicitation results using any level of formality.
7	Stakeholders	➤ Domain Subject Matter Expert ➤ Any Stakeholder
8	Output	➤ **Elicitation Results (confirmed)** – Integrated output that the business analyst and other stakeholders agree correctly reflects captured information and confirms it is relevant and useful as an input to further work.

2.1.4 Task 4: Communicate Business Analysis Information

1	Purpose	To ensure that the stakeholders have a shared understanding of business analysis information.
2	Description	➤ Appropriate information must be communicated to stakeholders at the right **time** and in **formats** that meet their needs. ➤ Consideration is given to expressing the information in **language, tone and style** that is appropriate to the **audience**. ➤ Communication of information is usually **bi-directional** and **iterative**. It involves determining recipients, explaining the content, providing right context and expecting an outcome out of it. ➤ Business analysts acts on any **discrepancies** that are identified and works on resolving them. This could be also due to the method of delivering the information as stakeholders may not be able to understand it.
3	Inputs	➤ **Business Analysis Information** – Any kind of information at any level of detail that is used as an input or output of business analysis work. This is a best input when the need is to be communicated as information to stakeholders. ➤ **Stakeholder Engagement Approach** – Describes stakeholder groups, roles, and general needs regarding communication of business analysis information.

4	Elements	➤ **Determine Objectives and Format of Communication** – The primary goal of developing a package is to **convey** information **clearly** and in **usable** format for continuing change activities.
		   ○ Business analysis information packages may be prepared for several reasons such as below:
		      ■ communication of requirements and designs to stakeholders,
		      ■ early assessment of quality and planning,
		      ■ evaluation of possible alternatives,
		      ■ formal reviews and approvals,
		      ■ inputs to solution design,
		      ■ conformance to contractual or regulatory obligations and
		      ■ maintenance for reuse.
		   ○ The package must have combination of material which can convey a cohesive and effective message as a

		whole. Such packages can be stored in different online or offline repositories including documents and tools.
		o Possible form of packages include:
		  ▪ **Formal Documentation** – Usually based on template used by organization to provide a stable, easy to use, long term record of information.
		  ▪ **Informal Documentation** – Documented as part of change process but not as part of formal organizational process.
		  ▪ **Presentations** – A high level overview to show understanding of goals of a change, functions of a solution or supported information for decision making purpose.
		➤ **Communicate Business Analysis Package** – The purpose of communicating the business analysis package is to provide **appropriate level of detail about the change** so they can understand the information it contains. Stakeholders are given the opportunity to review the package, comment as well as raise any concerns they may have. Communication can be done via following ways:
		  o **Group Collaboration** – Communicate the package to a group of stakeholders at same time. This allows immediate discussion about information and issues.
		  o **Individual Collaboration** – Used to communicate the package to a single stakeholder at a time. Very beneficial when an individual understanding is required.
		  o **Email or other non-verbal methods** – Best when to communicate highly matured and self-explanatory information to support it.

5	Guidelines & Tools	➤ Business Analysis Approach – Describes how the various information will be disseminated. Includes level of details, formality, communication frequency and its impact on geographically distributed stakeholders. ➤ Information Management Approach – Helps determine how the information will be packaged and communicated to stakeholders.
6	Techniques	➤ **Interviews** – Used to individually communicate information to stakeholders. ➤ **Reviews** – Used to provide stakeholders with an opportunity to express feedback, request changes, agree or provide

		approvals. Reviews can be used during **group** or **individual** collaboration. ➤ **Workshops** – Best fit for group collaboration and provides stakeholders with an opportunity to express feedback and to understand adjustments, responses, actions, gaining consensus and providing approvals.
7	Stakeholders	➤ End User ➤ Customer ➤ Domain Subject Matter Expert ➤ Implementation Subject Matter Expert ➤ Tester ➤ Any stakeholder
8	Output	➤ **Business Analysis Information (communicated)** – It is considered as communicated when target audience reaches to a state of understanding of its content and implications.

2.1.5 Task 5: Manage Stakeholder Collaboration

1	Purpose	To encourage stakeholders to work towards a common goal.

2	Description	➤ Managing stakeholder collaboration is an **ongoing** activity.
		➤ New stakeholders can be identified at **any point** during an initiative. As new stakeholders are identified, their role, influence and relationship to the initiative are analyzed. Each stakeholder's role, responsibility, influence, attitude, and authority may change over time.
		➤ Business analysts manages stakeholder collaboration to **capitalize** on positive reactions and **mitigate** or avoid negative reactions. Stakeholder's attitude need to be monitored and assessed to determine if it is affecting their participation in business analysis activities. Outcomes of poor relationships with stakeholders could be as follows:
		   o failure to provide quality information,
		   o strong negative reactions to setbacks and obstacles,
		   o resistance to change,
		   o lack of support and participation in business analysis work and ignorance of business analysis information.
		➤ A strong, positive and trust-based relationships need to be managed with stakeholders who:
		   o provides service to business analyst

		○ depends on the services provided by business analyst ○ participate in execution of business analysis tasks.
3	Inputs	➢ **Stakeholder Engagement Approach** – Describes the type of expected engagement with stakeholders and how they might need to be managed. ➢ **Business Analysis Performance Assessment** – Provides key information about effectiveness of business analysis tasks being executed, including those focused on stakeholder engagement.

4	Elements	➢ **Gain Agreement on Commitments** – Stakeholders may be participating in activities that involve investing time and commitments from resources. This needs to be identified and agreed upon as early as possible.
		○ Explicit understanding of expectations and desired outcomes of the commitment need to be communicated formally or informally. In case of issues with the terms and conditions of the commitments, effective **negotiation, communication and conflict-resolution skills** need to be used.
		➢ **Monitor Stakeholder Engagement** – Business analysts continually monitor participation and performance of stakeholders as well as risks.
		○ Continuous monitoring of participation and performance ensures that:
		  ▪ right subject matter experts are participating effectively,
		  ▪ stakeholder attitudes and interest are improving,
		  ▪ elicitation results are confirmed within time,
		  ▪ agreements and commitments are maintained
		○ Following types of risks are monitored:
		  ▪ stakeholders being diverted to other work,
		  ▪ elicitation activities not providing quality of information required,
		  ▪ delayed approvals
		➢ **Collaboration** – Stakeholders are more supportive of change if business analysts collaborate with them to allow the flow of information, ideas and innovations. Collaboration involves regular and frequent communication in form of free flow of information around obstacles and to promote a shared effort to resolve problems and achieve desired outcomes.

5	Guidelines & Tools	➢ Business Analysis Approach – Describes the nature and level of collaboration required from each stakeholder group. ➢ Business Objectives – Describe the desired direction needed to achieve the future state. ➢ Future State Description – Defines the future state and expected value it delivers while keeping focus on common goal. ➢ Recommended Actions – Communicating what should be done to improve the value of the solution can help to galvanize support and focus on common goal. ➢ Risk Analysis Results – Stakeholder related risks will need to be addressed to ensure stakeholder collaboration activities are successful.
6	Techniques	➢ **Collaborative Games** – Used to stimulate teamwork and collaboration by immersing participants in a safe and fun situation to explore and share the knowledge. ➢ **Lessons Learned** – Used to understand stakeholder's satisfaction or dissatisfaction and offer them an opportunity to help improve the working relationships. ➢ **Risk Analysis and Management** – Used to identify and manage risks. ➢ **Stakeholder List, Map, or Personas** – Used to determine who is available to participate in business analysis work and who needs to be consulted about different kinds of business analysis information.
7	Stakeholders	➢ All Stakeholders
8	Output	➢ **Stakeholder Engagement** – Willingness of stakeholders to engage in business analysis activities and interact with the business analyst when necessary.

2.2 Glossary

- **Requirements Management Tools** – Tools provide a continuous process of managing requirements and managing them throughout lifecycle of those requirements. Couple of examples of such tools are: IBM Rational Rose, IRIS Business Architect and Enterprise Architect.
- **Focus group:** It is used to identify and understand ideas from a group
- **Elicitation:** Is to draw forth or bring out something for further analysis and understanding. Requirement elicitation refers to a set of activities to extract business needs from the stakeholders
- **Scope:** Defines the extent of responsibility for a team. But it does not refer to the requirements or functionality scope. Scope of work in software world refers to the activities needed to be completed for a software project (or change).
- **Value:** The benefit resulting through a change. The benefit could be monetary or non-monetary
- **Sponsor:** A stakeholder who is responsible for initiating the effort to define a business need and develop a solution that meets that need. They authorize the work to be performed and control the budget and scope for the initiative.
- **RACI Matrix:** Responsible, Accountable, Consulted, and Informed matrix (RACI matrix): A tool used to identify the responsibilities of roles or team members and other stakeholders
- **Proof of concept (POC):** A proof of concept is a controlled test conducted to check the viability of a concept or to identify information. It's a type of experiments
- **Business analysis information package:** The primary goal of developing a package is to convey information clearly and in usable format for continuing change activities.
- **Informal documentation:** It may include text, diagrams, or matrices that are used during a change but are not part of a formal organizational process.
- **Formal documentation:** It may include text, diagrams, or matrices that are used during a change based on an organizational template

2.3 Exercises and Drills

Q1. Complete the crossword puzzle

Across

1. Elicitation type that involves identifying/discovering information unknown to stakeholders (11)

3. Elicitation type that involves direct interaction with stakeholders (13)

4. Technique which elicits information by viewing performance (11)

Down

2. Elicitation type that involves identifying/discovering information not directly known by stakeholders (8)

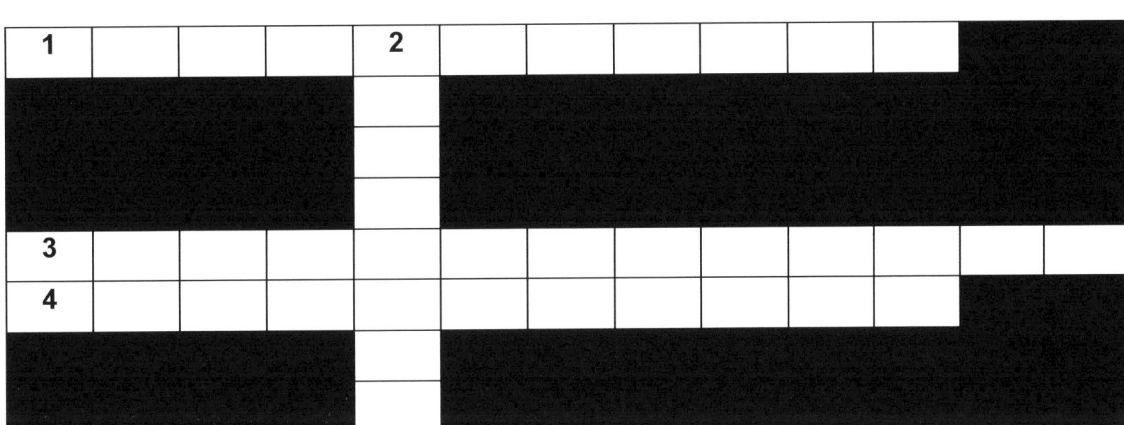

Q2. Match the following tasks with their respective description:

1. Prepare for elicitation	A. Describes the work performed to understand stakeholder needs and identify potential solutions
2. Conduct elicitation	B. Describes working with stakeholders to engage them in business analysis process and to ensure that business analyst can deliver outcomes needed

3. Confirm elicitation results	C. Ensures that stakeholders have the information they need to provide and that they understand the nature of activities they are going to perform. It also sets shared expectations regarding outcomes of the activity
4. Communicate business analysis information	D. Ensures that stakeholders have a shared understanding of outcomes of elicitation, that elicited information is recorded aptly, and that business analyst has the information sought from an elicitation activity
5. Manage stakeholder collaboration	E. Provides stakeholders with the information they need; at the time they need it

Q3. Match the following tasks with their respective description:

1. Understand the scope of elicitation	A. Draft versions of analysis models; existing system documents, business rules, organizational policies, etc.
2. Set up Logistics	B. Involves educating stakeholders on how and elicitation technique works, ensuring that there is buy-in from all necessary stakeholders
3. Secure Supporting Material	C. Allows business analysts to respond if any activity strays from intended scope. Also allows them to recognize if people and materials are not available in time, and when the activity is complete
4. Prepare stakeholders	D. Identify participants and their roles, locations, communication channels, techniques, scheduled resources like people, rooms and tools

Q4. Complete the crossword puzzle

Across

2. Used to elicit BA information from a group of people in a collaborative way(8)

3. Used to elicit BA information from many people in a relatively short period of time (6)

Down

1. Composed of pre-qualified individuals whose purpose is to discuss on a topic under the guidance of a trained facilitator (10)

4. used to elicit and validate stakeholders' needs through an iterative process that creates a model of requirements or designs (11)

Q5. Elicitation results (unconfirmed) is

I. Output of Confirm Elicitation Results task
II. Input to Conduct Elicitation task
III. Input to Confirm Elicitation Results task
IV. Output of Conduct Elicitation task

Choose the right option from below

    A. I and III

    B. II and IV

    C. III and IV

    D. None of the above

Q6: Match the terms in the first column with the second column

1. Individual collaboration	A. Information package which is not based on organizational templates
2. Formal documentation	B. Communication platform used to communicate the information package to a single stakeholder
3. Group collaboration	C. Information package which is based on templates used by the organization
4. Informal documentation	D. Communication platform used to communicate the information package to a group of relevant stakeholders at the same time

Answers to Exercises & Drills

Answer 1:

1 E	X	P	E	2 R	I	M	E	N	T	S		
				E								
				S								
				E								
3 C	O	L	L	A	B	O	R	A	T	I	V	E
4 O	B	S	E	R	V	A	T	I	O	N		
				C								
				H								

Answer 2: 1 – C, 2 – A, 3 – D, 4 – E, 5 – B

Answer 3: 1 – C, 2 – D, 3 – A, 4 – B

Answer 4:

	4 P		1 F			
	R		O			
	O		C			
	T		U			
2 W	O	R	K	S	H	O	P
	T		G			
	Y	3 S	U	R	V	E	Y
	P		O			
	I		U			
	N		P			
	G					

Answer 5: C

Answer 6: 1 – B, 2 – C, 3 – D, 4 - A

Chapter 3: Requirements Life Cycle Management

Requirements Life Cycle Management knowledge area describes the tasks that business analysts perform in order to **manage** and **maintain** requirements and design information from inception to retirement.

The purpose of requirements life cycle management is to maintain traceability between business, stakeholder and solution requirements and designs and solution implements them. It also involves control on the requirements and its implementation in actual solution.

Requirements life cycle **begins** with representation of business need as a requirement, **continues** through the development of a solution and ends when a solution and requirements that represent it are **retired**.

Requirements continue to provide value if managed properly and its management does not end once the solution is implemented. It is an ongoing activity.

Requirements may be in **multiple states** at one time.

The usage and application of each of the core concepts within the context of Requirements Life Cycle Management is as follows:

- **Change** – Manage how proposed changes to requirements and designs are evaluated during an initiative
- **Need** – Trace, prioritize and maintain requirements to ensure that the need is met
- **Solution** – Trace requirements and designs to solution components to ensure that the solution satisfies the need
- **Stakeholder** – Work closely with key stakeholders to maintain understanding, agreement, and approval of requirements and designs
- **Value** – Maintain requirements for reuse in future
- **Context** – Analyse the context to support tracing and prioritization activities

3.1 Requirements Life Cycle Management Tasks

- Task 1: Trace Requirements
- Task 2 : Maintain Requirements
- Task 3 : Prioritize Requirements
- Task 4 : Assess Requirements Changes
- Task 5: Approve Requirements

3.1.1 Task 1: Trace Requirements

1	Purpose	Requirements and designs at different levels are aligned to one another and to manage the effects of change to one level on related requirements.
2	Description	- Requirements traceability identifies and documents the lineage of each requirement, including its **backward** traceability, its **forward** traceability, and its **relationship** to other requirements. - **Traceability** is used to help ensure that the solution conforms to requirements and to assist in **scope, change, risk, time, cost, communication management**, to detect any **missing functionality** and to identify if the implemented functionality is **not supported** by any requirement. In addition, it also supports both **requirements allocation** and **release planning** by providing a direct line of sight from requirement to expressed need.
3	Inputs	- **Requirements** – May be traced to other requirements, solution components, visuals, business rules and other work products - **Designs** – May be traced to other requirements, solution components and other work products
4	Elements	- **Level of Formality** – Value delivered by tracing requirements, nature and use of traceability relationships created help to decide the formality level. When the requirements and related relationships grows, effort to trace them also increases significantly. - **Relationships** – Several types of relationships that business analyst considers when defining traceability approach: ○ **Derive** – Used when a requirement is derived from another requirement. For e.g., a solution requirement derived from a business or a stakeholder requirement

		<ul><li>○ **Depends** – Used when one requirement is dependent on another. Types of dependency relationships include:<ul><li>**Necessity** – When it makes **sense** to implement a particular requirement if a related requirement is also implemented</li><li>**Effort** – When a requirement is **easier** to implement if a related requirement is also implemented</li></ul></li><li>○ **Satisfy** – Relationship between an implementation element and the requirements it is satisfying</li><li>○ **Validate** – Relationship between a requirement and another element to identify whether solution fulfils the requirement.</li></ul><ul><li>➢ **Traceability Repository** – It is recommended to use **Requirements management tools** to reap benefits when we are tracing a large number of requirements as compared to manual approaches. Some examples of requirements management tools are IBM Rational Rose, JIRA, Rally, etc.</li></ul>
5	Guidelines & Tools	<ul><li>➢ Domain Knowledge – Knowledge of and expertise in business domain needed to support traceability</li><li>➢ Information Management Approach – Provides decisions form planning activities</li><li>➢ Legal / Regulatory Information – Describes legislative rules or regulations that must be followed</li><li>➢ Requirements Management Tools/Repository – Used to store and manage business analysis information</li></ul>
6	Techniques	<ul><li>➢ **Business Rules Analysis** – Used to trace business rules to requirements</li><li>➢ **Functional Decomposition** – Used to break down solution scope into smaller components for allocation</li><li>➢ **Process Modelling** – Used to visually show future state process and tracing requirements to the same</li><li>➢ **Scope Modelling** – Used to visually depict scope to the area of scope the requirement supports</li></ul>
7	Stakeholders	<ul><li>➢ Customers</li><li>➢ Domain Subject Matter Expert</li><li>➢ End User</li><li>➢ Implementation Subject Matter Expert</li><li>➢ Operational Support</li><li>➢ Project Manager</li><li>➢ Sponsor – Required to **approve** the various relationships</li></ul>

8			Output	➢ Suppliers ➢ Tester – Need to understand **how** and **where** requirements are implemented when creating test plans and test cases
8	Output	➢ **Requirements (Traced)** – Have clearly defined relationships to other requirements, solution components, or releases, phases or iterations within a solution scope ➢ **Designs (Traced)** - Have clearly defined relationships to other requirements, solution components, or releases, phases or iterations within a solution scope

3.1.2 Task 2: Maintain Requirements

1	Purpose	Retain requirement accuracy and consistency throughout and beyond the change during entire requirements lifecycle to support its reuse in other solutions

2	Description	➢ To maximize the benefits of maintaining and reusing requirements, the requirements should be:
		    o consistently represented
		    o reviewed and approved for maintenance using a standardized process that defines proper access rights and ensures quality
		    o easily accessible and understandable

3	Inputs	➢ **Requirements** – Includes goals, objectives, business, stakeholder, solution and transition requirements that need to be maintained throughout lifecycle ➢ **Designs** – Maintained throughout lifecycle as needed

4	Elements	➢ **Maintain Requirements** – After an approved change, requirements are kept **correct** and **current** for future initiatives. This is achieved via requirements management tools.
		    o Requirements need to be clearly **named**, **labelled**, **defined** and easily accessible to stakeholders.
		    o Relationships among requirements, sets of requirements and associated business analysis information is maintained to ensure the **context** and **original intent** of requirement is preserved.
		    o Repositories with accepted **taxonomies** assist in establishing and maintaining links between maintained requirements and facilitate requirements and designs traceability.

		➤ **Maintain Attributes** – Attributes such as requirement's **source**, **priority** and **complexity** aid in managing each requirement throughout lifecycle.
		➤ **Reusing Requirements** – Requirements for future initiatives need to be named, labelled, defined and stored in a manner easily accessible to stakeholders. Requirements at higher level of abstraction may be written with limited reference to specific solutions whereas those represented in **general manner** tend to be more reusable. Requirements that are intended for **reuse** reflect the **current state** of the organization. Requirements can be reused:
		    ○ within the current initiative
		    ○ within similar initiatives
		    ○ within similar departments
		    ○ throughout entire organization

5	Guidelines & Tools	➤ Information Management Approach – Indicates how requirements will be managed for reuse
6	Techniques	➤ **Business Rules Analysis** – Used to identify business rules that may be similar across the enterprise to facilitate reuse ➤ **Data Flow Diagrams** – Used to identify information flow ➤ **Data Modelling** – Used to identify data structure that may be similar across enterprise to facilitate reuse ➤ **Document Analysis** – Used to analyze existing documentation for reusing requirements ➤ **Functional Decomposition** – Identify requirements associated with components and available for reuse ➤ **Process Modelling** – Identify requirements associated with processes that are available for reuse ➤ **Use Cases and Scenarios** – Used to identify a solution component that may be utilized by more than one solution ➤ **User Stories** – Identify requirements associated with the story that may be available for reuse
7	Stakeholders	➤ Domain Subject Matter Expert ➤ Implementation Subject Matter Expert – Utilized maintained requirements when **developing regression tests** and **conducting impact analysis** for an enhancement ➤ Operational Support ➤ Regulator ➤ Tester
8	Output	➤ **Requirements (maintained)** – Defined once and available for long team usage as **organizational process assets** to be used in

		future initiatives. **A requirement that was not approved or implemented may be maintained for possible future initiative.** ➤ **Designs (maintained)** – May be reusable once defined.

3.1.3 Task 3: Prioritize Requirements

1	Purpose	Rank Requirements in the order of relative importance
2	Description	➤ Prioritization is the act of **ranking** requirements to determine their relative importance to stakeholders. ➤ Priority can refer to **relative value** of a requirement, or to the **sequence** in which it will be implemented. ➤ It is an **ongoing** process with priorities changing as context changes ➤ **Inter dependencies** between requirements are identified and used as basis for prioritization. ➤ It is critical exercise that seeks to ensure the maximum **value** is achieved.
3	Inputs	➤ **Requirements** – Any requirements in form of text, matrices or diagrams that are ready to prioritize ➤ **Designs** – Any design in form that are ready to prioritize.

4	Elements	➤ **Basis for Prioritization** – Typical factors that influence prioritization include:
		   ○ **Benefit** – Advantage accrued to stakeholders as a result of requirement implementation as measured against the goals and objectives for the change. **Conflict resolution and negotiation** may be employed to come to consensus on overall benefit.
		   ○ **Penalty** – Consequences that result from not implementing a given requirement. It may also refer to the **negative consequence** of not implementing a requirement that improves customer experience.
		   ○ **Cost** – Effort and resources needed to implement the requirement.
		   ○ **Risk** – Uncertainty about requirement not been met at all or requirement not delivering potential value. A proof of concept in form of **prototype** or **spike** is created to gain confidence in high risk options.

		<ul><li>○ **Dependencies** – Relationships between the requirements where one requirement cannot be fulfilled unless the other requirement is fulfilled.</li><li>○ **Time Sensitivity** – A date after which implementation of specific requirement loses value.</li><li>○ **Stability** – Likelihood that the requirement will change due to need to do further analysis or because stakeholders have not reached a consensus about it</li><li>○ **Regulatory or Policy Compliance** – Requirements to meet regulatory or policy demands which may take precedence over stakeholder interests.</li></ul><ul><li>➢ **Challenges of Prioritization** – **Relative value** is assessed as part of prioritization. There are chances that stakeholders might prioritize all requirements as high or may indicate priority to influence the result according to their desired outcome.</li><li>➢ **Continual Prioritization** – Priorities may shift as **context** evolves and as more **information** becomes available. Initially prioritization is done at higher level of abstraction and once requirements are further refined, it is done at more granular level.</li></ul>
5	Guidelines & Tools	<ul><li>➢ Business Constraints – Obligations or business policies that may define priorities</li><li>➢ Change Strategy – Provides information on costs, timelines and value realization which are used to determine priority of requirements</li><li>➢ Domain Knowledge – Understanding of business domain to support prioritization</li><li>➢ Governance Approach – Outlines the approach for prioritizing requirements</li><li>➢ Requirements Architecture – Understand the relationships with work products and other requirements</li><li>➢ Requirements Management Tools/Repository</li><li>➢ Solution Scope</li></ul>
6	Techniques	<ul><li>➢ **Backlog Management** – Compare requirements within backlog to be prioritized</li><li>➢ **Business Case** – Assess requirements against identified business goals and objectives</li><li>➢ **Decision Analysis** – Identify high value requirements</li><li>➢ **Estimation** – Produce estimates which can be base for prioritization</li></ul>

		➢ **Financial Analysis** – Assess the financial value of the requirements set and how timing of delivery will affect that value. ➢ **Interviews** – Gain an understanding of a small group of stakeholders that can provide a base for prioritization ➢ **Item Tracking** – Track issues raised by stakeholders ➢ **Prioritization** – Facilitate process of prioritization. ➢ **Risk Analysis and Management** – Understand the risks for the basis of prioritization ➢ **Workshops** – Gain an understanding of stakeholder's basis of prioritization
7	Stakeholders	➢ Customer ➢ End User – Verifies that prioritized requirements will deliver **value** from a customer ➢ Implementation Subject Matter Expert ➢ Project Manager ➢ Regulator ➢ Sponsor
8	Output	➢ **Requirements (prioritized)** – Ranked requirements available for additional work by making sure that requirements with **top most value** are addressed first. ➢ **Designs (prioritized)** – Ranked designs available for additional work.

3.1.4 Task 4: Assess Requirements Changes

1	Purpose	To evaluate the implications of proposed changes to requirements ad designs

2	Description	➢ This task is performed as new **needs** or possible **solutions** are identified.
		➢ Assessment is needed to determine whether a proposed change will increase **business value of the solution** and the necessary **action** that need to be taken for applying the same.
		➢ It is utmost necessary to **trace** back a proposed change to a need to understand the background. When assessing changes, proposed change is considered if it:
		    ○ aligns with overall strategy
		    ○ affects value delivered to business or stakeholder group

		<ul><li>impacts the time or resources required to deliver value</li><li>alters any risks, opportunities or constraints associated with overall initiative</li></ul>
3	Inputs	<ul><li>**Proposed Change** – Can be identified at any time and impact any aspect of business analysis work or deliverables completed to date.</li><li>**Requirements** – Identify the impact of proposed change</li><li>**Designs** – Assessed to identify impact of a proposed modification.</li></ul>
4	Elements	<ul><li>**Assessment Formality** – Formality of assessment process will be determined based on the information available, the importance of the change and governance process.<ul><li>**Predictive Approach** – It requires a **formal** assessment of proposed changes. There is a high chance of **rework** of already completed work due to impact of change as it is following a step by step approach in waterfall cycle.</li><li>**Adaptive Approach** – It requires **less formality** in assessment of proposed changes. Iterative and incremental implementation technique (**agile frameworks**) helps to minimize the impact of changes and in turn may reduce the need for formal impact assessment.</li></ul></li><li>**Impact Analysis** – This is conducted to **assess** and **evaluate** the effect of a change for which traceability is considered as a useful tool. Impact of proposed change must be assessed by considering:<ul><li>**Benefit** – Benefit that will be gained by accepting a change</li><li>**Cost** – Total cost to make the changes</li><li>**Impact** – Customer or business processes that are affected by the change</li><li>**Schedule** – Impact to existing delivery commitments</li><li>**Urgency** – Level of importance of the change</li></ul></li><li>**Impact Resolution** – All impacts and resolutions resulting from the change are to be documented and communicated to all stakeholders.</li></ul>
5	Guidelines & Tools	<ul><li>**Change Strategy** – Describes the purpose and direction of changes as well as identify critical components for change.</li><li>**Domain Knowledge** – Knowledge of business domain needed to assess proposed requirements changes.</li></ul>

		➢ Governance Approach – Provides guidance regarding the change control and decision-making processes ➢ Legal / Regulatory Information – Describes legislative rules or regulations that must be followed. ➢ Requirements Architecture – Examine and analyze requirement relationships to determine which requirement will be impacted by requested requirement change. ➢ Solution Scope – Considered to fully understand the impact of proposed change.
6	Techniques	➢ **Business Cases** – Required for justification of proposed change ➢ **Business Rules Analysis** – Used to assess changes to business policies and develop revised guidance. ➢ **Decision Analysis** – Help to facilitate the change management process ➢ **Document Analysis** – Analyze any existing documents that facilitate understanding of the impact of change ➢ **Estimation** – Determine the size of the change ➢ **Financial Analysis** – Financial impact of a proposed change ➢ **Interface Analysis** – Identify interfaces that can be affected by change ➢ **Interviews** – Used to gain understanding of impact on the organization and its assets ➢ **Item Tracking** – Used to track any issues or conflicts discovered during impact analysis ➢ **Risk Analysis and Management** – Determine the level of risk associated with the change ➢ **Workshops** – Understand the impact of change in group setting
7	Stakeholders	➢ Customer – Provides **feedback** on the impact of change will have on value. ➢ Domain Subject Matter Expert ➢ End User ➢ Operational Support ➢ Project Manager ➢ Regulator ➢ Sponsor ➢ Tester
8	Output	➢ **Requirements Change Assessment** – Recommendation to **approve**, **modify** or **deny** a proposed change to requirements.

		➤ **Designs Change Assessment** – Recommendation to approve, modify or deny a proposed change to one or more design components.

3.1.5 Task 5: Approve Requirements

1	Purpose	Obtain agreement on and approval of requirements and designs to proceed on business analysis work and/or solution construction.
2	Description	➤ Clear **communication** of requirements, designs and other business analysis information to key stakeholders is responsible for **approving** that information ➤ Business Analysts work with key stakeholders to gain consensus on new and changed requirements, communicate the outcome of discussion and track as well as manage the approval. ➤ Predictive approach perform approvals at the **end of phase** or during planned control meetings. ➤ Adaptive approach typically approve requirement when the solution matching those requirements is ready to be taken into construction phase.
3	Inputs	➤ **Requirements (verified)** – A set of requirements that have been matching sufficient quality to be used for further work ➤ **Designs** – A set of designs that are ready to be used for further specification and development.
4	Elements	➤ **Understand Stakeholder Roles** – Business analysts are responsible for obtaining stakeholder approvals and must be able to identify the parties holding **decision-making** responsibility versus those having **authority for sign-off** across the initiative. Example of same in agile world is product owner versus external stakeholders. ➤ **Conflict and Issue Management** – Stakeholder groups have a varying point of view and conflicting priorities. A conflict may arise among stakeholders due to varying interpretations of requirements. ○ Conflict resolution and issue management may occur **quite often** while aiming to secure sign off.

		➢ **Gain Consensus** – Business analysts are responsible for ensuring that stakeholders with approval authority **understand** and **accept** requirements. The approval may confirm that stakeholders see **sufficient value** that will be created by justifying investment in a solution. Risks need to be **identified** and **managed** via mitigation plan in case of lack of agreement.
		➢ **Track and Communicate Approval** – Requirements maintenance and tracking tool is used to record approval decisions and to keep accurate records of current approval status. Audit history of changes to requirements refers to following:
		    o what was changed
		    o who made the changes
		    o the reason for change
		    o when was the change made

5	Guidelines & Tools	➢ Change Strategy – Provides information in managing stakeholder consensus regarding stakeholder needs. ➢ Governance Approach – Identify the stakeholders who have authority and responsibility to approve business analysis information ➢ Legal / Regulatory Information – Legislative rules to be followed. ➢ Requirement Management Tools/ Repository – Tool to record requirements approvals ➢ Solution Scope – Must be considered while approving requirements.
6	Techniques	➢ **Acceptance and Evaluation Criteria** – Used to define approval criteria ➢ **Decision Analysis** – Used to resolve issues and gain agreement ➢ **Item Tracking** – Used to track issues identified during agreement process ➢ **Reviews** - Used to evaluate requirements ➢ **Workshops** – Used to facilitate obtaining approvals
7	Stakeholders	➢ Customer – May play an active role in **reviewing** and **approving** requirements to ensure needs are met ➢ Domain Subject Matter Expert ➢ End User – People who **use** the solution ➢ Operational Support ➢ Project Manager ➢ Regulator ➢ Sponsor

		➢ Tester
8	Output	➢ **Requirements (approved)** – Requirements which are agreed to by stakeholders and are ready for use. ➢ **Designs (approved)** – Agreed by stakeholders and ready for use.

3.2 Glossary

- **Traceability** – Traceability provides the ability of tracking the relationships between sets of requirements and designs. It helps to support change control by ensuring source of the requirement can be identified and those potentially affected by a change are known.
- **Forward Traceability** – This refers to tracing requirements and designs to the solution that will implement them.
- **Backward Traceability** – This refers to tracing requirements and designs back to stakeholder needs and related goals and objectives for verification purpose.
- **Change Control Board (CCB):** A group of stakeholders who discuss and make decisions regarding the treatment of change requests/ changing requirements
- **Requirements Traceability Matrix (RTM):** A matrix used to trace requirements relationships. It is a grid that links requirements from their origin to the deliverables that satisfy them
- **MoSCoW Analysis:** Must have, Should have, Could have, Won't have categorization of requirements based on priority
- **Impact analysis:** Performed to assess/ evaluate the effect of a change
- **Acceptance and evaluation criteria:** These are important techniques which are used to define the requirements approval criteria

3.3 Exercises and Drills

Q1. Match the following tasks with their respective description:

1. Trace requirements	A. Evaluate the implications of new and changing requirements
2. Maintain requirements	B. Ensure that requirements and design are accurate and consistent throughout the life cycle, and facilitates reuse in other solutions
3. Prioritize requirements	C. Obtain agreement on and approval of requirements and design elements
4. Assess requirements changes	D. Analyse and maintain relationships between requirements, design and solution components for impact analysis, coverage and allocation
5. Approve requirements	E. Rank requirements in the order of relative importance

Q2. Match the following relationships with their description:

1. Satisfy	A. Relationship between a requirement and a test case that can determine if a solution fulfils the requirement
2. Necessity	B. A requirement that is easy to implement only if another requirement is implemented
3. Validate	C. A requirement derived from another requirement which is usually on a different level of abstraction
4. Derive	D. Relationship between an implementation element and the requirement it is satisfying
5. Effort	E. A requirement that only makes sense to implement if another related requirement is also implemented
6. Subset	F. A requirement is decomposed from another requirement

Q3. Complete the below crossword:

Across

2. The process of analyzing and maintaining the relationships between requirements, designs, solution components, and other work products (7)
3. Name the relationships between requirements, when a requirement is easier to implement if a related requirement is also implemented.

Down

1. A point-in-time view of requirements that have been reviewed and agreed upon to serve as a basis of further development (8)
4. A place where things are stored and can be found

Q4. Match the following:

1. Maintain attributes	A. Requirements represented in a generic manner at high levels of abstraction
2. Reusing requirements	B. Eliciting information such as requirement's source, priority, complexity, etc.
3. Maintain requirements	C. Requirements must be clearly named, defined and accessible to stakeholders

Q5. Solve the crossword:

Risk analysis involves determining the 1 (down) of a risk event occurring and its 2 (across) on the project, should it materialize.

3 (across) and 4(down) are two techniques employed by Business Analysts to ensure consensus in case of conflicts among stakeholders during requirements prioritization.

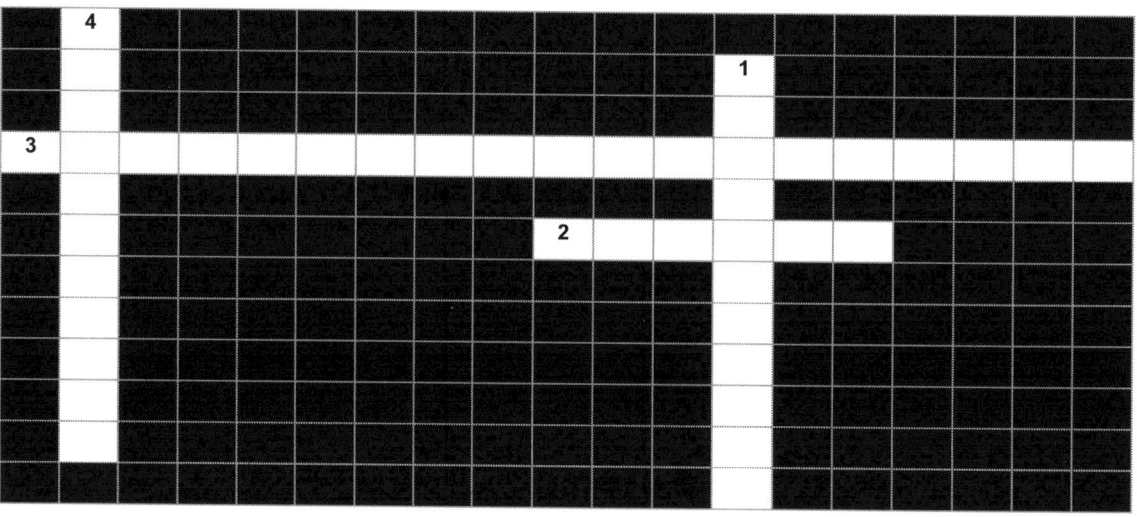

Answers to Exercises & Drills

Answer 1: 1 – D, 2 – B, 3 – E, 4 – A, 5 – C

Answer 2: 1 - D, 2 – E, 3 - A, 4 - C, 5 – B, 6 - F

Answer 3:

Answer 4: 1 - B, 2 – A, 3 - C

Answer 5:

Chapter 4: Strategy Analysis

Strategy Analysis knowledge area describes the business analysis work that is required to be carried out in order to identify a **business need**, enable the enterprise to address that need and align the resulting strategy for the change.

Strategic analysis focuses on defining the **future** and **transition** states needed to address the business need and the work required to achieve that state.

Strategy analysis should be performed as a **business need is identified**. This allows stakeholders to make the determination of whether to address that need or not. Strategy analysis is an **ongoing** activity that assesses any changes in that need, in its context, or any new information that may indicate a change to strategy may be required.

In case of change having predictable outcome, future state and possible transition states can typically be defined clearly and a clear strategy can be planned out. In case of an outcome of a change that is difficult to predict, strategy may need to focus more on mitigating risk, testing assumptions and changing the approach until business goals are identified or until the initiative has ended. A strategy may be captured in a **strategic plan, product vision, business case, product roadmap** or other artefacts.

Usage and application of each of the core concepts within the context of Strategy Analysis is as follows:

- **Change** – Define the future state and develop a change strategy to achieve the future state
- **Need** – Identify needs within the current state and prioritize needs to determine the desired future state
- **Solution** – Define the scope of the solution as part of developing a change strategy
- **Stakeholder** – Collaborate with stakeholders to understand the business need and to develop a change strategy and future state that will meet those needs
- **Value** – Examine the potential value of the solution to see if a change can be justified
- **Context** – Consider the context of the enterprise in developing a change strategy

4.1 Strategy Analysis Tasks

- Task 1: Analyze Current State
- Task 2 : Define Future State
- Task 3 : Assess Risks
- Task 4 : Define Change Strategy

4.1.1 Task 1: Analyse Current State

1	Purpose	To understand the reasons why an enterprise needs to change some aspect of how it operates and what would be directly or indirectly affected by change.
2	Description	<ul><li>The starting point for any change is an understanding of **why the change** is needed. Potential change is triggered by problems or opportunities that cannot be addressed without altering the current state.</li><li>Change always occurs in a context of existing stakeholders, processes, technology and policies which constitute the current state of the enterprise. The **current state** is explored in just enough detail to validate the need of a change or change strategy.</li><li>The scope of the current state describes the important existing characteristics of the environment. The current state of an enterprise is **rarely static** while a change is being developed and implemented.</li></ul>
3	Inputs	<ul><li>**Elicitation Results** – Used to define and understand the current state</li><li>**Needs** – The problem or opportunity faced by an enterprise or organization often launches business analysis work</li></ul>
4	Elements	<ul><li>**Business Needs** – **Problems** or **opportunities** faced by enterprise leading to strategic outcome are termed as business needs. An **issue** encountered in the organization usually triggers the evaluation of a business need.<ul><li>A business need may be identified at many different levels of enterprise:<ul><li>Achieving a strategic goal via **top-down** approach. This includes starting from the goal</li></ul></li></ul></li></ul>

definition and finding out required steps to achieve it by drilling it down to smallest possible.
- Problem with the current state of a process, function or system via **bottom-up** approach
- From **middle management** needing additional information to make sound decisions to meet business objectives
- In form of **external drivers** such as customer demands or business competition in marketplace

o The definition of business needs is frequently the most **critical** step in any business analysis effort. A **solution** must satisfy the business needs to be considered successful.

o The approach to determine a business need includes identification of **alternative solutions**, identifying **stakeholders** for consultation and solution **approaches** that will be evaluated.

o Business needs are always expressed from the **perspective of the enterprise, not that of any stakeholder**. Business needs will drive overall analysis of the **current state**.

o Factors that business analyst may consider for the solution:
- adverse impacts the problem is causing within the organization
- expected benefits from any potential solution
- how quickly the problem could potentially be resolved, or the opportunity could be taken
- the underlying source of the problem

➢ **Organizational Structure and Culture** – **Formal relationships** between people working in an enterprise is termed as organizational structure.

o Organizational culture is the **beliefs, values and norms** shared by the members of the organization which drive the actions taken by the organization.

o Business analysts perform a cultural assessment to:
- identify if the goals that need to be achieved need any cultural changes

- identify if stakeholders understand the value delivered as well as rationale behind current state
- ascertain if current state needs any change or is it in a satisfactory state

➢ **Capabilities and Processes** – Activities performed by enterprise are termed as capabilities and processes. It is due to these capabilities and processes, an enterprise can be a unique player in a particular area. They are measured by performance indicators that can be used to assess the benefits of the change. There are 2 views that enterprise may apply:
  o **Capability-Centric view** – This is applied when looking for innovative solutions that combine existing capabilities to produce a new outcome. It is very useful to identify the gaps while maintaining the functional hierarchy of the capabilities.
  o **Process-Centric view** – This is applied when an enterprise is looking for ways to improve the performance of current activities. The processes are organized in such a way that the change in fact increases performance.

➢ **Technology and Infrastructure** – Information systems used by the enterprise support people in executing processes, making decisions, and in interactions with suppliers and customers. The infrastructure describes the enterprise's environment with respect to physical components and capabilities.

➢ **Policies** – Policies define the **scope of decision making** at different levels of enterprise. They generally address routine operations rather than strategic change. The scope of solution space and any constraints on the type of action will be impacted by identification of relevant policies.

➢ **Business Architecture** – It is very important to understand how the elements of current state fit together to support one another in order to recommend changes that will be effective. Existing business architecture is a combination of **business** and **stakeholder** needs.

➢ **Internal Assets** - Tangible or intangible resources used in a current state are identified as enterprise assets. For e.g. patents, reputation, brand names and financial resources

		➤ **External Influencers** – Usually present constraints, dependencies or drivers on the current state. Sources include:
		  o Industry Structure
		  o Competitors
		  o Customers
		  o Suppliers
		  o Political and Regulatory Environment
		  o Technology
		  o Macroeconomic Factors

5	Guidelines & Tools	➤ Business Analysis Approach – Guides how the business analyst undertakes an analysis of current state ➤ Enterprise Limitation – Used to understand the challenges that exist within the enterprise ➤ Organizational Strategy – A set of goals and objectives that provide a vision of a future state ➤ Solution Limitation – Understand current state and challenges of existing solutions ➤ Solution Performance Goals – Measure the current performance of an enterprise or solution ➤ Solution Performance Measures – Describe the actual performance of existing solutions ➤ Stakeholder Analysis Results – Stakeholders contributing to an understanding and analysis of current state.
6	Techniques	➤ **Benchmarking and Market Analysis** – Provides an understanding of where the opportunities for improvement are in current state. Available frameworks to conduct this technique include 5 Force Analysis, PEST, STEEP, CATWOE ➤ **Business Capability Analysis** – Identifies gaps and prioritizes them in relation to value and risk ➤ **Business Model Canvas** – Provides an understanding of value proposition that enterprise satisfies for its customers, critical factors in delivering that value and resulting cost and revenue streams. ➤ **Business Cases** – Capture information regarding business need and opportunity ➤ **Concept Modelling** – Capture key terms and concepts in the business domain and define the relationships between them ➤ **Data Mining** – Used to obtain information on performance of enterprise ➤ **Document Analysis** – Analyse any existing documentation about the current state

- **Financial Analysis** – Understand the profitability of the current state and financial capability to deliver change
- **Focus Groups** – Solicits feedback from customers or end users
- **Functional Decomposition** – Breaks down complex systems or relationships in current state
- **Interviews** – Facilitate dialogue with stakeholders to understand the current state and any needs evolving from the same
- **Item Tracking** – Tracks and manages issues discovered about the current state
- **Lessons Learned** – Enables the assessment of failures and opportunities for improvement in past initiatives
- **Metrics and Key Performance Indicators** – Assesses performance of the current state of enterprise
- **Mind Mapping** – Explore relevant aspects of current state and factors affecting the business need
- **Observation** – May provide insights into needs within the current state which may have been missed previously
- **Organizational Modelling** – Describes the roles, responsibilities and reporting structure existing in current state organization
- **Process Analysis** – Identify opportunities to improve current state
- **Process Modelling** – Describes how work occurs within current solution
- **Risk Analysis and Management** – Identifies risks to current state
- **Root Cause Analysis** – Understanding of underlying causes of any problems in current state to clarify a need
- **Scope Modelling** – Helps define the boundaries on current state description
- **Survey or Questionnaire** – Gain an understanding of the current state from a large, varied, or disparate group of stakeholders
- **SWOT Analysis** – Evaluates the strengths, weaknesses, opportunities and threats to current state in enterprise
- **Vendor Assessment** – Assessment of vendors on making sure that commitments are met or if any changes are needed
- **Workshops** – Engage stakeholders to collaboratively describe the current state and their needs

7	Stakeholders	<ul><li>Customers – Makes **use** of existing solution and might have input about **issues** with a current solution</li><li>Domain Subject Matter Expert</li><li>End User – Directly **uses** a solution and might have input on **issues** with current solution</li><li>Implementation Subject Matter Expert</li><li>Operational Support</li><li>Regulator</li><li>Sponsor</li><li>Supplier</li><li>Tester</li></ul>
8	Output	<ul><li>**Current State Description** – The context of enterprise's scope, capabilities, resources, performance, culture, dependencies, infrastructure ad relationships between these elements</li><li>**Business Requirements** - The problem, opportunity or constraint which is defined based on an understanding of current state.</li></ul>

4.1.2 Task 2: Define Future State

1	Purpose	To determine the set of necessary conditions to meet business need
2	Description	<ul><li>Business analysts work to ensure that the **future state** of the enterprise is well defined, that it is achievable with the **resources** available and that key **stakeholders** have a shared consensus vision of the outcome. The future state will be defined at a level of detail that:<ul><li>allows to identify and assess competing strategies to achieve that future state</li><li>provides a clear definition of the outcomes that will satisfy the business needs</li><li>detail the scope of the solution space</li><li>allows for value associated with future state to be assessed and</li><li>enables consensus to be achieved among key stakeholders</li></ul></li><li>The future state description can describe the **new, removed and modified components** of enterprise. It can include</li></ul>

		changes to the **boundaries** of the organization, or it can be simple changes to **existing** components of an organization.
		➤ Changes may be needed to various components of enterprise such as business processes, functions, lines of business, organization structures, staff competencies, knowledge and skills, training, facilities, desktop tools, organization locations, data and information, application system and/or technology infrastructure.
		➤ Describing the future state allows stakeholders to understand the **potential value** that can be realized from a solution which can be used as part of the decision-making process regarding the change strategy.
		➤ For **predictable** approach, where outcome is predictable and where there are large number of possible changes that can increase value, the purpose of future state analysis is to gather sufficient information to make **best possible choices** amongst available options. This also requires to conduct **cost-benefit analysis** of the options.
		➤ For **adaptive** approach, where it is difficult to predict the value realized by a change, the future state may be defined by identification of appropriate **performance measures** and exploring multiple **options**.
3	Inputs	➤ **Business Requirements** – Problems, opportunities or constraints that the future state will address.

4	Elements	➤ **Business Goals and Objectives** – Business goals and objectives describe the ends that the organization is seeking to achieve.
		○ Goals and objectives can relate to changes that the organization wants to **accomplish**, or current conditions that it wants to **maintain**.
		○ Goals are **longer term, ongoing and qualitative statements** of a state or condition that the organization is seeking to establish and maintain. Certain examples of business goals are:
		  ▪ Create a new capability such a new product/service to gain competitive advantage
		  ▪ Improve revenue by increasing sales or reducing cost
		  ▪ Increase customer satisfaction
		  ▪ Increase employee satisfaction
		  ▪ Comply with new regulations

- Improve safety
- Reduce time to deliver a product or service

o As goals are analyzed, they are converted into more **descriptive, granular, specific objectives and linked to measures** that make it possible to assess if the objective can be achieved. A common test for assessing objectives is to ensure they are **SMART**:
- **Specific** – describing something that has observable outcome
- **Measurable** – Tracking and measuring the outcome
- **Achievable** – Testing the feasibility of effort
- **Relevant** – Aligning with enterprise's vision, mission and goals
- **Time-Bounded** – Define a timeframe that is consistent with the need

o **Example** – For an organization investing heavily in digital initiatives, **goal** can be to "increase traffic on online portal by enabling self-service" and **objective** can be to "increase traffic by 50% and reduce incident calls to call centre by 50% within 1 year".

➢ **Scope of Solution Space** – Decisions must be made about range of solutions that will be considered to meet the business goals and objectives. The scope of the solution space defines which kinds of options will be considered when investigating possible solutions, including changes to **organizational structure or culture, capabilities and processes, technology and infrastructure, policies, products or services** or even creating or changing **relationships** with organizations currently outside scope of enterprise.

o In case of multiple future states meeting the business needs, goals and objectives, it is necessary to determine which ones to be considered and that consideration will be dependent on **overall objectives of the enterprise, qualitative and quantitative value of each option, the time needed to achieve** each future state and the opportunity cost to enterprise.

➢ **Constraints** – Constraints describe aspects of current state and planned future state that may not be **changed** by the solution or mandatory elements of the design. Constraints may reflect any of the following:

- o budgetary restrictions,
- o time restrictions
- o technology & infrastructure
- o policies
- o limits on number of resources available
- o restrictions based on skills of team and stakeholders
- o a requirement that certain stakeholders may not be affected by implementation of the solution
- o compliance with regulations and
- o any other restriction

➢ **Organizational Structure and Culture** – The formal and informal working relationships that exist within the enterprise may need to change to facilitate the desired future state. In addition, changes to reporting lines can encourage teams to work more closely together to achieve goals and objectives.

➢ **Capabilities and Processes** – New or changed capabilities and processes will be needed to **deliver** new products and services, to **comply** with new regulations or to **improve** the performance of the enterprise.

➢ **Technology & Infrastructure** – There could be technical constraints imposed on the design of solution on basis of existing technology and infrastructure. **Technical constraints** may describe **restrictions** such as resource utilization, message size and timing, software size, maximum number of and size of files, records and data elements. It includes any **IT architecture standards** that must be followed.
- o A very good **example** of technical constraint could be "System should be able to show 50 transactions at a time". This describes the technical constraint on size of file retrieved by system from backend.

➢ **Policies** – Policies are a **common source of constraints** on a solution or on the solution space. Depending on approval levels, approach used to obtain approval, necessary criteria used to receive funding, business policies may mandate what solutions will be implemented.

➢ **Business Architecture** – Elements of future state must effectively support one another, and all contribute to meeting the business goals and objectives.

➢ **Internal Assets** – When analysing resources, business analysts examine the resources needed to maintain the current

		state and implement the change strategy and determine what resources can be used as part of desired future state.
		➢ **Identify Assumptions** – Assumptions must be identified and clearly understood, so that appropriate decisions can be made if the assumption later proves invalid. These assumptions need to be tested as early as possible so that a decision can be taken to either redirect or terminate an initiative. **Example** – Test environment must be available at start of the project.
		➢ **Potential Value** – Potential value must be evaluated to see if it is sufficient to justify a change. **The potential value of the future state is the net benefit of the solution after operating costs are accounted for**. It is possible that future state can show a decrease in value for certain stakeholder or at an enterprise level.
		    ○ When determining the future state, business analysts consider varying potential value from:
		        ▪ external opportunities revealed in assessing external influences
		        ▪ unknown strengths of new partners
		        ▪ new technologies or knowledge
		        ▪ potential loss of a competitor in a market and
		        ▪ mandated adoption of a change component
		    ○ Business case for the change should reflect the potential value in form of costs and benefits in case of no change is made.
		    ○ In most cases, future state will not address all of the **opportunities of improvement**. Those opportunities that are not addressed will be taken as **enhancements** in future analysis.
		    ○ In addition, the analysis should consider the acceptable level of **investment** to reach the future state. It helps to guide the selection of possible strategies.

5	Guidelines & Tools	➢ Current State Description – Provides the context within which the work needs to be completed. It is often used as a **starting point** for future state. ➢ Metrics and Key Performance Indicators (KPIs) – Key performance indicators and metrics will determine if the desired future start has been achieved ➢ Organizational Strategy – Describes the approach an organization will take to achieve the desired future state.

6	Techniques	
		➢ **Acceptance and Evaluation Criteria** – Used to identify what may make the future state acceptable or how options may be evaluated
		➢ **Balanced Scorecard** – Used to set targets for measuring the future state
		➢ **Benchmarking and Market Analysis** – Used to make decisions about future state business objectives
		➢ **Brainstorming** – Used to collaboratively come up with ideas for the future state.
		➢ **Business Capability Analysis** – Used to prioritize capability gaps in relation to value and risk
		➢ **Business Cases** – Used to capture the desired outcomes of the change initiative
		➢ **Business Model Canvas** – Used to plan strategy required to fulfil the value proposition to customers in desired future state
		➢ **Decision Analysis** – Used to compare different future state options and understand which one is the best?
		➢ **Decision Modelling** – Used to model complex decisions regarding future state options
		➢ **Financial Analysis** – Used to estimate potential financial returns to be delivered by a proposed future state
		➢ **Functional Decomposition** – Used to break down complex systems within the future state
		➢ **Interviews** – Used to talk to stakeholders to understand their future state they want to achieve
		➢ **Lessons Learned** – Used to determine which opportunities for improvement will be addressed and how the current state can be improved upon
		➢ **Metrics and Keys Performance Indicators (KPIs)** – Used to determine when the organization has succeeded in achieving business objectives
		➢ **Mind Mapping** – Used to develop ideas for the future state and understand relationships between them
		➢ **Organizational Modelling** – Used to describe the roles, responsibilities, reporting structures that would exist within the future state organization
		➢ **Process Modelling** – Used to describe how work would occur in the future state
		➢ **Prototyping** – Used to describe how work would occur in the future state

		➤ **Scope Modelling** – Used to define the boundaries of the enterprise in the future state ➤ **Survey or Questionnaire** – Used to understand stakeholder's desired future they want to achieve including needs they want to address and desired business objectives they want to meet ➤ **SWOT Analysis** – Used to evaluate strengths, weaknesses, opportunities and threats that may be exploited or mitigated by future state ➤ **Vendor Assessment** – Used to assess potential value provided by vendor solution options ➤ **Workshops** – Used to work with stakeholders to collaboratively describe the future state
7	Stakeholders	➤ Customers ➤ Domain Subject Matter Expert ➤ End User ➤ Implementation Subject Matter Expert ➤ Operational Support ➤ Project Manager ➤ Regulator ➤ Sponsor – **Authorizes** and ensures **funding** to support moving towards the future state. ➤ Supplier ➤ Tester
8	Output	➤ **Business Objectives** – Desired direction that the business wishes to pursue in order to achieve the future state. ➤ **Future State Description** – Future state description includes boundaries of the proposed, new, removed and modified components of the enterprise and the potential value expected from future state. ➤ **Potential Value** – The value that may be realized by implementing the proposed future state.

4.1.3 Task 3: Assess Risks

1	Purpose	To understand the undesirable consequences of internal and external forces on the enterprise during a transition to or once in the future state. An understanding of **potential impact** of those forces can be used to make a recommendation about a course of action.

2	Description	➢ Assessing risks includes **analyzing** and **managing** them. Risks might be related to the current state, a desired future state, a change itself, a change strategy, or any tasks being performed by the enterprise. ➢ The risks are analyzed for the possible **consequences** if the risk occurs, **impact** of those consequences, **likelihood** of the risk and **potential time frame** when the risk might occur. ➢ A **risk assessment** can include choosing to accept a risk if either the effort required to modify the risk or the level of risk outweighs the probable loss.
3	Inputs	➢ **Business Objectives** – Describing the desired direction needed to achieve the future state can be used to identify and discuss potential risks ➢ **Elicitation Results (confirmed)** – Understanding of what the various stakeholders perceive as risks to the realization of desired future state ➢ **Influences** – Factors inside the enterprise and factors outside of the enterprise which will impact the realization of the desired future state ➢ **Potential Value** – Describing the value to be realized by implementing the proposed future state provides a benchmark against which risks can be assessed. ➢ **Requirements (prioritized)** – Depending on their priority, requirements will influence the risks to be defined and understood as part of solution realization.
4	Elements	➢ **Unknowns** – When assessing a risk, there will be **uncertainty** in the likelihood of it occurring, and the **impact** if it does occur. Business analyst should be able to estimate the impact of unknown events if possible. o The lessons learned from **past changes** and **expert judgement** from stakeholders assist in guiding the team in deciding the impact and likelihood of risks for the current change. ➢ **Constraints, Assumptions and Dependencies** – If the constraint, assumption and dependency is related to an aspect of the change, it can be restated as a **risk** by identifying the event or condition and related consequences. ➢ **Negative Impact to Value** – Risks refer to uncertainties that may increase the chances of a negative impact of value. Business analysts clearly identify and express each risk and estimate its **likelihood** and **impact** to determine the level of

risk. Overall risk level can be quantified in **financial terms, or in amount of time, effort** or other measures.
- **Risk Tolerance** – It is the measure which shows the willingness to accept the uncertainty against value delivered out of it. There are three broad ways of describing attitude towards risk:
    - **Risk-aversion** – This refers to a state where risk is not acceptable. It includes avoiding the action that can cause risk or invest more to reduce the chance of risk.
    - **Neutrality** – Some levels of risk is acceptable, provided the course of action does not result in a loss even if the risks occur.
    - **Risk-seeking** – A state where risk is accepted against higher potential value.
- **Recommendation** – A change to current state of enterprise or to the strategy is required in order to manage risk. The recommendation usually falls into one of the following categories:
    - pursue the benefits of the change **regardless** of risk,
    - pursue the benefits of a change while investing in **reducing risk**,
    - seek out ways to **increase** the benefits of a change to **outweigh** a risk,
    - identify ways to **manage** and **optimize** opportunities,
    - do not pursue the **benefits** of the change.

5	Guidelines & Tools	<ul><li>Business Analysis Approach – Guides how the business analyst analyses risks.</li><li>Business policies – Define the limits within which decisions must be made.</li><li>Change Strategy – Provides the plan to transition from current state to the future state and achieve desired business outcomes.</li><li>Current State Description – Provides the context within which the work needs to be completed.</li><li>Future State Description – Determines risks associated with the future state</li><li>Identified Risks – Can be used as a starting point for more thorough risk assessment.</li><li>Stakeholder Engagement Approach – Understanding stakeholders helps identify and assess potential impact of internal and external forces.</li></ul>

6	Techniques	<ul><li>**Brainstorming** – Used to collaboratively identify potential risks for assessment</li><li>**Business Cases** – Used to capture risks associated with alternative change strategies.</li><li>**Decision Analysis** – Used to assess problems.</li><li>**Document Analysis** – Used to analyze existing documents for potential risks, constraints, assumptions and dependencies</li><li>**Financial Analysis** - Used to understand potential effect of risks on the financial value of solution.</li><li>**Interviews** – Used to understand what stakeholders might think be risks and related factors</li><li>**Lessons Learned** – Used as a foundation of past issues that might be risks</li><li>**Mind Mapping** – Used to identify and categorize potential risks and understand their relationships</li><li>**Risk Analysis and Management** – Used to identify and manage risks</li><li>**Root Cause Analysis** – Used to identify and address the underlying problem creating a risk</li><li>**Survey or Questionnaire** – Used to understand what stakeholders might think be risks</li><li>**Workshops** – Used to understand what stakeholders might think be risks</li></ul>
7	Stakeholders	<ul><li>Domain Subject Matter Expert</li><li>Implementation Subject Matter Expert</li><li>Operational Support</li><li>Project Manager</li><li>Regulator</li><li>Sponsor – Needs to understand risks as part of **authorizing** and **funding** change.</li><li>Supplier</li><li>Tester</li></ul>
8	Output	<ul><li>**Risk Analysis Results** – An understanding of the risks associated with achieving future state and the mitigation strategies which will be used to prevent them, reduce the impact of risk or reduce the likelihood of the risk occurring.</li></ul>

4.1.4 Task 4: Define Change Strategy

1	Purpose	To develop and assess alternative approaches to the change and then select the recommended approach.

2	Description	➤ Developing a change strategy is simpler when the **current** state and the **future** state are already defined because they provide some context of the change.
		➤ The change strategy clearly describes the nature of the change in terms of:
		    ○ context of the change
		    ○ identified alternative change strategies
		    ○ justification for why a change strategy is the best approach
		    ○ investment and resources required to work toward the future state
		    ○ how the enterprise will realize value after the solution is delivered
		    ○ key stakeholders in the change and
		    ○ transition states along the way
		➤ The change strategy might be presented as part of **business case, Statement of Work (SOW), an enterprise's strategic plan** or in other formats.
		➤ Various strategies are identified as part of defining change strategy and based on common decision pertaining to a situation, a particular strategy is selected and applied. This should be providing information on which parts of completed solution is going to provide value and needs a change.

3	Inputs	➤ **Current State Description** – Provides context about the current state and includes assessments of internal and external influences to the enterprise under consideration ➤ **Future State Description** – Provides context about the desired future state ➤ **Risk Analysis Results** – Describe identified risks and exposure of each risk ➤ **Stakeholder Engagement Approach** – Understanding stakeholder's communication and collaboration needs can help identify change related activities and should be included as part of change strategy.
4	Elements	➤ **Solution Scope** – The solution is the **outcome** of a change that allows an enterprise to satisfy a need. Best solution approach

is selected and justified as part of analysis of multiple solution options.
- The solution scope defines the **boundaries** of the solution and enables stakeholders to understand which new capabilities the change will deliver as well as how it will enable future state's goals. It also defines 'out of scope' solution components.
- The solution scope might be described in different ways, including the use of capabilities, technology, business rules, business decisions, data, processes, resources, knowledge and skills, models and descriptions of markets, functions, locations, networks, organizational structures, workflows, events, sequence, motivations or business logic.

➢ **Gap Analysis** – A gap analysis identifies the difference between **current** and **future** state using same technique. The gaps will be **addressed** in transition and future states.
- Gap analysis can help identify the gaps that prevent the enterprise from meeting **needs** and achieving **goals**. No change is required if no capability gaps are identified. In order to create the missing capabilities, a **change strategy** is needed.
- The capabilities analyzed in a gap analysis can include processes, functions, lines of business, organizational structures, staff competencies, knowledge and skills, training, facilities, location, data, application systems and technology infrastructure.

➢ **Enterprise Readiness Assessment** – The readiness assessment considers the enterprise's capacity to **make** the change, use and **sustain** the solution and **realize value** from the solution. The assessment also factors in:
- cultural readiness of the stakeholders
- operational readiness in making the change
- timeline from when the change is implemented to when value can be realized and
- resources available to support the change effort

➢ **Change Strategy** – A change strategy is a high level plan of key **activities** and **events** that will be used to transform the enterprise from current state to future state in form of sequence of projects or as improvement efforts.

- Several options are explored and described in enough detail to determine **feasibility**. Alternatives to those options are also identified through brainstorming and consulting subject matter experts. A preferred change strategy should be selected considering:
    - organizational readiness to make the change
    - major costs and investments needed
    - timelines to make the change
    - alignment to the business objectives
    - timelines for value realization and
    - opportunity costs of the change strategy
- The **options** considered and rejected are an important component of final strategy, providing stakeholders with an understanding of pros and cons of various approaches.
- If the **investment** for making the change is unbearable then the enterprise may skip this opportunity and look to invest in something else.
- The **potential value**, including the cost-benefit analysis is the key component to making a business case for the change.

➢ **Transition States and Release Planning** – Future state will need to be achieved over time rather than through a single change in many cases, meaning that enterprise will have to operate in one or more transition states.
- **Release planning** is concerned with determining which requirements to include in each release, phase or iteration of the change. **Business analysts** help **facilitate** release planning discussions to help stakeholders reach decisions.
- **Factors** guiding these decisions, are overall budget, deadlines or time constraints, resource constraints, training schedules and ability of the business to absorb the changes within a defined time frame by adhering to organizational constraints or policies.
- **Timing** of the implementation is also decided in order to cause minimal disruption to business activities and to ensure that all parties understand the impact of organization.

5	Guidelines & Tools	➢ Business Analysis Approach – Guides how the business analyst defines a change strategy

		➢ **Design Options** – Describe the various ways to satisfy the business needs. ➢ **Solution Recommendations** – Identifying the possible solutions which can be pursued in order to achieve the future state
6	Techniques	➢ **Balanced Scorecard** – Used to define the metrics that will be used to evaluate change strategy ➢ **Benchmarking and Market Analysis** – Used to make decisions about which change strategy is appropriate ➢ **Brainstorming** – Used to collaboratively come up with ideas for change strategies ➢ **Business Capability Analysis** – Used to prioritize capability gaps in relation to value and risk ➢ **Business Cases** – Used to capture information about the recommended change strategy that were assessed but not recommended ➢ **Business Model Canvas** – Used to define the changes needed to achieve potential value ➢ **Decision Analysis** – Used to compare different change strategies and choose an appropriate one ➢ **Estimation** – Used to determine timelines for activities within the change strategy ➢ **Financial Analysis** – Used to understand the potential value associated with change strategy and evaluate strategies against targets for return on investments. ➢ **Focus Groups** – Used to bring customers together to solicit their input on solution and change strategy ➢ **Functional Decomposition** – Used to break down components of the solution into parts ➢ **Interviews** – Used to talk to stakeholders to fully describe the solution scope and change scope and to understand their suggestions ➢ **Lessons Learned** – Used to understand what went wrong in past changes in order to improve change strategy ➢ **Mind Mapping** – Used to develop and explore ideas for change strategies ➢ **Organizational Modelling** – Used to describe organizational structure necessary for the change and is part of solution ➢ **Process Modelling** – Used to describe how work would occur in the solution scope or during the change. ➢ **Scope Modelling** – Used to define boundaries on solution scope and change scope descriptions.

		➤ **SWOT Analysis** – Used to make decision about which change strategy is appropriate ➤ **Vendor Assessment** – Used to determine whether any vendors are part of change strategy for implementation ➤ **Workshops** – Used to work with stakeholders to collaboratively develop change strategies
7	Stakeholders	➤ Customer ➤ Domain Subject Matter Expert ➤ End User ➤ Implementation Subject Matter Expert ➤ Operational Support ➤ Project Manager ➤ Regulator ➤ Sponsor – **Authorizes** and ensure **funding** for solution delivery and **champions** the change. ➤ Supplier ➤ Tester
8	Output	➤ **Change Strategy** – Approach that the organization will follow to guide change ➤ **Solution Scope** – Solution scope that will be achieved through execution of the change strategy

4.2 Glossary

- **Strategy** – A plan of action designed to achieve a long-term aim for an enterprise or for a function within enterprise.
- **Tactics** - Concrete steps or initiatives to achieve smaller steps or goals, part of a long-term plan. Strategy is a long-term vision and tactics represent short term actions.
- **PEST** – PEST analysis refers to an approach to widely analyze the Political, Economic, and Socio-Cultural and Technological changes in your business environment. PEST analysis looks at high level factors that has potential to influence a decision, market or any potential new business.
- **5 Forces Analysis** – The framework allows a business to identify and analyze the important forces that determine the profitability of an industry. Those 5 forces are – a) Competitive Rivalry, b) Threat of New Entrants, c) Threat of Substitutes, d) Bargaining Power of Buyers, e) Bargaining Power of Suppliers.
- **Business case** - It is a justification for investment. In other words, it is the evaluation of qualitative and quantifiable data to make a decision to move or not move forward with a particular solution to the proposed change. Comprises primarily of Cost, Benefit, Risk and Schedule aspects of the proposed change.
- **Assumptions** - Are factors that are believed to be true but have not been confirmed.
- **Constraints** - Are restrictions/ limitations on the delivery of the solution.
- **SWOT analysis** - Strengths, Weaknesses, Opportunities, and Threats Analysis is used to make decisions about which change strategy is appropriate.
- **Pilot testing** - It is a type of testing, which is conducted by a group of end users to ascertain the working of major functionality before its deployed on the production machine. Please note that doing a pilot is not the same as pilot testing.
- **Beta release** - Beta releases are early versions of the next major release. They follow the alpha releases.
- **Capability** - Capability refers to the potential and competency of an organization. A business analyst may evaluate an organization using capability centric view during strategy analysis

4.3 Exercises and Drills

Q1. Match the following tasks with their respective description:

1. Analyse current state	A. To determine the set of necessary conditions required to meet the business need
2. Define future state	B. To perform a gap analysis between the current and target state and then to select the best approach after having assessed various alternative approaches to the change
3. Assess risks	C. To understand the reason why a change is needed and what would be affected by the change
4. Define change strategy	D. To understand the uncertainties around the change and the consequences of such uncertainties

Q2. Match the following:

1. Business needs	A. Are the activities that an organization performs
2. Organizational structure	B. Suppliers, competitors, customers, technology, macroeconomic factors
3. External influencers	C. Are problems or opportunities or Compliance/ regulatory requirements
4. Organizational culture	D. Defines the formal relationships between people working in the organization
5. Capabilities and processes	E. Is the beliefs, values, norms shared by people working in an organization

Q3. Categorize the following under Goals and Objectives:

Long-term; Granular; Measurable; Qualitative; Time-bound; Descriptive; strategic in nature and high level

Goals	Objectives

Q4. Match the following risk tolerance attitudes with their description:

1. Risk aversion	A. Indicates that some level of risk is acceptable, provided it does not result in a loss even if the risk occurs
2. Neutrality	B. Indicates low tolerance to risks i.e. there is willingness to accept uncertainty
3. Risk seeking	C. Indicates that tolerance to risk is high i.e. there is unwillingness to accept much uncertainty

Q5. Complete the below crossword:

Across

2. High level plan of key activities and events that will be used to change the organization from current to future state

3. Defines the boundaries of the solution

4. Determines which requirements to include in each release, phase or iteration of the change

Down

1. Identifies the difference between current state and future state capabilities

Answers to Exercises & Drills

Answer 1: 1 – C, 2 – A, 3 – D, 4 – B

Answer 2: 1 – C, 2 – D, 3 – B, 4 – E, 5 – A

Answer 3:

Goals	Objectives
Long term	Time bound
Qualitative	Measurable (Quantifiable)
Strategic in nature and high-level	Granular and descriptive

Answer 4: 1 – C, 2 – A, 3 – B

Answer 5:

1. Gap Analysis
2. Change strategy
3. Solution scope
4. Release Planning

Chapter 5: Requirements Analysis and Design Definition

The Requirements Analysis and Design Definition knowledge area describes the tasks that business analysts perform to **structure** and **organize requirements** discovered during elicitation activities, **specify** and **model** requirements, **validate** and **verify** information, identify **solution options** that meet business needs, and estimate the **potential value** that could be realized for each solution option.

It covers the **incremental** and **iterative** activities ranging from the initial concept and exploration of the need through the transformation of those needs into a recommended solution.

Business analyst's role is instrumental in modelling needs, requirements, designs and solutions as well as conducting thorough analysis and communicating them with other stakeholders. The form, level of detail, and what is being modelled are all dependent on the **context**, **audience** and **purpose**.

Business analysts analyze the potential value of both requirements and designs. Solution options can be evaluated in order to recommend the best solution option that meets the need and brings the most value in collaboration with **implementation subject matter expert**.

Usage and application of core concepts within the context of Requirements Analysis and Design Definition are as follows:

- **Change** – Transform elicitation results into requirements and design in order to define the change.
- **Need** – analyze the need in order to recommend a solution that meets the needs.
- **Solution** – Define solution options and recommend the one that is most likely to address the need and has most value.
- **Stakeholder** – Tailor the requirements and designs so that they are understandable and usable by each stakeholder group.
- **Value** – Analyze and quantify the potential value of the solution options.
- **Context** – Model and describe the context in formats that are understandable and usable by all stakeholders.

5.1 Requirements Analysis and Design Definition Tasks

- ➤ Task 1: Specify and Model Requirements
- ➤ Task 2: Verify Requirements
- ➤ Task 3 : Validate Requirements
- ➤ Task 4 : Define Requirements Architecture
- ➤ Task 5: Define Solution Options
- ➤ Task 6: Analyze Potential Value and Recommend Solution

5.1.1 Task 1: Specify and Model Requirements

1	Purpose	To analyze, synthesize and refine elicitation results into requirements and designs.
2	Description	➤ This task describes the practices for **analyzing** elicitation results and **creating representations** of those results. ➤ The outputs are referred to as **requirements** when the focus of the specifying and modelling activity is on **understanding** the need and it is referred to as **designs** when the same activity is focused on **solution**. ➤ All business deliverables are referred to as requirements whereas the word 'design' is used specifically for technical designs. ➤ This task captures information about **attributes** or **metadata** about the requirements as well as the models used to represent the requirements.
3	Inputs	➤ **Elicitation Results (any state)** – Modelling can begin with any elicitation result and may lead to the need for more elicitation to clarify or expand upon requirements. **Elicitation and modelling may occur sequentially, iteratively or concurrently.**
4	Elements	➤ **Model Requirements** – A model is a descriptive way to convey information to a specific audience in order to support analysis, communication and understanding. o Models may also be used to confirm knowledge, identify information gaps and identify duplicate information. One or more of the following modelling formats are chosen:

- **Matrices** – A matrix is used in modelling a requirement or set of requirements that have a **complex but uniform structure** which can be broken down into elements that apply to every entry in table. Matrices are used for prioritizing requirements and recording requirements attributes and metadata. Data dictionaries, requirements traceability or gap analysis are the areas where matrices are applied.
- **Diagrams** – A diagram is a visual, often pictorial, representation of a requirement. It is used to depict **complexity** in a way that would be difficult to do with words. They can be used to define boundaries for business domains, to categorize and create hierarchies of items and to show components of objects such as data and their relationships.

○ Model categories can include:
  - **People and Roles** – Represent **organizations, roles and their relationships** within an enterprise and to a solution. Techniques include Organizational Modelling, Roles and Permissions Matrix and Stakeholder List, Map or Personas
  - **Rationale** – Represent **"why"** of a change. Techniques include Decision Modelling, Scope Modelling, Business Model Canvas, Root Cause Analysis and Business Rules Analysis.
  - **Activity Flow** – Represent a **sequence** of actions, events or a course that may be taken. Techniques include Process Modelling, Use Cases and Scenarios, and User Stories.
  - **Capability** – Focus on **features** or **functions** of an enterprise or a solution. Techniques include Business Capability Analysis, Functional Decomposition and Prototyping.
  - **Data and Information** – Represent the **characteristics** and the **exchange** the information within an enterprise or a solution. Techniques include Data Dictionary, Data Flow

			Diagrams, Data Modelling, Glossary, State Modelling, and Interface Analysis.
			➤ **Analyze Requirements** – Analysis of requirements is dependent on level of decomposition required, level of detail to be specified, knowledge of stakeholders, potential for misunderstanding and organizational standards. Information gathered is decomposed into components to further examine for:
			   o anything that must change to meet business need
			   o anything that should stay the same to meet the business need
			   o missing components
			   o unnecessary components,
			   o any constraints or assumptions that impact the components
			➤ **Represent Requirements and Attributes** – As part of specifying requirements, they can also be categorized according to the schema described in task Requirements Classification Schema. Categorizing requirements can help ensure the requirements are fully understood, a set of any type is complete, and that there is appropriate traceability between the types.
			➤ **Implement Appropriate Levels of Abstraction** – The level of requirement varies based on **type** of requirement and **audience** for the requirement. It is appropriate to produce different **viewpoints** of requirements to represent the same need for different stakeholders. Special care need to be taken to maintain the **meaning** and **intent** of the requirements over all representations.

5	Guidelines & Tools		➤ Modelling Notations/Standards – Allow requirements and designs to be precisely specified as is appropriate for the audience and purpose of the models. ➤ Modelling Tools – Software products that facilitate drawing and storing matrices and diagrams to represent requirements. ➤ Requirements Architecture – Requirements and interrelationships can be used to ensure models are complete and consistent. ➤ Requirements Life Cycle Management Tools – Software products that facilitate recording, organizing, storing and sharing requirements and designs.

		➤ Solution Scope – Boundaries of the solution provide boundaries for the requirements and design models.
6	Techniques	➤ **Acceptance and Evaluation Criteria** – Used to represent attributes of requirements. ➤ **Business Capability Analysis** – Represent features and functions of an enterprise ➤ **Business Model Canvas** – Describe the rationale for requirements ➤ **Business Rules Analysis** – Analyze business rules so that they can be specified and modelled alongside requirements. ➤ **Concept Modelling** – Used to define terms and relationships relevant to change and enterprise ➤ **Data Dictionary** – Used to record details about the data involved in the change ➤ **Data Flow Diagrams** – Used to visualize data flow requirements ➤ **Data Modelling** – Used to model requirements to show how data will be used to meet stakeholder information needs ➤ **Decision Modelling** – Used to represent the decisions in a model in order to show the elements of decision making required ➤ **Functional Decomposition** – Used to model requirements in order to identify constituent parts of an overall business function ➤ **Glossary** – Used to record the meaning of relevant business terms ➤ **Interface Analysis** – Used to model requirements in order to identify and validate inputs and outputs of the solution ➤ **Non-Functional Requirement Analysis** – Used to define and analyze the quality of service attributes ➤ **Organizational Modelling** – Used to allow business analysts to model the roles, responsibilities and communications within organization ➤ **Process Modelling** – Used to show the steps or activities that are performed in the organization ➤ **Prototyping** – Used to assist the stakeholders in visualizing the appearance and capabilities of a planned solution. ➤ **Roles and Permissions Matrix** – Used to specify and model requirements concerned with separation of duties among users and external interfaces ➤ **Root Cause Analysis** – Used to model root cause of a problem

		➢ **Scope Modelling** – Used to visually show a scope boundary
		➢ **Sequence Diagrams** – Used to specify and model requirements to show how processes operate and interact with one another
		➢ **Stakeholder List, Map or Personas** – Used to identify the stakeholders and their characteristics
		➢ **State Modelling** – Used to specify the different state of a part of the solution throughout a life cycle in terms of events
		➢ **Use Cases and Scenarios** – Used to model the desired behaviour of a solution by showing user interactions with the solution, to achieve a specific goal or accomplish a particular task.
		➢ **User Stories** – Used to specify requirements as a brief statement about what people do or need to do when using solution.
7	Stakeholders	➢ Any stakeholder – Business Analysts may choose to perform this task themselves and communicate the requirements to stakeholders for their review and approval.
8	Output	➢ **Requirements (specified and modelled)** – Any combination of requirements and designs in form of text, matrices and diagrams.

5.1.2 Task 2: Verify Requirements

1	Purpose	To ensure that requirements and designs specifications and models meet quality standards and are usable for the purpose they serve.
2	Description	➢ Verifying requirements ensures that the requirements and designs have been **defined** correctly and constitutes a **check** that they are ready for validation, and provides the information needed for further work to be performed.
		➢ A high-quality **specification** is a well written and easily understood by its intended **audience**. A high quality **model** represents **reality**.
		➢ The most important characteristic is **fitness for use** by the stakeholders who will use them for a particular purpose.
3	Inputs	➢ **Requirements (specified and modelled)** – Any requirement, design or set of those may be verified to ensure that text is well

4	Elements	structured, and that matrices and modelling notation are used correctly.
		
		 ➤ **Characteristics of Requirements and Designs Quality** – Acceptable quality requirements exhibit many of following characteristics:
		      o **Atomic** – Self-contained and capable of being understood independently
		      o **Complete** – Enough to guide further work and at appropriate level of detail for work to continue. The level of completeness required differs based on **perspective** or **methodology** and **point in life cycle** where the requirement is being examined or represented.
		      o **Consistent** – Aligned with the identified needs of the stakeholders and not conflicting with other requirements.
		      o **Concise** – Contains no extraneous and unnecessary content.
		      o **Feasible** – Reasonable and possible within the agreed upon risk, schedule, budget or considered feasible enough to investigate further through prototypes.
		      o **Unambiguous** – Requirement must be clearly stated in such a way to make it clear whether a solution does or does not meet the associated need.
		      o **Testable** – Able to verify the requirement has been fulfilled.
		      o **Prioritized** – Ranked, grouped or negotiated in terms of importance and value against all other requirements
		      o **Understandable** – Represented using common terminology of the audience
		
		 ➤ **Verification Activities** – Verification activities are typically performed iteratively throughout the requirement analysis process. They include:
		      o checking for **compliance** with organizational performance standards for business analysis, such as using right tools and methods,
		      o checking for **correct use** of modelling notations, templates or forms,
		      o checking for **completeness** within each model,
		      o **comparing** each model against other relevant models, checking for elements that are mentioned in one model

		but are missing in other models, and **verifying** that the elements are referenced consistently, ○ ensuring the terminology used in expressing the requirement is **understandable** to stakeholders and consistent with the used of those terms within the organization and **adding examples** where appropriate for clarification. ➤ **Checklists** – Checklists are used for **quality control** when **verifying** requirements and designs. ○ The purpose of checklist is to **ensure** that items determined to be important are included in the final requirements deliverables, or that **steps** required for the verification process are followed.
5	Guidelines & Tools	➤ Requirements Life Cycle Management Tools – Some tools have functionality to check for issues related to many of the characteristics such as atomic, unambiguous and prioritized.
6	Techniques	➤ **Acceptance and Evaluation Criteria** – Used to ensure that requirements are stated clearly enough to devise a set of tests that can prove that the requirements have been met. ➤ **Item Tracking** – Used to ensure that any problems or issues identified during verification are managed and resolved. ➤ **Metrics and Key Performance Indicators (KPIs)** – Used to identify how to evaluate the quality of requirements. ➤ **Reviews** – Used to inspect requirements documentation to identify requirements that are not of acceptable quality.
7	Stakeholders	➤ All Stakeholders – Business analyst in conjunction with the domain and implementation subject matter experts, has the primary responsibility for determining that the task has been completed.
8	Output	➤ **Requirements (verified)** – Set of requirements or designs that is of sufficient quality to be used as a basis for further work.

5.1.3 Task 3: Validate Requirements

1	Purpose	To ensure all the requirements and designs align to the business requirements and support the delivery of needed value.
2	Description	➤ Requirements validation is an **ongoing** process to ensure that stakeholder, solution and transition requirements align to the

		business requirements and that the designs satisfy the requirements.
		➤ The overall **goal** of implementing the requirements is to **achieve** the stakeholder's desired future state. Conflicts in needs, difference in views amongst stakeholders can be identified when requirements are validated.
3	Inputs	➤ **Requirements (specified and modelled)** – Validation applies to **any types** of requirements and designs. Validation activities may begin **before** requirements are completely **verified** but **cannot be completed** before requirements are completely verified.
4	Elements	➤ **Identify Assumptions** – If an organization is launching an unprecedented product/service, it may be necessary to make assumptions about **customer or stakeholder response** as there are no previous similar experiences on which to rely. o Stakeholders may be expecting certain benefits from requirements implementation. Such assumptions need to be recorded and detailed down so that associated **risks** can be managed. ➤ **Define Measurable Evaluation Criteria** – Business Analysts define the **evaluation criteria** that will be used to evaluate how successful the change has been after the solution is implemented. **Baseline metrics** might be established based on **current state**. Target metrics can be developed to reflect the achievement of the business objectives or some other measurement of success. ➤ **Evaluate Alignment with Solution Scope** – A requirement that does not deliver **benefit** to a stakeholder is a strong candidate for **elimination**. When requirements do not align, either the future state must be re-evaluated and the solution scope changed, or the requirement removed from the solution scope. Similarly, if a design cannot be validated to support a requirement, there might be a missing or misunderstood requirement, or the design must change.
5	Guidelines & Tools	➤ Business Objectives – Ensure the requirements deliver the desired business benefits. ➤ Future State Description – Helps to ensure the requirements that are part of the solution scope do help achieve the desired future state. ➤ Potential Value – Can be used a benchmark against which the value delivered by requirements can be assessed.

		➤ Solution scope – Ensures the requirements that provide benefit are within the scope of desired solution.
6	Techniques	➤ **Acceptance and Evaluation Criteria** – Used to define the quality metrics that must be met to achieve acceptance by a stakeholder. ➤ **Document Analysis** – Used to identify previously documented business needs in order to validate requirements. ➤ **Financial Analysis** – Used to define the financial benefits associated with requirements. ➤ **Item Tracking** – Used to ensure that any problems or issues identified during validation are managed and resolved. ➤ **Metrics and Key Performance Indicators (KPIs)** – Used to select appropriate performance measures for a solution, solution component or requirement ➤ **Reviews** – Used to confirm whether or not the stakeholder agrees that their needs are met. ➤ **Risk Analysis and Management** – Used to identify possible scenarios that would alter the benefit delivered by a requirement.
7	Stakeholders	➤ All Stakeholders – All project stakeholders are involved in this task. **Business analyst in conjunction with customer, end user and sponsors** has the primary responsibility for determining whether or not requirements are validated.
8	Output	➤ **Requirements (validated)** – Validated requirements and designs are those that can be demonstrated to deliver benefit to stakeholders and align with the business goals and objectives of the change. If a requirement or design cannot be validated, then it either doesn't benefit organization or doesn't fall within solution scope or both.

5.1.4 Task 4: Define Requirements Architecture

1	Purpose	To ensure that the requirements collectively support one another to fully achieve the objectives.

2	Description	➢ A requirements architecture fits the individual models and specifications together to ensure that all of the requirements form a **single whole** that supports the overall business objectives and produces a useful outcome.
		    o Requirements architecture is used to:
		        ▪ understand which **models** are appropriate for the domain, solution scope, and audience,
		        ▪ organize requirements into **structures** relevant to different stakeholders
		        ▪ illustrate how requirements and models **interact** with and **related** to each other and show how parts fit together into a meaningful whole,
		        ▪ ensure the requirements **work together** to achieve the overall objectives, and
		        ▪ make **trade-off decisions** about requirements while considering the overall objectives.
		    o Requirements architecture is focused on showing how elements work in harmony to support business requirements and to align the viewpoint of different stakeholders.
		    o **Traceability** is used to represent and manage these relationships. It proves that every requirement links back to an objective and shows how an objective was met.

3	Inputs	➢ **Information Management Approach** – Defines how the business analysis information will be stored and accessed. ➢ **Requirements (any state)** – Every requirement should be stated once and only once and incorporated into requirements architecture so that entire set may be evaluated for completeness. ➢ **Solution scope** – Must be considered to ensure the requirements architecture is aligned with solution boundaries.
4	Elements	➢ **Requirements Viewpoints and Views** – A viewpoint is a set of **conventions** that define how requirements will be represented,

how these **representations** will be organized and **related** to each other.
- Viewpoints provides templates for addressing the **concerns** of stakeholders. They include standards and guidelines for model types used for requirements, attributes that are included and used in models, model notations that are used and analytical approaches used to identify and maintain relationships among models.
- **No single viewpoint alone can form an entire architecture.** Each viewpoints has different model notations and techniques and each is important from solution perspective. Examples of viewpoints include:
  - Business process models,
  - Data models and information,
  - User interactions, including use cases and user experience,
  - Audit and security and
  - Business models.
- The actual requirements and design for a particular solution from a chosen viewpoint are referred to as a **view**. A collection of views makes up the **requirements architecture** for specific solution. The set of coordinated, complimentary views provides a basis for assessing the completeness and coherence of requirements.
- Overall, viewpoints tell what **information** they should provide for each stakeholder group to address their concerns, while views describe the actual requirements and designs that are produced.

➢ **Template Architectures** – An **architectural framework** is a collection of viewpoints that is standard across an industry, sector or organization. They can be treated as **predefined templates**. The framework can be populated with domain-specific information to form a collection of views if it is having accurate information populated in it.

➢ **Completeness** – An architecture helps ensure that a set of requirements is **complete**, **cohesive** and tells a **full story**. No requirements should be missing from the set, inconsistent with others, or contradictory to one another. All the **dependencies** between requirements need to be considered.

		<ul><li>○ Structuring requirements according to **viewpoints** ensure this completeness. Iterations of elicitation, specification and analysis activities can help identify gaps.</li></ul><ul><li>➢ **Relate and Verify Requirements Relationships** – Each relationship between requirements is examined by tracing requirements and to ensure that the relationships satisfy the following quality criteria:<ul><li>○ **Defined** – There is a relationship and the type is described.</li><li>○ **Necessary** – The relationship is necessary for understanding the requirements holistically.</li><li>○ **Correct** – Elements do not have the relationship described.</li><li>○ **Unambiguous** – There are no relationships that link elements I two different and conflicting ways.</li><li>○ **Consistent** – Relationships are described in the same way using the standard descriptions as defined in the viewpoints.</li></ul></li><li>➢ **Business Analysis Information Architecture** – The information architecture is a **component** of the requirements architecture because it describes **how** all of the business analysis information for a change relates.<ul><li>○ It defines **relationships** for types of information such as requirements, designs, types of models and elicitation results.</li><li>○ Understanding this type if information structure helps to ensure that the full set of requirements is **complete** by verifying the relationships are complete.</li></ul></li></ul>
5	Guidelines & Tools	<ul><li>➢ **Architecture Management Software** – Helps to manage the volume, complexity and versions of the relationships within the requirements architecture.</li><li>➢ **Legal / Regulatory Information** – Describes legislative rules or regulations that must be followed. They may impact requirements architecture or its outputs.</li><li>➢ **Methodologies and Frameworks** – A predetermined set of models and relationships between them to be used to represent different viewpoints.</li></ul>
6	Techniques	<ul><li>➢ **Data Modelling** – Describe the requirements structure as it relates to data.</li></ul>

		➤ **Functional Decomposition** – Used to break down an organizational unit, product scope into its component parts. ➤ **Interviews** – Used to define the requirements structure collaboratively ➤ **Organizational Modelling** – Used to understand the various organizational units, stakeholders and their relationships which might help define relevant viewpoints. ➤ **Scope Modelling** – Used to identify the elements and boundaries of the requirements architecture. ➤ **Workshops** – Used to define the requirements structure collaboratively.
7	Stakeholders	➤ Domain Subject Matter Expert, Implementation Subject Matter Expert, Project Manager, Sponsor, Tester – May assist in defining and confirming the architecture for requirements. ➤ Any stakeholder
8	Output	➤ **Requirements Architecture** – Requirements and interrelationships among them, as well as any contextual information that is recorded.

5.1.5 Task 5: Define Design Options

1	Purpose	To define the solution approach, identify opportunities to improve the business, allocate requirements across solution components, and represent design options that achieve the desired future state.
2	Description	➤ When designing a solution, there may be one or more **design options** identified which represent a way to satisfy a set of requirements and would be **tactical** rather than strategic. ➤ Trade-offs are made among design alternatives and the effect of them on delivery of value to stakeholders need to be assessed.
3	Inputs	➤ **Change Strategy** – Describes the approach that will be followed to transition to the future state. This may have some impact on design decisions in terms of what is feasible or possible. ➤ **Requirements (validated, prioritized)** – Only validated requirements are considered in design options. Requirements with highest priorities might deserve more weight in choosing solution components to best meet them as compared to lower priority requirements.

		➤ **Requirements Architecture** – A full set of requirements along with relationships is used in defining design options that can address the holistic set of requirements.
4	Elements	➤ **Define Solution Approaches** – The solution approach describes whether solution components will be created or purchased, or some combination of both. Proposed integration of components is considered in all the below design options. Solution approaches include: 　o **Create** – Solution components are newly constructed, assembled together or developed by experts as a response to the requirements set. This option includes **modifying** an existing solution. 　o **Purchase** – Solution components are selected from a set of offerings that fulfil requirements. These offerings are usually products or services **owned** and **maintained** by third parties. It is also referred to as **COTS** (Commercial off the shelf) solution. 　o **Combination of both** – Design options may include a combination of both creation and purchase of components. ➤ **Identify Improvement Opportunities** – As part of the process, a number of opportunities to improve the operation of the business may occur and are compared. Some common examples are: 　o **Increase Efficiencies** – Automate or simplify the work people perform which can increase consistency of behaviour thus reducing the likelihood of repetitive tasks by different stakeholders. 　o **Increase Access To Information** – Open up the gates for accessing information to staff who interact with customers and thus reducing need of specialists. 　o **Identify Additional Capabilities** – Highlight capabilities that have the potential to provide future value and can be supported by the solution. ➤ **Requirements Allocation** – Requirements allocation is the process of **assigning** requirements to solution components and releases to best achieve the **objectives** to maximize the **value** and **benefits** as well as to minimize **costs**. 　o The value of solution might vary depending on how requirements are implemented and when solution becomes **available** to stakeholders.

			<ul><li>Requirements allocation typically starts when a **solution approach** has been determined and continues until all requirements are allocated which is throughout design and implementation of a solution.</li></ul><ul><li>**Describe Design Options** – Design options are investigated and developed while considering the **desired future state**, and in order to ensure the design option is valid. **Solution performance measures** are defined for each design option. Design elements make up design components which contribute to design option. Design elements may describe:<ul><li>business policies and business rules,</li><li>business processes to be performed and managed,</li><li>people who operate and maintain the solution,</li><li>operational business decisions to be made,</li><li>software applications used in solution, and</li><li>organizational structures</li></ul></li></ul>
5	Guidelines & Tools		<ul><li>**Existing Solutions** – Existing products or services that are considered as a component of a design option.</li><li>**Future State Description** – Identifies desired state of the enterprise that design options will be part of and helps to ensure design options are viable.</li><li>**Requirements (traced)** – Define the design options that best fulfil known requirements</li><li>**Solution Scope** – Defines the boundaries when selecting viable design options.</li></ul>
6	Techniques		<ul><li>**Benchmarking and Market Analysis** – Used to identify and analyze existing solutions and market trends.</li><li>**Brainstorming** – Used to help identify improvement opportunities and design options.</li><li>**Document Analysis** – Used to provide information needed to describe design options and elements.</li><li>**Interviews** – Used to help identify improvement opportunities and design options.</li><li>**Lessons Learned** – Used to help identify improvement opportunities.</li><li>**Mind Mapping** – Used to identify and explore possible design options.</li><li>**Root Cause Analysis** – Used to understand the underlying cause of the problems being addressed in the change to propose solutions to address them.</li></ul>

		➢ **Survey or Questionnaire** – Used to help identify improvement opportunities and design options. ➢ **Vendor Assessment** – Used to couple the assessment of a third party solution with an assessment of the vendor to ensure the solution is viable. ➢ **Workshops** – Used to help identify improvement opportunities and design options.
7	Stakeholders	➢ Domain Subject Matter Expert – Provides the expertise within the business to provide **input** and **feedback** for the potential benefits of a solution. ➢ Implementation Subject Matter Expert - Provides inputs about the **constraints** of a solution and its **costs**. ➢ Operational Support ➢ Project Manager ➢ Supplier – Provides information on **functionality** associated with a particular design option.
8	Output	➢ **Design Options** – Describe various ways to satisfy one or more needs in a context. They may include solution approach, improvement opportunities and the components that define the option.

5.1.6 Task 6: Analyze Potential Value and Recommend Solution

1	Purpose	To estimate the potential value for each design option and to establish which one is most appropriate to meet the enterprise's requirements.
2	Description	➢ This task describes how to **estimate** and **model** the potential value delivered by a set of requirements, design, or design options. ➢ **Potential value** is analyzed many times over course of change. This includes consideration that there is uncertainty in the estimates. The analysis may be a planned event or it may be triggered by a modification to the context or scope of the change. ➢ Design options are evaluated by comparing the potential value of each option to other options. There may be no best option to recommend or there may be a clear best choice. ➢ In some case, this means to develop **proof of concept** and measure performance whereas in some case, all proposed designs may be **rejected** and more analysis may be needed to

		define a suitable design. At times, best recommendation is to **do nothing**.
3	Inputs	➢ **Potential Value** – Can be used as a benchmark against which the value delivered by a design can be evaluated. ➢ **Design Options** – Need to be evaluated and compared to one another to recommend one option for the solution.

4	Elements	➢ **Expected Benefits** – Expected benefits describe the **positive value** that a solution is intended to deliver to stakeholders. Value can be any positive outcome such as benefits, reduced risk, compliance with business policies or an improved user experience.
		  ○ Benefits are determined based on the **analysis** of the benefit that stakeholders **desire** and the benefit that is possible to **attain**.
		  ○ The total expected benefit is the net benefit of **all the requirements** a particular design option addresses. They are realized over a **period of time**.
		➢ **Expected Costs** – Expected costs include any potential **negative value** associated with a solution, including the cost to acquire the solution, any negative impacts it may have on stakeholders and the cost to maintain it over time.
		  ○ Expected costs can include timeline, effort, operating costs, purchase / implementation costs, maintenance costs, physical resources, information resources and human resources.
		  ○ **Opportunity cost** is considered when estimating the expected cost of change. Opportunity cost of any design option is equal to the value of the best alternative not selected.
		➢ **Determine Value** – The potential value of a solution to a stakeholder is based on the **benefits** delivered by that solution and the associated **costs**. Value can be positive or negative.
		  ○ Business analysts consider **potential value** from the points of view of stakeholders. Value to the **enterprise** is more heavily weighted than value for any individual group. An overall positive increase in value for the enterprise as a whole justifies proceeding with the change.
		  ○ Potential value is **uncertain value**. Many changes are proposed in terms of intangible or uncertain benefits, while costs are described as tangible, absolute and

might grow. Complete estimate is defined by comparing tangible and intangible costs alongside the tangible and intangible benefits. This should consider the **degree of uncertainty** pertaining at the time the estimates are made.

- **Assess Design Options and Recommend Solution** – Each design option is assessed based on the potential value it is expected to deliver.
    - There could be a need to re-evaluate design options to include better understanding of **cost of implementation** and to determine best **cost-to-benefit** ratio.
    - The best option(s) deemed to be the most **valuable** solution to address the need is deemed. In many cases, best recommendation could be to do nothing if none of the design options are worthwhile. Various factors taken into consideration to assess each design option are:
        - **Available Resources** – Limitations regarding amount of requirements that can be implemented based on the allocated resources.
        - **Constraints on Solution** – Regulatory requirements or business decisions may require that certain requirements be handled manually or automatically, or that certain requirements be prioritized above all others.
        - **Dependencies between Requirements** – Some requirements could have limited value but are needed to be delivered as they support high level requirements.

5	Guidelines & Tools	
		➤ Business Objectives – Used to calculate expected benefit
		➤ Current State Description – Provides the context within which the work needs to be completed and can be used to identify and quantify the value to be delivered from a potential solution.
		➤ Future State Description – Describes the desired future state that solution will be part of in order to ensure design options are appropriate.
		➤ Risk Analysis Results – Potential value of design options includes assessment of the level of risk associated with design options

		➢ Solution Scope – Defines the scope of the solution that is being delivered
6	Techniques	➢ **Acceptance and Evaluation Criteria** – Used to express requirements in form of acceptance criteria when assessing proposed solutions and determining whether a solution meets the defined business needs. ➢ **Backlog Management** – Used to sequence the potential value. ➢ **Brainstorming** – Used to identify potential benefits of requirements in collaborative manner. ➢ **Business Cases** – Used to assess recommendations against business goals and objectives. ➢ **Business Model Canvas** – Used as a tool to help understand strategy and initiatives. ➢ **Decision Analysis** – Used to support assessment and ranking of design options. ➢ **Estimation** – Used to forecast the costs and efforts of meeting the requirements as a step towards estimating the value. ➢ **Financial Analysis** – Used to evaluate the financial return of different options and choose best possible return on investment. ➢ **Focus Groups** – Used to get stakeholder input on which design options best meet the requirements. ➢ **Interviews** – Used to get stakeholder input on which design options meet the requirements. ➢ **Metric and Key Performance Indicators (KPIs)** – Used to create and evaluate the measurements used in defining value. ➢ **Risk Analysis and Management** – Used to identify and manage the risks that could affect the potential value of requirements. ➢ **Survey or Questionnaire** – Used to get stakeholder input on which design options best meet the requirements ➢ **SWOT Analysis** – Used to identify areas of strengths and weakness that will impact the solution. ➢ **Workshops** – Used to get stakeholder input on which design options best meet the requirements
7	Stakeholders	➢ Customer – Represents the market segments affected by the requirements and solutions and will be involved in **analyzing the benefits and costs** for the same. ➢ Domain Subject Matter Expert ➢ End User – Provides an **insight** into potential value of change. ➢ Implementation Subject Matter Expert ➢ Project Manager

8	Output	<ul><li>Regulator</li><li>Sponsor – **Approves** the expenditure of resources to purchase or develop a solution and approve its final recommendation.</li><li>**Solution Recommendation** – Identifies the suggested, most appropriate solution based on an evaluation of all defined design options. The recommended solution should maximize the value provided to the enterprise.</li></ul>

5.2 Glossary

- **Opportunity Cost** – Opportunity costs are alternative results that might have been achieved if the resources, time and funds devoted to one design option had been allocated to another design option. It refers to the benefits that could have been achieved by selecting an alternative change strategy.
- **COTS** – Commercial off the Shelf. COTS refer to the solution components purchased from market or shared from a partner to achieve the goal within solution space.
- **Validation** - Testing against the business requirements. Always done against a business problem or opportunity. User Acceptance Test is about validating the solution.
- **Verification** - Testing to check the quality of the documented requirements. Attempts to improve the quality of the requirements and the solution.
- **Design** - They represent a way of satisfying the set of requirements. Design includes the details of requirements
- **Requirements allocation** - The process of assigning requirements to solution components and releases in order to best achieve the business objectives.
- **Viewpoints** - This describes what information should be provided to each stakeholder group
- **Release planning** - Allocation of requirements to phases and iterations and the plan to achieve the business goals considering priorities

5.3 Exercises and Drills

Q1. Match the following tasks with their respective description:

1. Specify and model requirements	A. Structures all requirements and designs so that they work effectively as a cohesive whole to fully achieve the business objectives
2. Verify requirements	B. Identifies, explores and describes different possible ways of meeting the business need
3. Validate requirements	C. ensures that requirements and design specifications and models meet the quality standards
4. Define requirements architecture	D. Estimates the potential value of each design option and establishes the most appropriate one meeting the enterprise's requirements
5. Define solution options	E. Describes a set of requirements and design in detail
6. Analyze potential value and recommend solution	F. Ensures that a set of requirements and designs delivers business value and supports organizations goals and objectives

Q2. Complete the below crossword:

Across
1. The output is referred to as _____ when the focus of specifying and modelling activity is on understanding the business need
2. The output is referred to as _____ when the focus of specifying and modelling activity is on a solution

Down
3. Metadata about requirements are called _____.
4. A descriptive and visual way to convey information is called a _____.

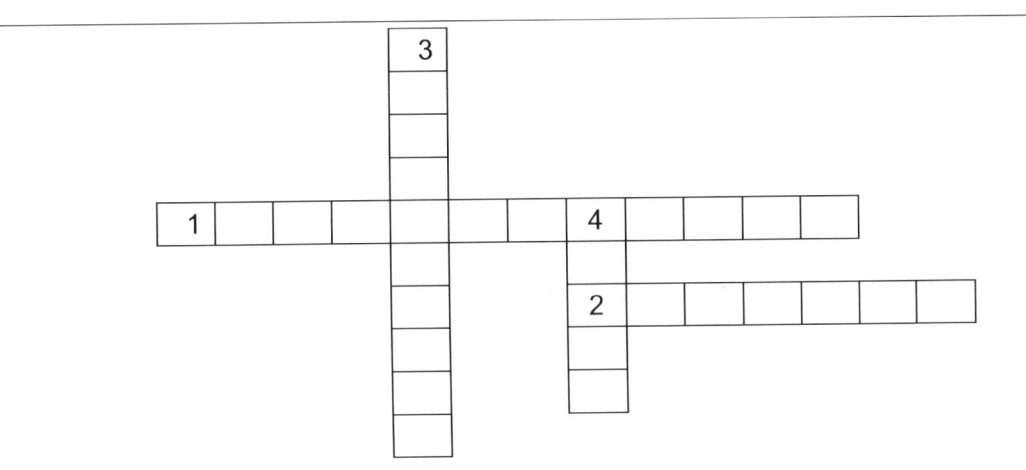

Q3. Categorize the following under Model formats and categories:

Rationale, Activity flow, Matrices, Capability, Diagrams, Data & Information, People & Roles

Model categories	Model formats

Q4. Match the following requirements characteristics with their description:

1. Atomic	A. Requirements are possible, reasonable to implement given all assumptions and constraints
2. Concise	B. All relevant requirements are represented and are not lacking any information
3. Testable	C. Requirements are self-contained and are capable of being understood independently of other requirements
4. Feasible	D. Requirements are without contradiction and the level of detail for all requirements is the same

5. Complete	E. There is a way to prove that each requirement has been met
6. Unambiguous	F. Contains no extraneous and unnecessary content
7. Consistent	G. Requirements must not be open to multiple interpretations

Q5. Categorize the following under the right group:

Doing things right, Doing right things, Checks quality standards, Ensures right stakeholder requirements are captured

Verification	Validation

Q6. Complete the crossword:

Across

2. A collection of views makes up the _____ for a solution

3. The actual requirements and designs for a solution from a chosen viewpoint

Down

1. A set of conventions that define how requirements will be represented, organized and related

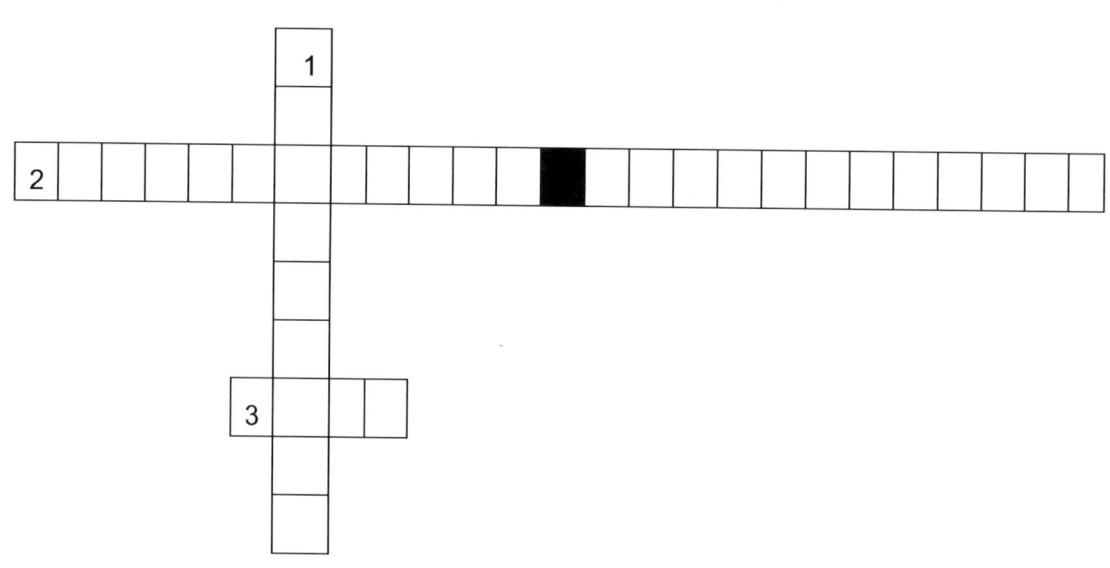

Answers to Exercises & Drills

Answer 1: 1 – E, 2 – C, 3 – F, 4 – A, 5 – B, 6 – D

Answer 2:

1. Requirements
2. Designs
3. Attributes
4. Model

Answer 3:

Model categories	Model formats
Rationale	Diagrams
Data & information	Matrices
Activity flow	
Capability	
People & Roles	

Answer 4:

1 – C, 2 – F, 3 – E, 4 – A, 5 – B, 6 – G, 7 - D

Answer 5:

Verification	Validation
Doing things right	Doing right things
Checks quality standards	Ensures right stakeholder requirements are captured

Answer 6:

1. Viewpoint
2. Requirements Architecture
3. View

Chapter 6: Solution Evaluation

The Solution Evaluation knowledge area describes the tasks that business analysts perform to **assess the performance** and **value delivered** by the solution in use by the enterprise, and to recommend removal of **barriers** or **constraints** that prevent the full realization of the value.

Solution Evaluation knowledge area focuses on an **existing solution**. This could be only be a partial solution, but the solution or solution component has already been **implemented** and is **operating** in some form.

Solution Evaluation tasks that support the realization of benefits may occur before a change is initiated, while current value is assessed after a solution has been implemented.

Solution Evaluation tasks can be performed on solution components such as:

- **Prototypes or Proofs of Concept** – Working but limited versions of a solution that demonstrates value.
- **Pilot or Beta Releases** – Limited implementations or versions of a solution used in order to work through problems and understand how well it actually delivers value before fully releasing the solution.
- **Operational Releases** – Full versions of a partial or completed solution used to achieve business objectives, execute a process, or fulfil a desired outcome.

Solution Evaluation describes the tasks that analyze the actual value being delivered, identifies limitations preventing the value to be realized and make recommendations to increase the value of the solution. It focuses generally on a **component of an enterprise** rather than entire enterprise.

Usage and application of core concepts within the context of Requirements Analysis and Design Definition are as follows:

- **Change** – Recommend a change to either a solution or the enterprise in order to realize the potential value of the solution.
- **Need** – Evaluate how a solution is fulfilling the need.
- **Solution** – Assess the performance of the solution, examine if it is delivering the potential value and analyze why value may not be realized by the solution.
- **Stakeholder** – Elicit information from the stakeholders about solution performance and value delivery.
- **Value** – Determine if the solution is delivering the potential value and examine why value may not be being realized.

- **Context** – Consider the context in determining the solution performance measures and any limitations within the context that may prohibit the value from being realized.

6.1 Solution Evaluation Tasks

➢ *Task 1: Measure Solution Performance*
➢ *Task 2 : Analyze Performance Measures*
➢ *Task 3 : Assess Solution Limitations*
➢ *Task 4 : Assess Enterprise Limitations*
➢ *Task 5: Recommend Actions to Increase Solution Value*

6.1.1 Task 1: Measure Solution Performance

1	Purpose	To define the performance measures and use the data collected to evaluate the effectiveness of a solution in relation to the value it brings.
2	Description	➢ Performance measures determine the **value** of a newly deployed or existing solution. ➢ The measures used depend on the **solution** itself, the **context** and how the organization defines **value**. ➢ Performance may be assessed through **key performance indicators** aligned with enterprise measures, goals and objectives for a project, process performance targets, or tests for a software application.
3	Inputs	➢ **Business Objectives** – The measurable results that the enterprise wants to achieve. Provides a benchmark against which solution performance can be assessed. ➢ **Implemented Solution (external)** – A solution that exists in some form.
4	Elements	➢ **Define Solution Performance Measures** – Business analysts ensure that any existing performance measures are **accurate**, **relevant** and elicit any additional performance measures identified by stakeholders. The type and nature of measurements are considered when choosing the **elicitation method**.

		<ul><li>Business goals, objectives and business processes, influence by third parties such as solution vendors, government bodies or other regulatory organizations are common sources of measures.</li><li>Solution measures may be **quantitative** (numerical, countable) or **qualitative** (can include attitudes, perceptions) or **both**, depending on value being measured.</li></ul>➤ **Validate Performance Measures** – Validating performance measures helps to **ensure** that the assessment of solution performance is useful. Business analysts validate performance measures and any influencing criteria with **stakeholders**. Decisions about which **measures** are used to evaluate solution performance often reside with the **sponsor**, but may be made by any stakeholder with decision-making authority. ➤ **Collect Performance Measures** – Business analyst consider following factors when collecting performance measures:<ul><li>**Volume or Sample Size** – A volume or sample size appropriate to the initiative is selected. Small sample size may lead to inaccurate conclusions whereas large sample size may not be practical to obtain.</li><li>**Frequency or Timing** – This may have an effect on the outcome</li><li>**Currency** – Most recent measurement represent correctly than older data.</li></ul>
5	Guidelines & Tools	➤ Change Strategy – Change strategy in use or used to implement the potential value. ➤ Future State Description – Boundaries of proposed new, removed or modified components of enterprise along with potential value expected from future state. ➤ Requirements (validated) – A set of requirements that have been analyzed and appraised to determine their value. ➤ Solution Scope – The solution boundaries to measure and evaluate.
6	Techniques	➤ **Acceptance and Evaluation Criteria** – Used to define acceptable solution performance. ➤ **Benchmarking and Market Analysis** – Used to define measures and their acceptable levels. ➤ **Business Cases** – Used to define business objectives and performance measures for a proposed solution.

		➤ **Data Mining** – Used to collect and analyze large amounts of data regarding solution performance.
		➤ **Decision Analysis** – Used to assist stakeholders in deciding on suitable ways to measure solution performance and acceptable levels of performance.
		➤ **Focus Groups** – Used to provide subjective assessments, insights and impressions of a solution's performance.
		➤ **Metrics and Key Performance Indicators (KPIs)** – Used to measure solution performance.
		➤ **Non-Functional Requirements Analysis** – Used to define expected characteristics of a solution.
		➤ **Observation** – Used either to provide feedback on perceptions of solution performance or to reconcile contradictory results.
		➤ **Prototyping** – Used to simulate a new solution so that performance measures can be determined and collected.
		➤ **Survey or Questionnaire** – Used to gather opinions and attitudes about solution performance.
		➤ **Use Cases and Scenarios** – Used to define the expected outcomes of a solution.
		➤ **Vendor Assessment** – Used to assess which of the vendor's performance measures should be included in the solution's performance assessment.
7	Stakeholders	➤ Customer
		➤ Domain Subject Matter Expert
		➤ End User – Contributes to the actual value realized by the solution in terms of solution performance. They may be consulted to provide reviews and feedback on areas such as workload and job satisfaction.
		➤ Project Manager
		➤ Sponsor
		➤ Regulator
8	Output	➤ **Solution Performance Measures** – Measures that provide information on how well the solution is performing or potentially could perform.

6.1.2 Task 2: Analyze Performance Measures

1	Purpose	To provide insights into the performance of a solution in relation to the value it brings.

2	Description	➤ The measures collected in the task 'Measure Solution Performance' require interpretation and synthesis to derive **meaning** and to have **actionable items**. Performance measures rarely trigger a decision about the **value** of a solution. ➤ In order to conduct meaningful analysis, business analysts require an understanding of potential value as well as need to consider variables such as goals and objectives of enterprise, key performance indicators (KPIs), the level of risk of the solution, the risk tolerance of stakeholders and enterprise.
3	Inputs	➤ **Potential Value** – Describes the value that may be realized by implementing the proposed future state. It can be used as a benchmark against which solution performance can be evaluated. ➤ **Solution Performance Measures** – Measures and provides information on how well the solution is performing or potentially could perform.
4	Elements	➤ **Solution Performance versus Desired Value** – A solution might be providing high performance but less value is generated whereas there could be some solutions having low performance but generating potential great value. In such cases, other measurements are collected and a **solution risk** is raised. ➤ **Risks** – New risks may be uncovered towards solution performance and to the enterprise. ➤ **Trends** – Time period is considered to guard against **anomalies** and **skewed trends**. Accurate depiction of solution performance to make decision can be provided by analyzing large enough sample size. ➤ **Accuracy** – The accuracy of performance measures is essential to the validity of their analysis. To be considered accurate and reliable, results of performance measures should be reproducible and repeatable. ➤ **Performance Variances** – Difference between **expected** and **actual** performance represents a **variance** that is considered when analyzing solution performance. **Root cause analysis** may be necessary to determine the underlying causes of significant variances within a solution.
5	Guidelines & Tools	➤ Change Strategy – Change strategy in use or used to implement the potential value. ➤ Future State Description – Boundaries of proposed new, removed or modified components of enterprise along with potential value expected from future state.

		➤ Risk Analysis Results – Overall level of risk and the planned approach to modifying individual risks. ➤ Solution Scope – The solution boundaries to measure and evaluate.
6	Techniques	➤ **Acceptance and Evaluation Criteria** – Used to define the acceptable solution performance through acceptance criteria. The degree of variance from these criteria will guide the analysis of that performance. ➤ **Benchmarking and Market Analysis** – Used to observe the results of other organizations employing similar solutions. ➤ **Data Mining** – Used to collect data regarding performance, trends and variances from expected performance levels and understand patterns and meaning in that data. ➤ **Interviews** – Used to determine expected value of a solution and its perceived performance from a group ➤ **Metrics and Key Performance Indicators (KPIs)** – Used to analyze solution performance on judging how well a solution contributes to achieving goals. ➤ **Observation** – Used to observe a solution in action. ➤ **Risk Analysis and Management** – Used to identify, analyze, develop plans to modify risks and to manage risks on an ongoing basis. ➤ **Root Cause Analysis** – Used to determine underlying cause of performance variance. ➤ **Survey or Questionnaire** – Used to determine expected value of solution and its perceived performance.
7	Stakeholders	➤ Domain Subject Matter Expert ➤ Project Manager ➤ Sponsor – Can identify **risks**, provide **insights** into data and potential value of a solution. Makes **decision** about significance of expected versus actual solution performance.
8	Output	➤ **Solution Performance Analysis** – Results of analysis of measurements collected and recommendations to solve performance gaps and leverage opportunities to improve value.

6.1.3 Task 3: Assess Solution Limitations

1	Purpose	To determine the factors internal to the solution that restrict the full realization of value.

2	Description	<ul><li>Assessing solution limitations identifies the **root causes** for under-performing and ineffective solutions and solution components.</li><li>Assess Solution Limitations is closely **linked** to the task **Assess Enterprise Limitations**.</li><li>These tasks may be performed concurrently, and internal and external factors are to be identified which will limit value. Assessment of such factors internal to the solution is focused via this task.</li><li>Assessment is performed at **any time** during solution life cycle. It may occur on a solution component during its development, on a completed solution prior to full implementation or on an existing solution that is currently working within an organization.</li></ul>
3	Inputs	<ul><li>**Implemented Solution (external)** – A solution that exists. The solution should be in some form, may not be in operational use, or it may be a prototype.</li><li>**Solution Performance Analysis** – Results of the analysis of measurements collected and recommendations to solve for performance gaps and leverage opportunities to improve value.</li></ul>
4	Elements	<ul><li>**Identify Internal Solution Component Dependencies** – Solutions often have internal dependencies that limit the performance of the entire solution to the performance of least effective component. Business Analysts identify dependencies about solution components and determine if there is anything about those dependencies that limit solution performance and value realization.</li><li>**Investigate Solution Problems** – **Problem analysis** is conducted to identify the source of problem if the solution is consistently producing outputs which are not effective.<ul><li>Problems are identified in a solution or solution component by examining instances where the outputs are below an **acceptable level of quality** or where the **potential value** is not being realized. Problems may be indicated by an inability to meet a stated goal, objective, or requirement or may be failure to realize a benefit that was projected to increase solution value.</li></ul></li><li>**Impact Assessment** – All the identified problems are reviewed in order to assess the **effect** they have on the operation of organization or the ability of the solution to **deliver** its potential value.</li></ul>

			o Above action requires determining the **severity** of the problem, the probability of **re-occurrence** of the problem, the **impact** on the business operations and the **capacity** of the business to absorb the impact. o Business analysts identify which problems must be resolved, mitigated through actions, or which can be accepted as well as assess risks to the solution and potential limitations of the solution. This risk assessment is specific to the solution and its limitations.
5	Guidelines & Tools		➢ Change Strategy – Change strategy in use or used to implement the potential value. ➢ Risk Analysis Results – The overall level of risk and the planned approach to modifying the individual risks. ➢ Solution Scope – The solution boundaries to measure and evaluate.
6	Techniques		➢ **Acceptance and Evaluation Criteria** – Used both to indicate the level at which acceptance criteria are met or anticipated to be met or not met by the solution. ➢ **Benchmarking and Market Analysis** – Used to assess if other organizations are experiencing the same solution challenges and determine how they are addressing it. ➢ **Business Rules Analysis** – Used to illustrate current business rules and the changes required to achieve the potential value of the change. ➢ **Data Mining** – Used to identify factors constraining performance of solution. ➢ **Decision Analysis** – Used to illustrate the current business decisions and the changes required to achieve potential value of the change. ➢ **Interviews** – Used to help perform problem analysis. ➢ **Item Tracking** – Used to record and manage stakeholder issues related to why the solution is not meeting the potential value. ➢ **Lessons Learned** – Used to determine what can be learned from the inception, definition and construction of the solution to have been impacted its ability to deliver value ➢ **Risk Analysis and Management** – Used to identify, analyze and manage risks to solution and potential limitations restricting the realization of potential value.

		➤ **Root Cause Analysis** – Used to identify and understand the combination of factors and their underlying causes that led to solution being unable to deliver its potential value. ➤ **Survey or Questionnaire** – Used to help perform problem analysis.
7	Stakeholders	➤ Customer ➤ Domain Subject Matter Expert ➤ End User – Contributes to the **actual value** realized by the solution in terms of solution performance. They may be consulted to provide **reviews** and **feedback** on areas such as workload and job satisfaction. ➤ Tester ➤ Sponsor – Responsible for **approving** potential **value** of the solution as well as approving **change** to potential value. ➤ Regulator
8	Output	➤ **Solution Limitations** – A description of the current limitations of the solution including constraints and defects.

6.1.4 Task 4: Assess Enterprise Limitations

1	Purpose	To determine how factors external to the solution are restricting value realization.
2	Description	➤ Solutions may depend on environmental factors that are within an enterprise or external to the enterprise. Enterprise limitations may include factors such as culture, operations, technical components, stakeholder interests or reporting structures. ➤ Assessing enterprise limitations identifies **root causes** and describes how enterprise factors **limit** the value realization. ➤ This assessment may be performed at any time during solution life cycle on a solution component during development, on a completed solution prior to implementation or on an existing solution.
3	Inputs	➤ **Current State Description** – The current internal environment of the solution including environmental, culture and internal factors influencing the solution limitations. ➤ **Implemented (or Constructed) Solution (external)** – A solution that exists. The solution should be in some form, may not be in operational use, or it may be a prototype.

4	Elements	

		➢ **Solution Performance Analysis** – Results of the analysis of measurements collected and recommendations to solve for performance gaps and leverage opportunities to improve value.
		➢ **Enterprise Culture Assessment** – The beliefs, norms and values shared by the members of an enterprise define the enterprise culture.
		    ○ Cultural assessment is performed to:
		        ▪ identify whether or not stakeholders understand the reasons why a solution exists,
		        ▪ find out if the solution is going to be providing beneficial value to stakeholders
		        ▪ identify cultural changes that are required to realize value of the solution
		    ○ Enterprise culture assessment helps to identify, evaluate the acceptance of solution is used to identify, evaluate the extent to which culture can accept a solution. It also shows readiness for enterprise to judge its ability and willingness to adapt to these cultural changes. Internal and external stakeholders are evaluated to:
		        ▪ Identify the depth of understanding and willingness to accept the solution,
		        ▪ assess cost-benefit analysis along with potential value from the solution and
		        ▪ determine the activities that are needed to ensure awareness and understanding of solution.
		➢ **Stakeholder Impact Analysis** – This is conducted to find out how the solution is going to affect a particular stakeholder group. Following factors are considered during stakeholder impact analysis:
		    ○ **Functions** – Processes performed by stakeholder which includes usage of solution in form of input provided by stakeholder to a process, usage of solution to execute the process and outputs received from the process
		    ○ **Locations** – Stakeholders may be in disparate locations which will impact the way they will use the solution and their ability to realize the value of the solution.

		<ul><li>**Concerns** – Issues, risks and overall concerns the stakeholders have with the solution.</li></ul><ul><li>**Organizational Structure Changes** – This refers to organizational changes and its structure that is impacted by a solution. The use of a solution and the ability to adopt a change can be enabled or blocked by **relationships** among stakeholders, **reporting** structure to allow a solution to perform effectively, assessment of organizational **hierarchy** to support the solution, informal relationships within an organization and impact the ability of a solution to deliver potential value.</li><li>**Operational Assessment** – This identifies which **processes** and **tools** within the enterprise are adequately equipped to benefit from the solution and if assets are in place to support it. Following factors are considered while conducting an operational assessment:<ul><li>policies and procedures</li><li>capabilities and processes that enable other capabilities</li><li>skill and training needs,</li><li>HR practices,</li><li>risk tolerance and management approaches and</li><li>tools and technology that support a solution.</li></ul></li></ul>
5	Guidelines & Tools	<ul><li>Business Objectives – Considered when measuring and determining solution performance.</li><li>Change Strategy – Used or in use to implement the potential value.</li><li>Future State Descriptions – Boundaries of proposed new, removed or modified components as well as potential value expected from future state.</li><li>Risk Analysis Results – Overall level of risk and planned approach to modify individual risks.</li><li>Solution Scope – Solution boundaries to measure and evaluate.</li></ul>
6	Techniques	<ul><li>**Benchmarking and Market Analysis** – Used to identify existing solution and enterprise interactions.</li><li>**Brainstorming** – Used to identify organizational gaps or stakeholder concerns.</li><li>**Data Mining** – Used to identify factors constraining performance of the solution.</li><li>**Decision Analysis** – Used to assist in making an optimal decision under conditions of uncertainty.</li><li>**Document Analysis** – Used to gain an understanding of the culture, operations, and structure of the organization.</li></ul>

		➢ **Interviews** – Used to identify organizational gaps or stakeholder concerns. ➢ **Item Tracking** – Used to ensure that issues are not neglected or lost and that issues identified by assessment are resolved. ➢ **Lessons Learned** – Used to analyze previous initiatives and how the enterprise interacted with the solution. ➢ **Observation** – Used to witness the enterprise and solution interactions to identify impacts. ➢ **Organizational Modelling** – Used to ensure identification of any changes to organizational structure that need to be addressed. ➢ **Process Analysis** – Used to identify possible opportunities to improve performance. ➢ **Process Modelling** – Illustrate the current business processes or changes that must be made in order to achieve potential value of the solution. ➢ **Risk Analysis and Management** – Used to consider risks in areas of technology, finance and business. ➢ **Roles and Permissions Matrix** – Used to determine roles and associated permissions to stakeholders as well as stability of end users. ➢ **Root Cause Analysis** – Used to determine if underlying cause may be related to enterprise limitations. ➢ **Survey or Questionnaire** – Used to identify organizational gaps or stakeholder concerns. ➢ **SWOT Analysis** – Used to demonstrate how a change will help the organization maximize strengths and minimize weakness and to assess strategies developed to respond to identified issues. ➢ **Workshops** – Used to identify organizational gaps or stakeholder concerns.
7	Stakeholders	➢ Customer ➢ Domain Subject Matter Expert ➢ End User ➢ Regulator ➢ Sponsor – **Authorizes** and ensures **funding** for solution delivery. Act as a **champion** to resolve problems identified as part of organizational assessment.
8	Output	➢ **Enterprise Limitation** – Current limitations of the enterprise including the impact of solution performance on enterprise.

6.1.5 Task 5: Recommend Actions to Increase Solution Value

1	Purpose	To understand the potential value and future value, differences between them, factors that create that difference and to provide recommendation on action plan to align both values.
2	Description	➢ The goal of the task is to **improve solution performance** and **increase value realization**. ➢ It focuses on understanding the performed assessments, understand common patterns and identify alternatives and actions to achieve above mentioned goal. ➢ Recommendations identify how a solution can be **replaced**, **changed** via enhancements or **retired** after a particular time. This includes long term effects and contributions of the solution to stakeholders and may include recommendations to adjust the organization to achieve above goal.
3	Inputs	➢ **Enterprise Limitation** – A description of current limitations of enterprise including how the solution performance is impacting the enterprise. ➢ **Solution Limitation** – A description of current limitations of the solution including constraints and defects.

4	Elements	➢ **Adjust Solution Performance Measures** – Appropriate measures need to be identified in order to identify and define more appropriate measures to tune the performance of the solution in order to support fulfilment of **business goals** and **objectives**.
		➢ **Recommendations** – Recommendations are provided for the situation where solution performance is lower than expected. Some common examples of the same are as follows:
		    o **Do Nothing** – In case of the situation where the change is not possible with the **resources** available or in the allotted **time frame**, **value** of the change is relatively low than the effort that are put in for the change, or when the **risk** around change is significantly high, it is recommended to do nothing.
		    o **Organizational Change** – Organizational change management generally refers to a **process** and set of **tools** for managing change at an organizational level. These changes could be around providing recommendations for changes to **organizational structure**, making new **information** available to

stakeholders and create new **skills** required to operate the solution. Possible recommendations include:

- **Automating or simplifying work people perform** – Identifying tasks that can be automated, work activities and business rules that can be reviewed and analyzed for re-engineering, outsourcing or changes in responsibilities.
- **Improving access to information** – Greater amount and better quality of information available to decision makers and regular staff.

○ **Reduce Complexity of Interfaces** – Reducing the complexity of interfaces that come into picture due to transfer of work between systems or between people can enhance better understanding. This can be achieved by better analyzing **API interfaces**.

○ **Eliminate Redundancy** – Reduce the cost of solution implementation by identifying common needs that can be met by a single solution. This can be achieved by conducting process re-engineering via **lean principles**.

○ **Avoid Waste** – Change processes to completely remove those activities that do not add value or that do not contribute to the final product directly. Again this can be achieved via applying **lean** principles.

○ **Identify Additional Capabilities** – Solution options may be providing certain capabilities which are not providing immediate potential value but will provide future value for sure. Solution can support rapid development and implementation of the same. This can be achieved via performing **Capability Gap Analysis**.

○ **Retire the Solution** – Replacement of the solution may be needed because **technology** has reached end of its life, **services** are being insourced or outsourced, or the solution is not fulfilling the **goals** for which it was created. Additional factors that may impact the decision include:

- **Ongoing costs versus initial investment** – Ongoing cost for existing solution increases over time whereas newer alternatives will have

		higher investment cost and less maintenance cost over time. ▪ **Opportunity Cost** – Potential value that can be realized and achieved by pursuing alternative courses of action. ▪ **Necessity** – It is feasible to maintain the solution component until it is providing appropriate value. At a certain point, it becomes impractical to maintain and continue with it. ▪ **Sunk Cost** – Describes the money and effort already committed to an initiative. While deciding on future action, this investment is effectively irrelevant as it cannot be recovered. Decisions should be based on **future investment** required and **future benefits** that can be gained.
5	Guidelines & Tools	➤ Business Objectives – Considered in evaluating, measuring and determining solution performance. ➤ Current State Description – Provides the context within which work needs to be completed. ➤ Solution Scope – Solution boundaries to measure and evaluate.
6	Techniques	➤ **Data Mining** – Used to generate predictive estimates of solution performance. ➤ **Decision Analysis** – Used to determine the impact of acting on any of the potential value or performance issues. ➤ **Financial Analysis** – Used to assess the potential costs and benefits of a change. ➤ **Focus Groups** – Used to determine if solution performance measures need to be adjusted and uses to identify potential opportunities to improve performance. ➤ **Organizational Modelling** – Used to demonstrate potential change within organization's structure. ➤ **Prioritization** – Used to identify relative value of different actions to improve solution performance. ➤ **Process Analysis** – Used to identify opportunities within related processes. ➤ **Risk Analysis and Management** – Used to evaluate different outcomes under specific conditions.

		➢ **Survey or Questionnaire** – Used to gather feedback from a wide variety of stakeholders to determine if the value has been met or exceeded.
7	Stakeholders	➢ Customer ➢ Domain Subject Matter Expert ➢ End User ➢ Regulator ➢ Sponsor – Authorizes and ensures funding for implementation of any recommended actions.
8	Output	➢ **Recommended Actions** – Recommendation of what should be done to improve the value of the solution within the enterprise.

6.2 Glossary

- **API** – Refers to application programming interface. It is a set of functions that allows creation of applications that access the features or data of other systems. In short, it acts as a communication medium for two software programs.
- **Capability Gap Analysis** – It is referred to change management. Due to given change in an organization, capability gap analysis helps to identify the differences between current state and desired future state in area of capabilities owned by individuals.
- **Lean** – This refer to creation of perfect value for customers by using perfect process and having zero waste.
- **Solution performance metrics** - These are the criteria (qualitative or quantifiable) by which the performance of the solution will be measured
- **Proof of concept (POC)** - A working but limited versions of a solution that demonstrate value.
- **Operational Release** - Full versions of a partial or completed solution used to achieve business objectives, execute a process, or fulfil a desired outcome.
- **Implementation** - Implementation refers to post-sales process of guiding a client from purchase to use of the software or hardware that was purchased. This includes requirements analysis, scope analysis, customizations, systems integrations, user policies, user training and delivery.
- **Key Performance Indicators (KPIs)** - A Key Performance Indicator is a measurable value that demonstrates how effectively a company is achieving key business objectives. Organizations use KPIs at multiple levels to evaluate their success at reaching targets.

- ➤ **Scope** - Scope of work defines the extent of work in a software project e.g. what is in scope (to be done) and what's out-of-scope. Scope is not same as requirements
- ➤ **online transaction processing system (OLTP)** - OLTP systems record business interactions as they occur in the day-to-day operation of the organization, and support querying of this data to make inferences.
- ➤ **Environmental Factors** - In business analysis, the word 'environmental' can sometimes be used refer to all external factors that affect a business (just like in environmental analysis), from Political to Legal, and everything in between.
- ➤ **Sunk Cost** - A sunk cost is a cost that has already been incurred and cannot be recovered. A sunk cost differs from future costs that a business may face, such as decisions about inventory purchase costs or product pricing.

6.3 Exercises and Drills

Q1. Match the following tasks with their respective description:

1. Measure solution performance	A. Determines factors internal to the solution that restrict the full realization of value
2. Analyze performance measures	B. Identifies and defines actions an enterprise can take to increase the value that can be delivered by a solution
3. Assess solution limitations	C. Provides insights into the performance of a solution in relation to the value it brings
4. Assess enterprise limitations	D. Determines the most appropriate way to assess the performance of a solution
5. Recommend actions to increase solution value	E. Determines factors external to the solution that restrict the full realization of value

Q2. Match the following stages of development with their description:

1. Prototypes or Proof of Concept (PoC)	A. limited implementations/ versions of a solution before fully releasing the solution
2. Pilot or Beta releases	B. Full versions of a partial/ completed solution used to achieve business objectives, execute a process, or fulfil a desired outcome
3. Operational releases	C. Working but limited versions of a solution that demonstrate value

Q3. Complete the crossword:

Across

1. Describes the value that may be realized by implementing the proposed solution

Down

2. The measurable results that the enterprise wants to achieve

3. Difference between actual and expected performance

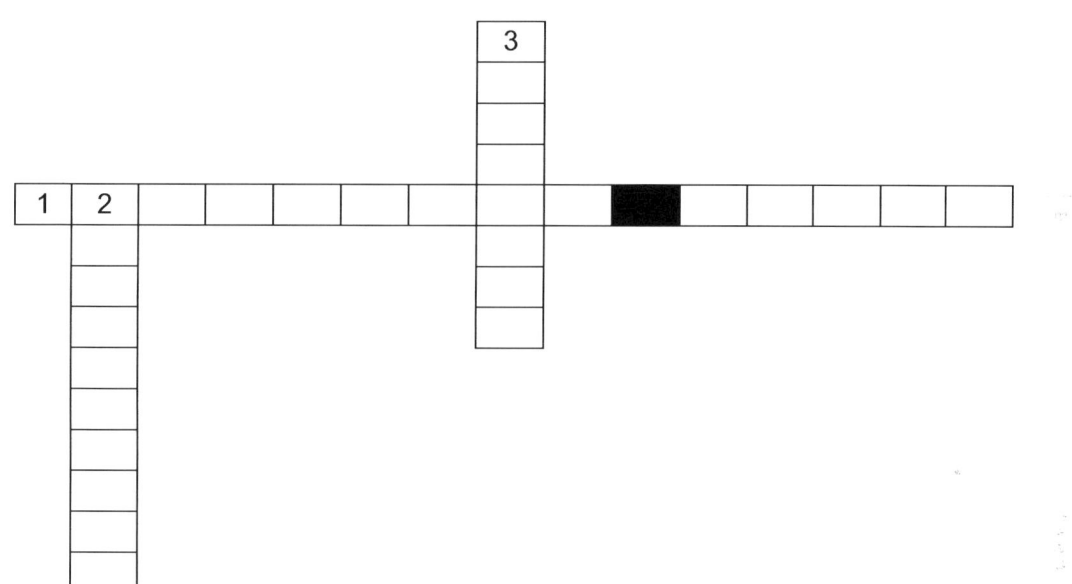

Q4. Match the following:

1. Sunk cost	A. Common needs of different stakeholders that can be met with a single solution
2. Opportunity cost	B. Potential value that could be realized by pursuing alternative initiatives
3. Avoid waste	C. Value of a change is low vis-à-vis the effort required to make the change
4. Eliminate redundancy	D. Money and effort already committed to an initiative
5. Do nothing	E. Remove those activities completely which do not add value to the final product

Answers to Exercises & Drills

Answer 1: 1 – D, 2 – C, 3 – A, 4 – E, 5 – B

Answer 2: 1 – C, 2 – A, 3 – B

Answer 3:

    1. Potential value

    2. Objectives

    3. Variance

Answer 4: 1 – D, 2 – B, 3 – E, 4 – A, 5 – C

Chapter 7 - Techniques

7.1 Acceptance and Evaluation Criteria

1	Purpose	<ul><li>Acceptance criteria are used to define requirements, or conditions that must be met for accepting solution by stakeholders.</li><li>Evaluation criteria is the metric form of judgement to assess set of requirements to choose between multiple solutions.</li></ul>
2	Description	<ul><li>Acceptance and evaluation criteria define measures of **value** attributes to be used for assessing and comparing solutions and alternative designs as well as they can be applied at all levels of a project.</li><li>Acceptance criteria describe the **minimum** set of requirements that must be met in order to consider a solution worth implementing. It is typically used when only **one** possible solution is being evaluated and is expressed as pass or fail.</li><li>Evaluation criteria define a set of **measurements** which allow for ranking of solutions and alternative designs according to value that will be provided. Attributes that cannot be measured directly are evaluated using expert judgement.</li><li>The solutions with lower costs and better performance gets rated as highest while evaluating solution options whereas the solution having maximum cost limits, better user acceptance tests and minimum performance requirements are given high priority while accepting a solution.</li></ul>
3	Elements	<ul><li>**Value Attributes** – Value attributes are agreed-upon decomposition of value proposition that are described as qualities that the solution should possess or avoid. Business analysts may design tools and instructions for recording and performing the assessment as well as recording the outcomes of the same. Some examples of value attributes include:<ul><li>ability to provide information specifically, to perform specific operations,</li><li>performance and responsiveness characteristics,</li><li>applicability of the solution in specific situations,</li><li>availability of specific features and capabilities and usability, security, scalability and reliability</li></ul></li></ul>

		➢ **Assessment** – A solution must be in a measurable format in order to assess it against acceptance and evaluation criteria. ○ **Testability** – Requirements are broken down into atomic form so that acceptance criteria can be shown in a testable form and are written in form of statements which can be verified as true or false. Generally applied through user acceptance testing. ▪ Usually there are various approaches to write acceptance criteria in Agile methodology. Some of them are – Behaviour driven development (**BDD**) where acceptance criteria is written in form of **Gherkin** language (Given, when, then) and ▪ Test driven development (**TDD**) where tests are written first which must fail and then code is written to make it work. ○ **Measures** – Evaluation criteria focuses on an approach if the necessary value to satisfy stakeholder needs is provided via parameters that can be measured against a continuous or discrete scale. It is measured using benchmarking and expert judgment techniques.
4	Usage Considerations	➢ **Strengths** – ○ Agile methodologies require requirements to be written in form of testable acceptance criteria. ○ Acceptance criteria is necessary to express contractual obligations. It provides a way to assess requirements on agreed-upon criteria. ○ Evaluation criteria provides the ability to assess diverse needs based on agreed upon criteria. ○ It also assist in delivery of expected return on investment and help in defining priorities. ➢ **Limitations** – ○ Acceptance criteria may express contractual obligations and can be difficult to change. ○ Evaluation criteria could be a challenge to be accepted for differing needs among diverse stakeholders.

7.2 Backlog Management

Backlog refers to product backlog in agile methodology which is a list of ideas, information about functionalities, features and requirements gathered and recorded from stakeholders, customers and product management team in form of epics and user stories. Epics refer to high level features and user stories refer to functionalities that need to be delivered as part of that feature.

1	Purpose	Record, track, and prioritize remaining work items.
2	Description	➢ Backlog occurs when the volume of work items to be completed exceeds the capacity of teams to complete them. There may be more than one backlog focusing on type and priority of work. ➢ Items at top of backlog have highest priority and business value in a managed backlog and are best candidates to be picked up next. ➢ Periodic review of backlog is necessary to confirm to needs and hence make changes to the priority. As a result, it is reviewed at periodic planned intervals. The review session is called as **Backlog Refinement Session**. ➢ If a backlog is growing, then it could be increase in demand or drop in productivity. ➢ A declining backlog refers to drop in demand or improvements in production process.

3	Elements	➢ **Items in the Backlog** – Backlog items can be any kind of item that has any work associated with it. It can contain various items such as use cases, user stories, functional requirements, non-functional requirements, change requests, planned rework, etc.
		    ○ If an item is adding value to the stakeholder, then it needs to be added in backlog. There are rules and policies to which everyone adheres to in order to add anything to backlog.
		    ○ Responsibility to add or remove item lies usually with product owner and he/she is liable to interact with other stakeholders to get their inputs.
		➢ **Prioritization** – Items in backlog can be prioritized depending on stakeholder's priorities and dependencies between the items.

			o Items when added initially are prioritized using high, medium or low category. o High priority items are then prioritized using a numerical ranking base such as **story points** for user stories. ➢ **Estimation** – The level of detail used to describe the backlog item may vary. Items at top of backlog are usually described in more detail, with accurate estimate about their size and complexity which in turn help in determining cost and effort to implement them. o An item when initially added to backlog has very less information which is enough for anyone to understand it and initiate work on the same. **Story points** are allocated to the items in order to proceed with its development. o An individual item's relative priority may rise and lead to a need for review as work progresses on it. ➢ **Managing changes to backlog** – New requirements or changes to requirements are identified and added to backlog and reviewed against the items in backlog. Depending on capacity, size and capacity, items are picked up by teams. o Items are removed from backlog when a decision is made to not to work on them or are completed. o In case of changes to stakeholder needs, less time and effort estimates based on re-assessment and defects raised, the items that are removed can be re-added to backlog.
4	Usage Considerations		➢ **Strengths** o Very good approach to understand the highest priority work items as they are on top of backlog. o Only items from top of backlog are elaborated and estimated in detail, keeping the items near the bottom to receive less attention. o Can be effective medium to understand which items will be worked on, which will not be touched and which can be scoped out for stakeholders. ➢ **Limitations** o Sometimes large backlog can be hard to manage. o Good experience is required to know the art of breaking down items into enough details for accurate estimation.

		o A lack of detail in the items can result in lost information.

7.3 Balanced Scorecard

Balanced Scorecard is a performance metric used to identify and improve various internal functions of a business and their resulting external outcomes. It is a metric tool to provide feedback to organizations.

1	Purpose	Manage performance in any business model, organizational structure or business process.

2	Description	➤ Balanced scorecard is a **strategic planning and management** tool used to measure organizational **performance** beyond traditional financial measures.
		➤ It is outcome focused and provides a **balanced view** of an enterprise by implementing strategic plan as well as making sure that **drivers** of value creation are tuned in order to create sustainable performance.
		➤ It is applicable to any level – enterprise, organizational functional or at a level of a project.
		➤ It is comprised of 4 dimensions:
		   o Learning and Growth,
		   o Business process,
		   o Customer,
		   o Financial.

3	Elements	➤ **Learning and Growth Dimension** – Includes measures regarding employee training and learning, product and service innovation and corporate culture. Metrics guide use of funds, knowledge sharing and technology enhancements. There are usually 3 objectives for this perspective and related metrics to measure them *[Source – Aleksey Savkin, BSC Designer, Learning & Growth Perspective of Balanced Scorecard, Nov 9, 2016]*. They are as follows: o **Employee capabilities** – This includes employees obtaining the skills to support the strategy mentioned in scorecard and to gain a better understanding of company's major aspects such as sales, etc. Some of those metrics could be –

- Number of training hours passed
- Exam score
- **Information system capabilities** – Identify and list down information systems which are needed to execute the strategy effectively. Some of metrics for measuring them could be –
    - Resources in form of time and money saved
    - Improving customer retentions.
- **Strategy awareness and motivation** – Address some typical motivation and alignment issues via sessions that will explain strategy to employees and involve them in its execution. Some of metrics measuring them could be –
    - Resources and time spent on training to improve strategy awareness
    - Average score of strategy awareness survey.

➢ **Business Process Dimension** – Include process related metrics that shows the overall operations for enterprise and if their product meets customer needs. As part of this, following strategies are applied to ensure operation and stability of business is maintained *[Source – Aleksey Savkin, BSC Designer, Internal Processes Perspective of Balanced Scorecard, Oct 30, 2016].*
- **Product Leadership Strategy** – Includes developing new products, innovating existing products and improving speed to market. Example – "Develop BPAY function in mobile app in order to satisfy the biller pay need of a customer and achieve financial goal".
- **Customer Intimacy Strategy** – Includes customer relationship management system, support services provided and customer's interactions with the company. Example – "Update the website to engage customers better and reduce calls to call centre".
- **Operational Excellence Strategy** – Includes decreasing operation costs and cycle time, ensuring high standards of quality and delivery time by optimizing their supply chain. Example – "Decrease time to market for innovative and competitive solution from 1 month to 1 week"

		➢ **Customer Dimension** – Metrics focus on customer focus, customer satisfaction rate and delivery of value to them. This helps to capture how properly customer needs are met, how satisfy the customer is with the product and if quality has been met for the delivery of products/services.
		    o As part of this, question 'Is the company meeting customer's expectations?' is answered.
		    o There are various **metrics** considered as part of this which are – customer satisfaction, customer retention, new customer acquisition, market share and on time delivery to customer.
		    o Examples – "CSAT (customer satisfaction) rate has increased from 80% to 90% as customers started using mobile app".
		➢ **Financial Dimension** – This is to identify the financially necessary things to realize the strategy. The question around whether company is achieving financial goals is answered as part of this perspective in balanced scorecard.
		    o **Metrics** used here ROI, operating income, return on assets, sales growth and cash flow from operations.
		    o **Examples** – "Due to launch of mobile app, operating margin has been reduced from 50% to 40% and sales have increased 2 times since last month".
		➢ **Measures or Indicators** – Lagging indicators provide results of actions already taken whereas leading indicators provide similar level of information but for future performance.
		    o **Examples** are as follows – Lagging indicator is around number of training hours put in by a person whereas lagging indicator is around the exam success rate which is conducted post training.

4	Usage Considerations	➢ **Strengths**
		    o Facilitate holistic and balanced planning and thinking.
		    o Various types of goals can be tied to programs with success measures to achieve them.
		    o Strategic, tactical and operational teams are more easily aligned in their work.
		    o Encourages forward thinking and competitiveness.
		➢ Limitations
		    o Lack of clear strategy makes aligning difficult.
		    o Can be seen as a single tool for strategic planning only.

		o Can be misinterpreted as a replacement of strategic planning, execution and measurement.

7.4 Benchmarking and Market Analysis

Benchmarking and market analysis is evaluation of business operations and processes in order to strive for operational excellence and competitive advantage.

1	Purpose	To improve organizational operations, increase customer satisfaction and increase value to stakeholders.
2	Description	➤ Benchmarking focuses on **comparison** of existing organizational practices against best-in-class practices. ➤ Objective is to **evaluate** existing performance for enterprise and ensure that the enterprise is operating efficiently. ➤ Market Analysis focuses on **researching** customers to understand their needs, factors impacting the needs and competition related to same in market. ➤ The objective is to **acquire** information to support decision making process and to determine when to exit a market.

3	Elements	➤ **Benchmarking**
		   o Benchmarking includes:
		      ▪ identifying areas to be studied,
		      ▪ identifying enterprise that are leaders in specific sectors,
		      ▪ conducting a survey to understand their practices,
		      ▪ using Request for Information to gather information about capabilities,
		      ▪ arranging visits to best-in-class organization,
		      ▪ determining gaps between current and best practices and develop a project proposal to implement best practices
		➤ **Market Analysis**
		   o Market Analysis includes:
		      ▪ identify customer preferences,
		      ▪ opportunities that provide more value to stakeholders, competitors and related operations,

			<ul><li>market trends,</li><li>define appropriate business strategies,</li><li>gather market data,</li><li>usage of existing resources,</li><li>review data to determine trends and draw conclusions</li></ul>
4	Usage Considerations		➤ **Strengths** 　o Benchmarking provides organizations with information about new and different methods to improve organizational performance. 　o Helps to identify best practices by its competitors in order to meet competition. 　o Helps to identify why similar companies are successful and their success factors. 　o Market analysis can target specific groups to answer specific questions. 　o Market analysis expose weaknesses within a certain company. 　o It also helps to identify differences in product offerings and services that are available from a competitor. ➤ **Limitations** 　o Benchmarking is time consuming and hence organization may not have expertise to conduct analysis. 　o It cannot produce innovative solutions because it involves comparing them with existing ones. 　o Market analysis can be time consuming and expensive and results may not be visible. 　o Without market segmentation, it may not product expected results about competitor's product/service.

7.5 Brainstorming

Brainstorming is a group creativity activity to gather list of ideas in order to solve a specific problem.

1	Purpose	To foster creative thinking about a problem. Overall aim is to produce new ideas and to derive themes for further analysis.

2	Description	➢ It is a technique intended to produce a broad and diverse set of options via ideas.
		➢ It focuses on discussion about a topic or a problem and then coming up with many possible solutions for it.
		➢ It is best applied in group as it draws on experience and creativity of all members.
		➢ In case of appropriate facilitation, this could be fun, engaging and productive exercise.
		➢ **Preparation**
		   o Define Area of Interest
		   o Determine Time Limit
		   o Identify Participants
		   o Establish Evaluation Criteria
		➢ **Session**
		   o Share Ideas
		   o Record Ideas
		   o Build on each other's ideas
		   o Elicit as many ideas as possible
		➢ **Wrap-Up**
		   o Discuss and Evaluate
		   o Create List
		   o Rate Ideas
		   o Distribute final list

3	Elements	➢ Preparation
		   o Develop a clear and concise definition of interest area
		   o Determine a time limit for group to generate ideas.
		   o Identify facilitator and participants in the session. Aim for 6-8 participants only.
		   o Set expectations and get buy-in from participants on process.
		   o Establish criteria for evaluating and rating the ideas.
		➢ Session
		   o Share new ideas without any criticism.

		<ul><li>Visibly record all ideas.</li><li>Encourage participants to be creative and build on ideas of others.</li><li>Don't limit the number of ideas as goal is to gather as many as possible within defined time limit.</li></ul> ➢ Wrap-up <ul><li>After defined time limit, discuss and evaluate the ideas using predetermined evaluation criteria.</li><li>Create a condensed list of ideas, combine them wherever appropriate and eliminate duplicates.</li><li>Rate the ideas and distribute final list of ideas.</li></ul>
4	Usage Considerations	➢ **Strengths** <ul><li>Ability to elicit a lot of ideas in short time period.</li><li>Non-judgemental environment encourages creative thinking.</li><li>Can be useful to reduce tension between participants.</li></ul> ➢ **Limitations** <ul><li>It is solely dependent on participant's creativity and willingness to participate.</li><li>Politics within organization and amongst people can limit it to some extent.</li><li>It must be agreed to avoid debating on ideas raised during the session.</li></ul>

7.6 Business Capability Analysis

Business capability analysis describe the assessment of abilities of an enterprise to act or transform something that helps the business to achieve a goal or objective and to identify performance gaps.

1	Purpose	To provide a framework for scoping and planning by generating a shared understanding of outcomes, identifying alignment with strategy and providing a scope and prioritization filter.
2	Description	➢ **Business capability analysis** describes what an enterprise is able to do in order to achieve a business goal or objective. ➢ **Performance gaps** are identified by doing assessment of existing capabilities and product development efforts are taken to improve the performance or to deliver an altogether new one.
3	Elements	➢ **Capabilities** – It is an ability of enterprise to perform or transform something that helps to achieve a business goal or objective. A good **example** of a capability is to allow customer to transact via internet banking platform. o Each capability focuses on outcome or purpose of doing an activity such as transformation and is shown uniquely on capability map. ➢ **Using Capabilities** – Capabilities impact different levels of value through increasing revenue, reducing cost, improving service and can be shown via a tool on capability assessment. For example, internet banking platform can help to increase revenue as it will allow self-servicing and reduce operational cost. ➢ **Performance Expectations** – Capabilities can be assessed to identify explicit performance expectations. Performance gap which is termed as difference between current and desired performance is identified when an improvement is made on capability. ➢ **Risk Model** – Risks could be in the performance of the capability or in lack of performance can usually can be business risk, technology risk, organizational risk and market risk. Example for business risk could be enabling a new platform to customers without thorough testing. Example of technology risk could be launching a platform with newer

		technologies. Organizational risk example could be opening up a new functionality without being compliant to regulations. ➢ **Strategic Planning** – Business capability assessment can product a set of recommendations which the enterprise need to apply in order to accomplish its strategy and provide a base for product roadmap as well as release planning. ➢ **Capability Maps** – They provide a graphical view of elements involved in business capability analysis as part of capability map shown on a larger capability grid.

4	Usage Considerations	➢ **Strengths**
		   o Provides a shared articulation of outcomes which help create a very focused and aligned initiatives.
		   o Helps align business initiatives across multiple aspects of organization.
		   o Useful when assessing ability of organization to offer new products
		➢ Limitations
		   o Requires an organization to agree to collaborate on this model.
		   o It could fail to deliver on goals of alignment if created unilaterally or in vacuum.
		   o Requires a broad collaboration in defining the capability model and value framework.

7.7 Business Cases

Business case is a documented argument that is intended to convince a decision maker to approve some kind of action.

1	Purpose	A business case provides a justification for a course of action based on the benefits to be realized by using the proposed solution, as compared to the cost, effort to acquire it and live with it.
2	Description	<ul><li>A business case captures the rationale for undertaking a change.</li><li>The amount of time and resources spent on business case should be proportional to the size and importance of its potential value.</li><li>A business case is used to<ul><li>define business need,</li><li>determine the desired outcomes,</li><li>assess constraints, assumptions and risks and</li><li>recommend a solution</li></ul></li></ul>
3	Elements	<ul><li>**Need Assessment** – The need is the driver for business case. Business goals and objectives that are relevant and are linked to a strategy of enterprise need to be met. The need assessment identifies the problem or potential opportunity as well as alternatives are provided to solve the problem or take an advantage of an opportunity that needs assessment.</li><li>**Desired Outcomes** – The desired outcomes describe the state which should result if the need is fulfilled. Measurable outcomes to determine business case success are to be included. Desired outcomes should be revisited at defined milestones and is independent of the recommended solution.</li><li>**Assess Alternatives** – The business case identified and assesses various alternative solutions which may include different technologies, processes, or business models. The 'do-nothing' alternative should be assessed and considered for recommended solution. Each alternative should be assessed in terms of:<ul><li>**Scope** – Organizational boundaries, system boundaries, product lines clearly define what will be included and what will be excluded.</li><li>**Feasibility** – Organizational and technical feasibility should be assessed for each alternative.</li></ul></li></ul>

		<ul><li>○ **Assumptions, Risks and Constraints** – Assumptions are agreed to facts which may influence on the initiative. Constraints are limitations that may restrict possible alternatives. Risks are potential problems that have a negative impact on the solution.</li><li>○ **Financial Analysis and Value Assessment** – This includes an estimate of the costs to implement and operate the alternative and quantified financial benefit from implementing the alternative. Benefits of non-financial nature are also important and add significant value to the organization.</li></ul><ul><li>➢ **Recommended Solution** – It is the most desirable way to solve the problem or opportunity. This also includes estimates of cost and duration to implement the solution. Measurable benefits/outcomes will be identified to assess the performance and success of the solution.</li></ul>
4	Usage Considerations	<ul><li>➢ **Strengths**<ul><li>○ Provides a combination of facts, issues and analysis required to make decisions regarding change.</li><li>○ Provides a detailed financial analysis of cost and benefits.</li><li>○ Provides guidance for ongoing decision making.</li></ul></li><li>➢ **Limitations**<ul><li>○ May be biased depending on authors</li><li>○ Not updated frequently once funding is secured.</li><li>○ Contains assumptions regarding costs and benefits that may prove invalid doing detailed investigation.</li></ul></li></ul>

7.8 Business Model Canvas

Business model canvas is a business tool used to visualize all the building blocks of business. It includes customers, route to market, value proposition and finance part within business.

1	Purpose	A business model canvas describes how an enterprise creates, delivers and captures value for and from its customers

2	Description	➤ A business model canvas is comprised of **nine building blocks** which intend to deliver value:
		    o Key Partnerships,
		    o Key Activities,
		    o Key Resources,
		    o Value Proposition,
		    o Customer Relationships,
		    o Channels,
		    o Customer Segments,
		    o Cost structure,
		    o Revenue Streams
		➤ A business model canvas serves as a **blueprint** for **implementing** a strategy.
		➤ As **diagnostic** tool, business model canvas helps to look into current state of the business especially from investments in various areas such as resources, time and effort.
		➤ As **planning and monitoring** tool, business model canvas helps to provide guideline and framework for understanding inter-relationships and dependencies among groups and initiatives.

3	Elements	➤ **Key Partnerships** – An effective key relationships can lead to more formalized relationships such as mergers and acquisitions. Benefits for the same include:
		    o optimization and economy,
		    o reduction of risk and uncertainty,
		    o acquisition of particular resources and activities,
		    o lack of internal capabilities
		➤ **Key Activities** – Key activities can be classified as:
		    o **Value-add** – Features and business activities for which customer is willing to pay. Example for this could be launching peer to peer payment on mobile app for which customer is happy to pay.

- **Non-value-add** – Activities for which customer is not willing to pay. Example for this could be longer SLA's on customer complaints due to outsourcing of same to external vendors.
- **Business non-value-add** – Characteristics included in offering, costs associated with doing business for which customer is not willing to pay. A very good example of this could be enabling e-statements on banking platform.

➤ **Key Resources** – Resources can be classified as:
- **Physical** – Applications, locations, etc.
- **Financial** – Cash and lines of credit to find a business model.
- **Intellectual** – Any proprietary aspects that enable a business model to thrive.
- **Human** – People needed to execute a particular business model.

➤ **Value Proposition** – It represents what a customer is willing to exchange for having their needs met.

➤ **Customer Relationships** – Customer relationships are classified as customer acquisition and customer retention. These relationships can be formal or informal too.

➤ **Channels** – Channels are different ways an enterprise interacts with and delivers value to its customers. Enterprise uses channels (communication oriented – marketing, delivery oriented – distribution channel, sales channels, partnering channels) to:
- raise awareness about their offerings,
- help customers evaluate the value proposition,
- allow customers to purchase a good or service,
- help enterprise deliver on value proposition and provide support

➤ **Customer Segments** – Grouping customers with common needs and attributes can help to address the needs of each segment. Customer segments are based on:
- different needs for each segment,
- varying profitability between segments,
- different distribution channels,
- formation and maintenance of customer relationships

➤ **Cost Structure** – Enterprise always have an associated cost for any entity, product or activity and it always tries to reduce

			the costs so that profitability can be increased and same funds can be used to create better value for the organization and customers.
			➤ **Revenue Streams** – A revenue stream is a method by which revenues comes into an enterprise from each customer segment in exchange for the realization of value proposition. Revenue could be resulting from a one-time purchase of a goods/service or recurring revenue from periodic payments for a good, service or ongoing support. Types of revenue streams include:
			    o **Licensing or Subscription Fees** – Customer pays for the right to access a particular asset.
			    o **Transaction or Usage Fees** – Customer pays each time they use a good or service.
			    o **Sales** – Customer is granted ownership rights to specific product.
			    o **Lending, Renting or Leasing** – Customer has temporary rights to use an asset.

4	Usage Considerations		➤ **Strengths**
			    o Simple to use and easy to understand.
			    o Widely used framework to understand and optimize business models.
			➤ **Limitations**
			    o Does not account for alternative measures of value
			    o Primary focus on value propositions does not provide a holistic insight for business strategy.
			    o Does not include strategic purpose of enterprise within canvas.

7.9 Business Rules Analysis

Business rules are the constraints and conditions that define the operation of business. Business rules analysis is conducting analysis of such business rules alongside business requirements.

1	Purpose	It is used to identify, express, validate, refine and organize the rules that shape day-to-day business behaviour and guide operational business decision making.

2	Description	➢ Business policies and rules guide the day-to-day operation of the business and its processes and shape operational business decisions.
		➢ A business **policy** is a directive concerned with broadly controlling, influencing or regulating the actions of an enterprise and people in it.
		➢ A business **rule** is a specific, testable, directive that serves as a criterion for guiding behaviour and making decisions.
		➢ A business rule must be practicable and is always under control of the business.
		➢ Analysis of business rules involves capturing business rules from sources, expressing them clearly, validating them and organizing them to align with business goals.
		➢ Sources of business rules may be explicit or tacit. Basic principles for business rules includes:
		   o basing them on standard business vocabulary to enable domain subject matter experts,
		   o expressing them on how they will be enforced,
		   o defining them at the atomic level and in declarative format,
		   o separating them from processes they support,
		   o mapping them to decisions that rule supports,
		   o maintaining them in a manner such that they can be monitored and adapted as business evolves over time

3	Elements	➢ Business rules require consistent use of business terms, a glossary of definitions and an understanding of structural connections. ➢ There should be reuse of existing terminology from external industry associations or internal glossaries.

- Business rules should be used independently of any implementation technology.
- Whenever there is a change to existing solution or new solutions emerge, existing business rules need to be challenged and made sure that they still meet business goals.
- **Definitional Rules** – Definitional rules shape concepts, or produce knowledge or information. They provide accurate information about some concept and supplementing it with definition.
    - Definitional rules are about operational knowledge of an organization.
    - They cannot be **violated** but they can be misapplied.
    - These rules often prescribe how information may be derived, inferred or calculated based on information available to the business.
    - An inference or calculation may be the result of multiple rules, each building on something inferred or calculated by some others. At times, these rules are used to make operational business decisions during some process or upon some event.
    - **Example** – A customer must be considered as 'Privilege customer' if they are ready to invest more than 5 lacs per year.
- **Behavioural Rules** – These rules are **people** rules. Such rules are created to serve to shape the daily business activities.
    - These rules are the ones which organization chooses to enforce as a matter of **policy**, often to reduce risk or enhance productivity.
    - These rules are intended to guide the **actions** of people working within the organization, or people who interact with it.
    - Behavioural rules may be determining how to carry out specific actions and provide conditions under which a particular action can be done correctly.
    - Such rules can be **violated** directly. There is a need to enforce the rules via detailed analysis which can lead to additional rules too. If the rules are not applied with an active enforcement, then it will just serve as a guidelines.

		o Various levels of enforcement may be specified such as – allow no violations, override by authorized actor, override with explanation and no active enforcement. o **Example** – An order must not be placed if the customer details are not matching to those recorded on file with financial organization.
4	Usage Considerations	➢ **Strengths** o When enforced and managed by single enterprise wide engine, changes to business rules can be implemented quickly. o A centralized repository creates the ability to reuse business rules. o They provide structure to govern business behaviours. o Clearly defining and managing business rules allows organizations to make changes to policy without altering process. ➢ **Limitations** o May produce lengthy list of business rules which could lead to ambiguity. o When combined, business rules may be contradicting to one another and can produce unanticipated results. o Business rule will only be accurate provided available vocabulary is sufficiently rich.

7.10 Collaborative Games

Collaborative games encourage participants in an elicitation activity to collaborate in building a joint understanding of problem or a solution.

1	Purpose	Collaborative games encourage participants in an elicitation activity to collaborate in building a joint understanding of problem or a solution.
2	Description	➢ Collaborative games refer to several structured techniques inspired by game play and are designed to facilitate collaboration. ➢ Each game includes rules to keep everyone focused and is used to share knowledge and experience of the participants in a given area, identify assumptions and explore knowledge. ➢ Collaborative games often benefit from involvement of a neutral facilitator whose job is to keep game moving forward and to help ensure that all participants play a role.

3	Elements	➢ **Game Purpose** – Each game has a purpose to serve which help to either better understand a problem or stimulate creative solutions. Facilitator makes sure that participants in the game understand that purpose and work towards the successful realization of that purpose.
		➢ **Process** – There is 3 step process or set of rules followed in this game. They are as follows:
		    ○ **Step 1** – Opening step where participants get involved, learn about the game and generate ideas.
		    ○ **Step 2** – Exploration step where they engage with one another and look for connections between their ideas.
		    ○ **Step 3** – Closing step where ideas are assessed and participants find out which ideas are useful and productive.
		➢ **Outcome** – Facilitator and participants work through results and determine any decisions or actions that need to be taken as part of learning.
		➢ **Examples of Collaborative Games** – Some examples are:
		    ○ Product Box – Construct a box for the product so that it can be sold in store. This help to identify features of product which are known in marketplace.

			○ Affinity Map – Writing features on sticky notes and assign them to other features appearing similar to original ones. Helps to identify related or similar features or themes. ○ Fishbowl – One group speaks and another group documents their observations by listening to them. Helps to identify hidden assumptions.
4	Usage Considerations		➢ **Strengths** ○ May reveal hidden assumptions or differences in opinion. ○ Encourages creative thinking by stimulating alternative mental process. ○ Challenges participants who are normally quiet to take an active role. ○ This helps to expose business needs which are not been thought of or are not met. ➢ **Limitations** ○ Sometimes serious participants can feel uncomfortable with the playful nature of games. ○ Games can be time consuming especially if the objectives or outcomes are not clear. ○ False sense of confidence can be reached in the conclusions reached.

7.11 Concept Modelling

A model that develops the meaning of core concepts for a problem domain, explains their collective structure, and specifies the appropriate vocabulary needed to communicate about it consistently.

1	Purpose	Set up business vocabulary needed to consistently and thoroughly communicate the knowledge of a domain.

2	Description	➢ Initiation done based on **glossary** which typically focuses on core noun concepts of a domain. Such models are free of data or implementation biases and emphasize rich vocabulary.
		➢ A correct choice of **terms** and **words** need to be done in communications where highly precisions and unique differences are to be identified.
		➢ A concept model is different from data model and therefore include vocabulary which is far rich as it is specific to knowledge intensive domains. Such models can be rendered graphically too.
		➢ Concept models can be effective where
		    o enterprise seeks to retain and communicate core knowledge,
		    o initiative needs to capture large number of business rules,
		    o there is resistance from stakeholders about perceived technical nature of models, definitions or diagrams,
		    o innovative solutions are sought when re-engineering business processes,
		    o enterprise faces regulatory or compliance challenges.

3	Elements	➢ **Noun Concepts** – Noun concepts are simply 'givens' for the space. ➢ **Verb Concepts** – Provide basic structural connections between noun concepts with help of wordings that can be referenced unambiguously. At times they are derived, inferred by definitional rules which lead to new knowledge or information. ➢ **Other Connections** – Standard connections include categorizations, classifications, partitive connections and roles.

4	Usage Considerations	<ul><li>**Strengths**<ul><li>A business-friendly way of communication with stakeholders about precise meanings.</li><li>Independent of data design biases and limited business vocabulary.</li><li>Proves highly useful white collar, knowledge rich business processes.</li><li>Helps ensures that large number of business rules and complex decision tables are free of ambiguity.</li></ul></li><li>**Limitations**<ul><li>Too high expectations set on relatively short notice.</li><li>Requires a specialized skill set based on ability to think abstractly.</li><li>Knowledge and rule focus may be foreign to stakeholders.</li><li>Sometimes require tooling to support real time use of business terminology.</li></ul></li></ul>

7.12 Data Dictionary

IBM Dictionary of computing defines data dictionary as

"A centralized repository of information about data such as meaning, relationships to other data, origin, usage, and format"

A data dictionary is also referred to as metadata repository. It comprises of information about the primitive and composite data elements.

A landline number is an example of a composite data element and it comprises of primitive data elements like ISD Code, STD Code, Area code etc.

Data dictionary is a set of information describing the contents, format and structure of a database and the relationship between its elements.

1	Purpose	It is used to standardize a definition of a data element and enable a common interpretation of data elements.
2	Description	➢ It is a document standard definitions of data elements, their meanings and allowable values. ➢ A data dictionary contains definitions of each data element and is used to standardize meanings and usage of data elements between solutions and stakeholders. ➢ It is also referred to as metadata repositories and are used to manage data within the context of a solution. Moreover they can be manually maintained in form of spreadsheet or via automated tools.

3	Elements	➢ **Data Elements** – Data dictionary contains definitions of each primitive data element, explains how they can be combined into composite data elements and describe characteristics such as definition, their meanings and allowable values.
		➢ **Primitive Data Elements** – Following information need to be recorded for each primitive data element:
		   o **Name** – Unique name for data element.
		   o **Aliases** – Alternate names for the data elements.
		   o **Values / Meanings** – A list of acceptable values for the data element. Usually shown as enumerated list or as a description of allowed formats for the data.

		<ul><li>○ **Description** – Definition of data element in context of solution.</li></ul><ul><li>➢ **Composite Elements** – Composite structures include:<ul><li>○ **Sequences** – ordering of primitive data elements within the composite structure.</li><li>○ **Repetitions** – Whether one or more data may be repeated multiple times.</li><li>○ **Optional Elements** – May or may not occur in particular instance of the composite element.</li></ul></li></ul>
4	Usage Considerations	<ul><li>➢ **Strengths**<ul><li>○ Provides all stakeholders with a shared understanding of format and content of relevant information.</li><li>○ Single repository of corporate metadata promoting the use of data throughout organization.</li></ul></li><li>➢ **Limitations**<ul><li>○ Requires regular maintenance else metadata could become obsolete or incorrect.</li><li>○ Requires time and effort to complete maintenance in a consistent manner.</li><li>○ May have limited value across enterprise unless it is used in multiple scenarios.</li></ul></li></ul>

7.13 Data Flow Diagrams

Data flow diagram is a graphical representation of the data flowing through an information system.

1	Purpose	Data flow diagrams shows where data comes from, which activities consume it and process it as well as if the output results are stored or utilized by another activity or external entity.
2	Description	➢ Data flow diagrams depict the **transformation** of data using the transactional data across the boundaries of a system. ➢ A data flow diagram illustrates **movement** of data between external entities and processes. The output from one external or process is an input to another. ➢ The data flow diagram shows **permanent** or **temporary repositories** where data is stored or retained for certain time. ➢ As part of multiple layers of abstraction, highest level diagram is a **context** diagram which represents the system as a whole. ➢ Further drilling down, **level 1** diagram shows the processes related to the system with the respective input data, output transformed data and data stores. At this level, internal partitions of work and data flowing between the partitions is shown. Each of these partitions can be decomposed further as part of level 2 and 3 diagrams if required. Only additional flows and stores are defined as part of this. ➢ **Logical** data flow diagrams represent the future or essential state showing transformations to be occurring irrespective of current physical limitations. ➢ **Physical** data flow diagrams model all the data stores, printers, forms, devices and other manifestations of data representing current state or 'to-be' state.

3	Elements	➢ **Externals (Entity, Source, Sink)** – An external refers to an object which is capable of producing or receiving data outside the system which is under analysis.
		    o Externals are sources and/or destinations of the data.
		    o There should be at least one data flow going to or coming from it.
		    o Usually shown as rectangle with a noun representation within context level diagrams.
		➢ **Data Store** – A data store is a collection of data where it can be stored for future use. There should be at least one or more

			data flow going in and coming out of it. It is represented as either two parallel lines or an open-ended rectangle with a label. ➢ **Process** – It can be a manual or automated activity performed to transform the data into an output. There must be at least one data flow going to it and one coming out from it. It is represented as a circle or rectangle with round corners. ➢ **Data Flow** – The movement of data between an external, process, and a data store is represented by data flows. Every data flow will connect to or from a process that transforms input into an output. They are represented as a line with an arrow displayed between processes. It is named using a noun.
4	Usage Considerations		➢ **Strengths** o Good to use as a discovery technique for processes or data and for verification of functional decompositions or data models. o Very good to define the scope of system helping for estimations of the effort needed to study the work. o Very easy to understand. o Helps to identify duplicated data elements. o Illustrates connections to other systems. o Helps define the boundaries of system. o Can be used as part of system documentation. o Helps to explain the logic behind data flow within system. ➢ **Limitations** o This can become complex and difficult for stakeholders to understand. o Different methods of notation or symbols could create challenges. o No idea about sequence of activities. o Process or stakeholders are not focused as part of this.

7.14 Data Mining

Data mining is practice of examining large pre-existing databases to generate new information.

1	Purpose	Improve decision making by finding useful patterns and insights from data.

2	Description	➤ It is an analytic process to **examine** large amount of data and summarize it in such a way that useful **patterns** or **relationships** are discovered.
		➤ Outcome of this technique is a **mathematical** model or equation that describe underlying patterns or relationships and which can be deployed for human decision making as well as for automated decision making systems.
		➤ In **supervised** investigation, generally a question is posed and an answer is expected to drive the decision making.
		➤ In **unsupervised** investigation, data mining usually emerges with discovery of patterns which emerge and are considered for business decisions. In general term this covers descriptive, diagnostic and predictive techniques:
		   o **Descriptive** – Clustering makes it easy to see patterns in set of data.
		   o **Diagnostic** – Understand the reason why a pattern exists.
		   o **Predictive** – Regression or neural networks can show likelihood of something to be true in future.

3	Elements	➤ **Requirements Elicitation** – Goal of data mining is identified either in terms of decision requirements or identified business decision.
		   o Top down data mining exercise is conducted with formal decision making process.
		   o Bottom up pattern discovery looks into insights that can be placed on existing decision models.
		   o They are productive when used in agile environment and assist in rapid iteration, confirmation and deployment.
		➤ **Data Preparation: Analytical Dataset** – These tools work on analytical dataset. It is formed by merging records from multiple tables or sources into a single wide dataset.
		   o The data can be extracted into a physical file or it may be a virtual file kept on database to be analyzed.
		   o Data volumes can be very large resulting in the need to work with samples or to work in data store so that data does not have to be moved around.
		➤ **Data Analysis** – Data is analyzed once it is available. This step is often the longest and most complex in data mining

		effort and is focused for automation. Mostly the work is around identifying typical characteristics in the data.
		➤ **Modelling Techniques** – Analytical dataset and calculated characteristics are fed into below mentioned algorithms which are either unsupervised or supervised. Couple of examples are:
		    o classification and regression trees, C5 and other decision tree analysis techniques,
		    o linear and logistic regression,
		    o neural networks,
		    o support sector machines and predictive scorecards
		➤ **Deployment** – Data mining models can be deployed to support a human decision making or to support automated decision making systems.
		    o Data mining results may be presented using visual metaphors or identified as potential business rules that can be deployed using a business rules management system.
		    o Some may lead to mathematical formulas which can be deployed as an executable and can be used to generate SQL or code for deployment.

4	Usage Considerations	➤ **Strengths**
		    o Reveal hidden patterns and create useful insight during analysis.
		    o Can be integrated into system design.
		    o Can be used to eliminate human bias by using the data to determine the facts.
		➤ **Limitations**
		    o Applying some techniques without an understanding can result in erroneous correlations.
		    o Access to big data mining tool sets can lead to accidental misuse.
		    o Many techniques and tools need specialist knowledge to work with.
		    o Many techniques used advanced math in background and hence they are not transparent to all stakeholders.
		    o Results may be hard to deploy if the decision they want to influence is poorly understood.

7.15 Data Modelling

Data modelling involves showing a progression from conceptual to logical to physical model and how data items relate to each other at different levels.

1	Purpose	A data model describes the entities, classes or data objects relevant to a domain, the attributes that are used to describe them and the relationships among them to provide a common set of semantics for analysis and implementation.

2	Description	➢ A data model usually shown in form of diagram supported by text descriptions shows elements that are important, attributes associated with them and relationships between them.
		➢ They are frequently used in **elicitation** and **requirement analysis** and **design** as well as **support** implementation and continuous improvement. Several variations of data models are:
		    ○ Conceptual data model – Being independent of any solution or technology, it is used to represent how the business perceives its information.
		    ○ Logical data model – Abstraction of conceptual data model applying rules of normalization to manage integrity of data and relationships and is associated with design of a solution.
		    ○ Physical data model – Is used to describe how a database is physically organized.
		➢ Logical and physical **entity relationship diagrams (ERD)** would be used to implement a relational database.
		➢ Similar level of logical and physical **class diagram** would be used to support object oriented software development.
		➢ **Object** diagrams can be used to illustrate particular instances of entities from a data model.

3	Elements	➢ **Entity or Class** – An entity can be something physical, organizational, and something abstract or an event based.
		    ○ Entities are referred to as **classes** in class diagrams.
		    ○ A class contains **attributes** and has **relationships** with other classes.
		    ○ In addition, it also contains functions or **operations** that provide information on what the class is meant to do. Every class will have a **unique identifier**.

			➤ **Attribute** - It defines a particular level of information associated with an entity including how much information can be captured in it, allowable values and type of information it represents. It can include values as:
			    ○ **Name** – A unique name for the attribute. Other names can be captured as aliases.
			    ○ **Values/Meanings** – A list of acceptable value for the attribute. It could be an enumerated list or a description of allowed formats for the data.
			    ○ **Description** – Definition of the attribute in context of the solution.
			➤ **Relationship or Association** – The relationship between entities provides **structure** of the data model and its specification indicate the number of **min** or **max occurrences** allowed on each side of the relationship. This is referred to as cardinality. Typical values are zero, one or many for above.
			    ○ For class model, **association** term is used instead of relationship and multiplicity is used instead of cardinality.
			➤ **Diagrams** – The diagram in a data model is called an entity relationship diagram whereas it is called class diagram in class model.
			➤ **Metadata** – The data model contains metadata describing what the entities represent, when and why they were created or changed, how they should be used and how often they need to be used, when and by whom.

4	Usage Considerations		➤ **Strengths**
			    ○ Can be used to define and communicate a consistent vocabulary.
			    ○ Review of logical data model helps to ensure the data correctly represents the business need.
			    ○ Provides a consistent approach to analyzing and documenting data and its relationships.
			    ○ Flexibility of different level of details for respective audience.
			    ○ Formal modelling of the information may expose new requirements as inconsistencies are identified.
			➤ **Limitations**
			    ○ May be unfamiliar to people from non-IT background.

		o May extend across multiple functional areas of organization which can be beyond the knowledge base for individual stakeholders.

7.16 Decision Analysis

Decision Analysis refers to a systematic, quantitative and interactive approach to addressing and evaluating important choices confronted by organizations.

1	Purpose	Formally assesses a problem and possible decisions in order to determine the value of alternate outcomes under condition of uncertainty.

2	Description	➢ A decision is an act of choosing a **single course of action** from several uncertain outcomes with different values. The outcome may be a financial value, score or a relative ranking.
		 ➢ Decisions are often difficult to assess when the problem is poorly defined, action towards outcome is not understood, external factors are underestimated or value of the outcome is not understood.
		 ➢ **Effective** decision analysis requires an understanding of values, goals and objectives, nature of the decision to be made, areas of uncertainty affecting decision and consequences of potential decision. Decision analysis approaches use following **activities**:
		    o Define problem statement
		    o Define Alternatives
		    o Evaluate Alternatives
		    o Choose Alternative to Implement
		    o Implement Choice

3	Elements	➢ **Components of Decision Analysis** – General components include: o **Decision to be made or Problem Statement** – Brief description of what the question or problem is about.

			o **Decision Maker** – Person responsible for final decision.
			o **Alternative** – A possible course of action.
			o **Decision Criteria** – Evaluation criteria used to evaluate the alternatives.
			➤ **Decision Matrices** – 2 types of decision matrices: Simple decision matrix and weighted decision matrix.
			   o Simple decision matrix – Checks whether each alternate meets each criterion being evaluated and then totals the number of criteria matched for each alternate.
			   o Weighted decision matrix – Assesses options in which each criterion is weighted based on importance. Higher the weighting, the more important the criterion. Alternates are ranked per criterion on a scale of 1-5.
			➤ **Decision Trees** – Allows for assessment of responses to uncertainty to be factored across multiple strategies. It includes decision nodes referring to different strategies, chance nodes defining uncertain outcomes and terminator or end nodes which identify a final outcome of the tree.
			➤ **Trade-offs** – Relevant when a decision problem involves multiple, conflicting objectives. Effective methods includes elimination of dominated alternatives and ranking objectives on similar scale.

4	Usage Considerations		➤ **Strengths**
			   o Provides a prescriptive approach for determining alternate options.
			   o Helps stakeholders under pressure to assess options based on criteria.
			   o Assess honestly the importance placed on different alternate outcomes to avoid false assumptions.
			   o Construct appropriate metrics to compare both financial and non-financial outcome evaluation criteria.
			➤ **Limitations**
			   o Information to conduct proper decision analysis may not be available and hence many decisions

		which are made immediately may not consider formal or informal process. ○ Some decision analysis models need specialized knowledge.

7.17 Decision Modelling

Decision model is an intellectual way of perceiving, organizing and managing business logic behind a business decision.

1	Purpose	Shows how repeatable business decisions are made.
2	Description	➢ Decision models show how **data** and **knowledge** are combined to make a specific decision. ➢ **Straightforward** decision models use a single decision table or decision tree to show how a set of business rules operating on a common set of data elements combine to create a decision. ➢ **Complex** decision models break down decisions into individual components so that each piece of decision can be separately described and modelled. ➢ A **comprehensive** decision model shows where the business rules come from and represents decisions as analytical insight. These rules may be definitional or behavioural.
3	Elements	➢ **Types of Models and Notations** – Decision tables are showing all the rules required to make an atomic decision. Complex decisions require the combination of multiple simple decisions showing dependency or via notations into a network. There are 3 key elements involved: - **decision**, **information** and **knowledge**. ○ **Decision Tables** – A decision table is a compact, tabular representation of a set of **rules** which use a specific set of input values to determine a particular outcome by using a defined set of business rules. ▪ Each row is a rule and each column represent one of the conditions of that rule. ▪ When all the conditions are met for the input data, then specified outcome is selected.

		<ul><li>There are one or more condition columns mapping to one or more specified data elements and to one or more action or outcome columns.</li></ul><ul><li>**Decision Trees** – Another way to represent the set of **business rules**. Each path on decision tree node is a single rule, branches show the conditions that must be met to continue down the branch. It is very effective to represent customer segmentation related rule sets.</li><li>**Decision Requirements Diagrams** – A visual representation of the **information**, **knowledge** and **decision** making involved in complex business decision. Such diagrams contain of elements such as decisions, input data, business knowledge models and knowledge sources. As part of diagrams, solid arrows represent the information requirements for a decision whereas broken, dashed, rounded arrows shows knowledge sources. This is authority of a person.</li></ul>
4	Usage Considerations	➢ **Strengths**<ul><li>Decision models are easy to share and support impact analysis.</li><li>Multiple perspectives can be shared when a diagram is used.</li><li>Simplifies complex decisions from the process.</li><li>Allows for reuse as it assists in managing large number of rules in decision tables by grouping them by decision.</li><li>Good models to work for rules based automation, manual or business intelligence projects.</li></ul>➢ **Limitations**<ul><li>Adds a second level diagram for modelling processes that contain decisions which adds unnecessary complexity.</li><li>Only limits the rules capturing decision.</li><li>May not involve behavioural business rules in a straightforward fashion.</li><li>Cuts across organizational boundaries that make the necessary sign off difficult to achieve.</li></ul>

7.18 Document Analysis

Document Analysis is technique around assessment of existing documents which are interpreted to give meaning around an assessment area of interest

1	Purpose	Elicit business analysis information including understanding requirements, examining available materials or existing organizational assets.
2	Description	➢ Document analysis is done to gather **background** information in order to understand the context of business need or to validate how a solution has been implemented. ➢ **Data mining** is an approach to document analysis which is used to analyze data in order to determine patterns, opportunities and related changes. ➢ By understanding and doing in depth analysis of the material such as wide variety of source materials, business rules, validation on existing solution and its implementation in current form will be understood. This helps to bridge the knowledge gaps when subject matter experts are no longer present or are absent during elicitation process.

3	Elements	➢ **Preparation** – While assessing documents for analysis, business analysts consider:
		    ○ whether or not source content is genuine and content is understandable as well as easily conveyed to stakeholders
		    ○ defining data to be mined grouped by logical relationships.
		➢ **Document Review and Analysis** – This includes conducting a detailed review of content and associated notes, identifying if there are any conflicts or duplicates and noting any gaps in knowledge which may need to be revisited again for additional research.
		➢ **Record Findings** – Consideration need to be given to the information elicited through document analysis to see if the content and level of detail is appropriate for intended audience and if the material can be transformed into any visual aids to improve understanding.

4	Usage Considerations	➢ **Strengths**

		<ul><li>Existing source material may be used as basis for analysis and no new content need to be created.</li><li>Existing resources can be used as a point of reference against the results of other requirements elicitation techniques.</li><li>Findings can be presented in formats that permit ease of review and reuse.</li></ul> ➤ **Limitations** <ul><li>Existing documentation may be out of date or invalid.</li><li>Authors may not be available for questions.</li><li>Primarily helpful only for evaluation of current state and can be very time consuming if have to go through wide range of sources which can lead to confusion.</li></ul>

7.19 Estimation

Estimation is the process of identifying and reaching to an estimate or an approximate value that is usable for some purpose from any kind of data.

1	Purpose	Used to forecast effort and cost involved in pursuing a course of action.
2	Description	➤ Estimation is used to support decision making by predicting attributes such as: <ul><li>cost and effort to pursue a course of action,</li><li>expected solution benefits,</li><li>project cost,</li><li>business performance,</li><li>potential value anticipated from a solution,</li><li>costs of creating and operating a solution,</li><li>potential risk impact</li></ul> ➤ The outcome of the estimations is sometimes expressed as a **single number** or a **range** having min and max value with a probability of occurrence. This is defined as **confidence interval**. ➤ Estimation is an **iterative** process and can include an assessment of its associated level of uncertainty.

3	Elements	➢ **Methods** – Common estimation methods include:
		   o **Top down** – examining components at a high level in a hierarchy.
		   o **Bottom up** – using lowest level element to examine the work in detail and summing across to provide an overall estimate.
		   o **Parametric Estimation** – Parametric model of element attributes being estimated.
		   o **Rough Order of Magnitude (ROM)** – High level of estimate having a varying confidence interval based on limited information.
		   o **Rolling Wave** – Repeated estimates throughout an initiative or project providing detailed estimates for near term activities and extrapolated for remainder of the initiative.
		   o **Delphi** – Uses a combination of expert judgement and history. There are several variations on this process, but they all include individual estimates, sharing the same with experts and having several rounds of estimation until consensus is reached. An average of three estimates is used.
		   o **PERT** – 3 values are given to each component of the estimate – a) Optimistic based on best case scenario, b) Pessimistic based on worst case scenario and c) Most likely value. PERT value is computed as a weightage average = (Optimistic + Pessimistic + (4 X most likely))/6.
		➢ **Accuracy of the Estimate** – It is a measure of uncertainty that evaluates how close an estimate is to the actual value measured later. Shown as ratio of width of confidence interval to its mean value and then expressed as a %.
		   o In case where little information is available, ROM estimate is delivered that is having high level of uncertainty.
		   o Definitive estimate is made for real world data. Such estimates are more accurate and used for predicting timelines, budgets, etc.
		   o Combination of above 2 is made for lot of initiatives where ROM is calculated for next iteration of work and definitive calculated for remainder of work.

		➢ **Sources of Information** – Common sources of information include:
		    ○ **Analogous Situations** – Using an element that is like the element being estimated.
		    ○ **Organization History** – Previous experiences of organization with similar work.
		    ○ **Expert Judgement** – Leveraging the knowledge of individuals about the element being estimated. It relies on expertise of those who have performed the work in the past, internal and external to organization.
		➢ **Precision and Reliability of Estimates** – Measure of agreement between estimates relates to precision of the same. Level of agreement can be determined by measuring the imprecision metric such as variance.
		    ○ **Reliability** of an estimate is reflected in variation of estimates made by different methods of estimating.
		➢ **Contributors to Estimates** – The estimators of an element are frequently those responsible for that element. Sometimes organization has a group that performs estimation for much of the work whereas in some cases it may call on an external expert to review estimate if high level of confidence is needed.

4	Usage Considerations	➢ **Strengths**
		    ○ Provides a rationale for an assigned budget or size of a set of elements.
		    ○ Teams making change without any estimate can be lead to unrealistic budget or schedule of work.
		    ○ Having estimate done by team of individuals provide closer predictor of the actual value.
		    ○ Updating estimate over work cycle helps ensure success and incorporates knowledge.
		➢ **Limitations**
		    ○ If organization or local knowledge is not there, estimates can vary widely from actual values.
		    ○ Usage of one estimation method may lead stakeholders to have unrealistic expectations.

7.20 Financial Analysis

Financial Analysis is a process of evaluating business, projects and related elements as well as finance related entities to determine their performance and suitability.

1	Purpose	It is used to understand the financial aspects of an investment, solution or solution approach.
2	Description	<ul><li>Financial analysis considers total **cost of the change** as well as total **costs** and **benefits** of **using** and **supporting** the solution.</li><li>It is an assessment of expected financial viability, stability and benefit realization of an investment option.</li><li>It is used to make solution recommendation for an investment based on analysis of<ul><li>**initial cost** and **time** frame in which costs are incurred,</li><li>expected financial **benefits** and time to achieve it,</li><li>**ongoing costs** of using and supporting solution,</li><li>**risks** associated with change initiatives,</li><li>**ongoing risks** to business value of using that solution</li></ul></li><li>A comparison of financial analysis results on investment options is made to make decisions.</li><li>In addition, it also helps to deal with uncertainty by assessing if the required business value will be delivered by a particular change initiative. In case financial analysis results show that information is not supporting initial solution recommendation, then the change initiative will be stopped.</li></ul>
3	Elements	<ul><li>**Cost of the change** – It is the expected cost of building or acquiring the new solution and expected costs of transitioning the enterprise from current to future state.</li><li>**Total Cost of Ownership (TCO)** – It is the cost to acquire or purchase a solution, use a solution, support the solution for a foreseeable future combined to help understand the potential value of the solution.</li><li>**Value Realization** – Value realized over time, so called as planned value, could be expressed as a cumulative value over specific time period.</li></ul>

- **Cost-Benefit Analysis** – It is the prediction of the expected total benefits minus expected total costs resulting in an expected net benefit.
    - **Assumptions** about the factors making up costs and benefits should be stated clearly so that better prediction can be made.
    - **Time period** should look far enough in future that the solution is in full use, and the planned value is being realized. Helps to understand costs and when expected value should be realized.
- **Financial Calculations** – They help to understand the perspectives about how and when different investments will deliver value. Financial software including spreadsheets provide functions to correctly perform these calculations.
    - **Return on Investment** – It is expressed as a percentage measuring the net benefits divided by the cost of the change. Formula to calculate ROI is – (Total benefits – cost of investment) / Cost of investment. Higher the ROI, better will be the investment.
    - **Discount Rate** – It is assumed interest rate used in present value calculations. A larger discount rate is used for time periods more than few years to reflect greater uncertainty and risk.
    - **Present Value** – Present day value is used to calculate benefits by comparing the effects of different rates and time periods. Formula to calculate present values is – Sum of (net benefits in that period / (1 + Discount Rate for that period)) for all periods of cost-benefit analysis. Present value is expressed in **currency**. Higher the present value, greater the total benefit.
    - **Net Present Value (NPV)** – It is the benefits minus the original cost of investment. It is expressed in **currency**. Higher the NPV, better the investment.
    - **Internal Rate of Return (IRR)** – IRR is interest rate at which an investment breaks even and is usually used to determine if the change or solution approach is worth investing in. The minimum threshold against which IRR is compared and organization expects to earn from its investments is called **hurdle rate**. If IRR

			< hurdle rate, investment should not be made. Higher IRR means better investment. IRR calculation based on interest rate at which NPV is 0 – NPV = (-1 X original investment) + Sum of (net benefit for that period / (1 + IRR) for all periods) = 0. ○ **Payback Period** – It provides a projection on time period required to generate enough benefits to recover the cost of the change and is expressed in years or years and months.
4	Usage Considerations		➢ **Strengths** ○ Help to objectively compare different investments from different perspectives. ○ Assumptions and estimates built into benefits and costs so they may be challenged or approved. ○ Reduces the uncertainty of a change or a solution by identification and analysis of factors influencing investment. ○ If anything changes during a change initiative, it can help to re-evaluate the recommended solution. ➢ **Limitations** ○ Some costs and benefits are difficult to quantify financially. ○ As it is forward looking, uncertainty is expected about costs and benefits. ○ Positive financial numbers may give false sense of security as not all information may be covered.

7.21 Focus Groups

Focus group is a group of selected people gathered to participate in a planned discussion about a particular topic or area of interest.

1	Purpose	Focus group is a means to elicit ideas and opinions about a specific product, service or opportunity in an interactive group environment.
2	Description	➢ A focus group is composed of pre-qualified **participants** whose objective is to discuss and comment on a topic within a context. ➢ A trained **moderator** manages the preparation of the session, helps and advises in selecting participants and facilitate the session. ➢ It may also serve to assess **customer satisfaction** with a product or service. ➢ A focus group is a form of **qualitative** research. **Difference** between **focus group** and **brainstorming** is that focus group is more structured and focused on participant's perspectives concerning a specific topic and it is not an interview session but rather a discussion during which feedback is collected on specific subject.
3	Elements	➢ **Focus Group Objective** – A clear objective to set the purpose of the group. ➢ **Focus Group Plan** – It ensures that all stakeholders are aware about the purpose and agree on expected outcomes and makes sure that session meets those objectives. A plan defines activities that include purpose, location, logistics, participants, budget, timelines and outcomes. ➢ **Participants** – A focus group has typically 6 to 12 attendees. If more participants are needed, then more than one focus group is required. ➢ **Discussion Guide** – A guide provided to moderator with a prepared script of specific questions and topics for discussion that meets the objective of the session. ➢ **Assign a Moderator and Recorder** – Moderator is an unbiased representative of feedback process focusing on engaging all participants with adaptability and flexibility. Recorder takes notes to ensure participant's opinions are accurately recorded.

		➤ **Conduct the Focus Group** – Moderator guides the discussion and recorder captures the group's comments. ➤ **After the Focus Group** – Results of focus group are transcribed as soon as session has ended. Business analyst looks for trends in responses and creates a report that summarizes the results.

4	Usage Considerations	➤ **Strengths**
		  o Ability to elicit data from group of people in single session.
		  o Effective to learn people's attitudes and desires
		  o Creation of environment where participants can consider their personal view.
		  o Online focus group sessions can be recorded easily and played back.
		➤ **Limitations**
		  o Participants may be unwilling to discuss sensitive topics in a group setting.
		  o Data collected may not be consistent with how people behave.
		  o In case of homogeneous group, responses may not have complete set of requirements.
		  o A skilled moderator is needed to manage this.
		  o Sometimes may be hard to schedule group for same date and time.
		  o Difficult for moderator to assess attitudes in an online focus group as it limit interaction between participants. One vocal participant can consume full time.

7.22 Functional Decomposition

Functional decomposition is a process of taking a complex process and breaking down into smaller and simpler parts.

1	Purpose	It helps manage complexity and reduce uncertainty by breaking down processes, systems or deliverables into simpler constituent parts and allowing each part to be analyzed independently.
2	Description	➢ Functional decomposition approaches the analysis of complex systems and concepts by considering them as a set of collaborating or related functions, effects and components. ➢ The isolation of components help to reduce complexity and allows scaling, tracking and estimating the work effort for each of them. ➢ It also helps to evaluate each sub component's success by relating it to other larger or smaller components. Any sub component can have only one parent component when developing the functional hierarchy.
3	Elements	➢ **Decomposition Objectives** – They drive the process of decomposition, and define what to decompose, how to do it and to what depth it needs to be done. Objectives include measuring, managing, designing, analyzing, estimating and forecasting, reusing, optimizing, substituting and encapsulating the problem area. ➢ **Subjects of Decomposition** – Functional decomposition applies to wide variety of subjects like business outcomes, work to be done, business process, functions, business units, solution components, activities, products and services as well as decisions. ➢ **Level of Decomposition** – The objective of decomposition is to have understanding and details to proceed as well as apply the results of decomposition in execution of other tasks. Therefore the level of decomposition helps in defining where to stop in order to achieve above objective. ➢ **Representation of Decomposition Results** – Diagramming techniques that can be used to represent functional decomposition includes tree diagrams, nested diagrams, use

		case diagrams, flow diagrams, state transition diagrams, cause-effect diagrams, decision trees, mind maps, component diagrams and decision models/notations.

4	Usage Considerations	➢ **Strengths**
		   o Makes complex endeavours by breaking down into feasible parts.
		   o Provides a structured approach to build understanding of complex matters.
		   o Simplifies measurement and estimation of work involved.
		➢ **Limitations**
		   o Missing or incorrect information may cause a need to revise the results.
		   o Many systems cannot be fully represented by simple relationships.
		   o Exploring all decompositions could be challenging and time consuming task.
		   o Involves deep knowledge of subject and collaboration with stakeholders for effective decomposition.

7.23 Glossary

Glossary refers to an alphabetical list of terms in a particular area of knowledge with the definitions for those terms.

1	Purpose	A glossary defines key terms relevant to business domain.
2	Description	➢ Glossaries provide a list of terms and related definitions in form of common language that can be used to communicate and exchange ideas. ➢ It is organized and continuously accessible to all stakeholders.

3	Elements	➢ A glossary is a list of terms with definitions and related common synonyms. A term is included in the glossary when:
		   o a term is unique to a domain,
		   o there are multiple definitions for the term,
		   o definitions implied is outside of term's common use,
		   o there is reasonable change of misunderstanding

		➢ Glossary creation should take place in early stages of a project in order to facilitate knowledge transfer and understanding. ➢ A point of contact responsible for maintenance and distribution of the glossary is identified. ➢ When developing a glossary definitions should be clear, concise and brief, acronyms should be spelled out, access should be available easily and editing of glossary should be limited to specific stakeholders.

4	Usage Considerations	➢ **Strengths**
		   o Promotes common understanding of the business domain and better communication.
		   o Capturing definitions provides a single reference and encourages consistency.
		   o Simplifies writing and maintenance of business analysis information.
		➢ **Limitations**
		   o A glossary requires an owner to perform timely maintenance.
		   o It may be challenging for different stakeholders to agree on a single definition for a term.

7.24 Interface Analysis

Interface Analysis is a technique allowing an individual to define the requirement on how solution and its components interact with each other as well as with outside world.

1	Purpose	Interface analysis is used to identify where, what, why, when, how and for whom information is exchanged between solution components.
2	Description	<ul><li>An interface is a connection between two components or solutions. Interface types include:<ul><li>user interfaces including human users,</li><li>people external to solution,</li><li>business processes,</li><li>data interfaces between systems,</li><li>application programming interfaces,</li><li>any hardware devices</li></ul></li><li>Interface analysis defines and clarifies who will be consumer for the interface, what information is being exchanged through the interface, when information will be exchanged, where the exchange will occur, purpose of the interface and approach of implementation of interface.</li><li>Early identification of interfaces helps in deciding **functional coverage** to meet needs and which **stakeholders** will benefit from various components of the solution.</li></ul>
3	Elements	<ul><li>**Prepare for Identification** – A context diagram can reveal high level interfaces between different parts of solution components. Results of analysis shows the frequency of usage of interfaces and any key issues that need to be resolved in order for solution to be created.</li><li>**Conduct Interface Identification** – Interfaces are identified which are needed in future state for each stakeholder or system that interacts with the system. Business analyst describes the functions of interface, assess the frequency of the interface usage, evaluate which type of interface may be appropriate and elicit initial details about interface.</li><li>**Define Interfaces** – Requirements are primarily focused on describing the **inputs** to and **outputs** from that interface, any validation **rules** that govern those inputs and outputs, and events that might trigger interactions.</li></ul>

		o Interface defines **user workflow** between solution components and management objectives for the interface. o Interface definition includes name for it, coverage or span of the interface, exchange method between two entities, message format and exchange frequency.
4	Usage Considerations	➢ **Strengths** o Increased functional coverage is provided by early analysis of interfaces. o Clear specification of interfaces provide a structured means of allocating requirements, business rules and constraints to solution. o Avoids over analysis of fine detail due to broad application of same. ➢ **Limitations** o Not much insight provided in other aspects of solution as internal components are not touched as part of analysis.

7.25 Interviews

Interview is a technique of formal meeting between two people where questions are asked on an area in order to obtain relevant information about the same.

1	Purpose	An interview is a systematic approach designed to elicit business analysis information from a person or group of people by talking to interviewees, asking relevant questions and documenting the responses. It is used for establishing relationships, building trust, increase stakeholder involvement or build support for a proposed solution.
2	Description	➢ It is a common technique to elicit requirements. ➢ One-on-one interviews are most common whereas interviewer can also conduct a group interview where it is very important to carefully elicit responses from each participant. ➢ Two basic types of interviews used to elicit business analysis information: o **Structured Interview** – Interviewer has predefined set of questions.

		<ul><li>○ **Unstructured Interview** – No predetermined format and questions may vary based on interviewee response and interactions.</li></ul><ul><li>➤ Successful interviewing depends on factors such as:<ul><li>○ level of understanding of the domain by interviewer,</li><li>○ experience of the interviewer in conducting interviews,</li><li>○ skill of interviewer in documenting discussions,</li><li>○ readiness of the interviewee to provide information relevant to topic,</li><li>○ degree of clarity in interviewee's mind about goal of interview</li><li>○ rapport of interviewer with the interviewee</li></ul></li></ul>
3	Elements	<ul><li>➤ **Interview Goal** – Overall purpose of conducting interviews must be clear and focus on individual goals for each interview that an interviewee can provide must be clearly expressed and communicated.</li><li>➤ **Potential Interviewees** – Based on goals, project manager, project sponsors and other stakeholders can help to identify potential interviewees.</li><li>➤ **Interview Questions** – **Open ended** questions can be used to elicit requirements in form of a dialogue and cannot be answered in yes/no fashion. This helps to uncover information about those areas which are not known.<ul><li>○ **Closed ended** questions are used to elicit response in form of yes, no or specific number. It can be used to clarify or confirm a previous answer.</li><li>○ Interview questions are often organized based on **priority** and **significance** as well can be compiled in an interview guide where interviewee's responses are easily recorded.</li></ul></li><li>➤ **Interview Logistics** – Ensuring a successful interview requires attention to logistics that include **location** of interview, whether or not to **record** interview, whether or not **sending questions** to interviewee in advance and how the results will be **summarized** to avoid identifying individual interviewees when the results are to be kept confidential.</li><li>➤ **Interview Flow** – Opening the interview includes describing the **purpose** of interview, confirming the interviewee's **roles**, explaining how the information will be recorded and shared.<ul><li>○ The interviewer maintains **focus** on established goals and predefined questions, considers the willingness of</li></ul></li></ul>

		interviewees to participate, manages concern raised and arranges for their follow up, actively listens and verified information provided and takes notes or record interviews wherever needed. o **Closing** interviews includes asking the interviewees for overlooked areas, providing contact information to follow up, summarizing the session, outlining the process on usage of interview results and thanking interviewees for their time. ➢ **Interview Follow-Up** – It is important for interviewer to organize information and confirm results with interviewees to point out any missed or incorrectly recorded items.

4	Usage Considerations	➢ **Strengths**
		    o Simple direct technique that encourages participation by and establishes rapport with stakeholders.
		    o Enables observation of non-verbal behaviour.
		    o Interviewer can ask follow up and probing questions to confirm their understanding.
		    o Maintains focus through usage of clear objectives for the interview and allows interviewees to express opinions in private.
		➢ **Limitations**
		    o Training as well as significant time is required to plan and conduct effective interviews.
		    o Requires considerable commitment and involvement of participants.
		    o Resulting documentation may be subject to interviewer's interpretation based on level of clarity.
		    o There is a risk of unintentionally leading interviewee.

7.26 Item Tracking

Item Tracking is a technique of tracking the items identified as part of discussion to a closure.

1	Purpose	Item tracking is used to capture and assign responsibility for issues and stakeholder concerns that pose an impact to the solution.
2	Description	➢ It is an organized approach to address stakeholder concerns.

		➢ Viability of stakeholder concern is checked when it is initially raised. ➢ Item tracking tracks the item from initial recording of identified concern till closure of the same including its degree of impact. Throughout the lifecycle, item tracking record is assigned to one or more stakeholder and is shared with all stakeholders to ensure transparency, visibility into the status and progress of items in record.
3	Elements	➢ **Item Record** – Each record item may contain all or any of the **attributes** for item tracking. These attributes are item identifier, summary, category, type, date identified, identified by, impact, priority, resolution date, owner, resolver, agreed strategy, status, resolution updates and escalation matrix. These attributes are usually available in format of a form within tool where items can be recorded. Good **examples** of such tools are JIRA from Atlassian, HP's Quality centre. ➢ **Item Management** – Organizational processes and stakeholder needs drive resolution of each and every item. When dependencies are identified, resolution efforts need not be duplicated and should progress in coordination. ➢ **Metrics** – Key performance indicators are identified and used to resolve the items tracked. By reviewing the output, stakeholders can determine how well items are getting resolved by proper resources, initiative is progressing and item tracking process is being utilized.

4	Usage Considerations	➢ **Strengths**
		   o Ensures concerns around requirements resolved to stakeholder's satisfaction.
		   o Allow stakeholders to rank the importance of outstanding items.
		➢ **Limitations**
		   o Sometimes the recording of data may outweigh actual benefits that could be realized.
		   o Time is spent on this which could be used somewhere else in better efforts.

7.27 Lessons Learned

Lessons Learned technique is actually a feedback loop for finding out improvements around concerned areas.

1	Purpose	Main purpose of lessons learned process is to compile and document successes, opportunities for improvements, failures and recommendations for future projects.
2	Description	➢ A lessons learned session which is also known as retrospective helps identify changes to business analysis process and deliverables or successes which can be incorporated into future work. ➢ These sessions could be either **formal** facilitated meetings with set agendas and meeting roles or **informal** working sessions. ➢ **Formal** sessions are conducted in form of sprint retrospective towards end of each iteration in agile methodology where teams visit their processes, technology used, approach being followed, communication as well as collaboration strategy and try to find out improvements in concerned areas. This is managed and decided mutually by all team members. It is one of the best **feedback loop mechanism** for agile team. ➢ **Informal** sessions can be conducted at any time or at any checkpoint within SDLC methodology.
3	Elements	➢ Sessions can include a review of business analysis activities, final solution or service or product, automation or technology that was introduced or eliminated, impact to organizational process, performance expectations, positive or negative variances, root causes impacting performance results and recommendations for approaches.

4	Usage Considerations	➢ **Strengths**
		   o Useful in identifying opportunities and assist in building team morale after a difficult period.
		   o Reinforces positive experiences and successes.
		   o Reduces risks for future and provide tangible value or metrics.
		   o Recognizes strengths or shortcomings with project structure or tools that were used.
		➢ **Limitations**

		<ul><li>Honest discussion may not occur if participants try to blame each other.</li><li>Participants may not be ready to discuss problems and as a result a proactive facilitator may be required to keep discussion on track.</li></ul>

7.28 Metrics and Key Performance Indicators (KPIs)

Metrics and Key Performance Indicators (KPIs) refer to a measurement value and related metric which demonstrates how effectively a company is achieving key business objectives.

1	Purpose	This technique is useful to measure the performance of solutions and related components.
2	Description	<ul><li>A **metric** is a quantifiable level of an indicator to measure progress. **Example** of a metric is as follows:<ul><li>Suppose we are tracking monthly sales over 6 month's period between July 2017 and January 2018. Total monthly sales for 7/17 – 1/18 is our metric.</li></ul></li><li>An **indicator** identifies a specific numeric measurement that represents the degree of progress towards achieving a goal. **Example** is as follows:<ul><li>Continuing on above example, a proper indicator of performance could be 'Total monthly sales to budget for 7/17 – 1/18'</li></ul></li><li>A **key performance indicator** is one that measures progress towards a strategic goal. **Example** of this is 'To increase monthly sales by 20%'.</li><li>Metrics and reporting are key components of monitoring and evaluation. Monitoring is a continuous process of data collection used to determine how well a solution that is implemented is matching the expected results.</li><li>**Evaluation** is a systematic and objective assessment of a solution both to determine its status and effectiveness in meeting objectives over time and identify ways to improve the solution to meet objectives.</li></ul>

			➤ Top most priorities for evaluation and monitoring system are intended goals, inputs, outputs and related activities.

3	Elements		➤ **Indicators** – An indicator displays result of analyzing one or more specific measures for addressing a concern about a need, value in a table or graphical form.
			    o A good indicator has six characteristics:
			        ▪ **Clear** – Precise and unambiguous. Continuing on above example, 'monthly sales' is clear as an indicator.
			        ▪ **Relevant** – Appropriate to concern. Monthly sales is relevant to the sales team as an indicator.
			        ▪ **Economical** – Not costly to obtain. Monthly sales can be calculated based on extraction of sales report from a tool.
			        ▪ **Adequate** – Provides a sufficient basis to assess performance. Monthly sales is adequate to understand existing sales target and determine the same for future.
			        ▪ **Quantifiable** – Independently validated. Monthly sales can be quantified against a target.
			        ▪ **Trustworthy and Credible** – Based on evidence and research. Previous year's sales performance can be taken into consideration to compare monthly sales.
			    o In addition to above, stakeholder's interests are also very important as they might need certain indicators that provide more information.
			    o In cases where all factors are not available to measure, substitutes are identified and used.
			➤ **Metrics** – Quantifiable level of indicators that are measured at a specified point in time. It can be a specific point, threshold or range and can be measured multi-yearly, annually, quarterly or monthly.
			➤ **Structure** – In order to establish a monitoring and evaluation system, **data collection procedure** which covers collection of samples and related frequencies, **data analysis** procedure which covers analyzing collected data for patterns, **reporting** procedure which looks at report templates and means as well as frequency to deliver reports

		to stakeholders and **baseline data** which looks about recent performance to measure progress from that point onwards is needed. ○ In addition, factors such as **reliability, validity and timeliness** are required to assess quality of indicators. ➤ **Reporting** – Reports compare baseline, current and target metrics to calculate difference presented in absolute and relative terms.

4	Usage Considerations	➤ **Strengths**
		    ○ Helps to allow stakeholders to understand the extent to which a solution meets an objective.
		    ○ Indicators, metrics and reporting also facilitate linking goals to objectives, supporting solutions and tasks.
		➤ **Limitations**
		    ○ Sometimes excessive amount of data gathered can lead to distraction of team members and unnecessary costs.
		    ○ Individuals can act to increase their performance on only those metrics which are used to assess their performance.

7.29 Mind Mapping

Mind Mapping is a technique to capture and link ideas on a particular topic leading to logical information.

1	Purpose	Mind mapping is used to articulate and capture thoughts, ideas and information.
2	Description	➤ It is a form of a **note** taking that captures ideas and information using graphs, images and connected relationships to apply structure and logic to information. ➤ A mind map has **central idea** which have linked secondary ideas and connections between them via single keyword. ➤ Mind maps are used to think through and generate ideas on complex concepts, explore relationships between problem

		areas and present a consolidated view of complex concepts or problems.
3	Elements	➢ **Main Topic** – Main topic is the thought or concept that is being articulated and is positioned in centre to show associations from other topics. ➢ **Topics** – These are thoughts or concepts that further articulate the main topic and is expressed through a connected line and a keyword associated with it. ➢ **Sub-topics** – Sub topics are related to main topic and are associated via a branch and keyword associated with it. ➢ **Branches** – Associations between main topic, topics and sub-topics. ➢ **Keywords** – Single words used to articulate nature of association of topics connected by a branch. ➢ **Colour** – Colours are used to show associations and provides a best way to suit their mode of thinking. ➢ **Images** – Images can be used to express larger volumes of information to encourage creativity and innovations through ideas and thoughts.
4	Usage Considerations	➢ **Strengths** 　o Used as an effective collaboration and communication tool. 　o Summarizes complex thoughts to show overall structure and associations facilitate understanding and decision making. 　o Enable creative problem solving and is helpful in preparing and delivering presentations. ➢ **Limitations** 　o Can be misused as a brainstorming tool. 　o Shared understanding of mind map may be difficult to communicate.

7.30 Non-Functional Requirements Analysis

Non-Functional Requirements Analysis is a technique for identifying quality attributes of requirements focusing on operations of a system.

1	Purpose	Non-functional requirements analysis examines the requirements for a solution that define how well the functional requirements must perform. It specifies criteria that is needed to judge operation of a system rather than specific behaviours.
2	Description	➢ Non-functional requirements referred to as **quality** attributes are associated with system solutions, process and people aspects of solution. ➢ They **supplement functional** requirements and identify **constraints** on those requirements as well as describe quality **attributes** a solution must exhibit when based on functional requirements. ➢ These kinds of requirements are generally expressed in textual formats as **declarative statements** or in **matrices**. ➢ A very good **example** of them is 'System must be able to send accounts back within 5 seconds'.

3	Elements	➢ **Categories of Non-Functional Requirements** – Common categories include:
		    ○ **Availability** – Degree to which solution is operable and accessible when it is used.
		    ○ **Compatibility** – Degree to which solution operates effectively with other components of solution.
		    ○ **Functionality** – Solution functions meeting user needs.
		    ○ **Maintainability** – Ease with which solution can be modified to adapt to changes in environment.
		    ○ **Performance Efficiency** – Degree to which a solution performs with minimum consumption of resources.
		    ○ **Portability** – Ease of transferring solution components from one environment to another.
		    ○ **Reliability** – Ability of solution to perform its required functions under specific conditions for a specified period of time.

- **Scalability** – Degree with which solution can be extended or evolved.
- **Security** – Aspects of solution protecting solution content from malicious access.
- **Usability** – Ease with which a user can learn and adapt to make use of the solution.
- **Certification** – Constraints on solution that are necessary to meet standards or regulations.
- **Compliance** – Regulatory, financial or legal constraints on solution.
- **Localization** – Attention to context looking towards dealing with local languages, laws, currencies.
- **Service Level Agreements** – Constraints of organization being served by the solution which is formally agreed to by both parties (provider and consumer/user) of solution.
- **Extensibility** – Ability of solution to incorporate new functionality.

➢ **Measurement of Non-Functional Requirements** – Non-functional requirements must be quantified and verified using appropriate measure of success. Measurement of same can be done based on source of requirement.
- A good **example** of **measurable** non-functional requirement is – "The system must be able to respond within 5 seconds in 80% of scenarios".
- **Example** of requirement impacted by **source** is "Certification requirements are generally specified in measurable detail using standard such as ISO certification."

➢ **Context of Non-Functional Requirements** – Context is dynamic by nature and such requirements may need to be adjusted or removed completely. It is always best to understand the relative stability of context in order to conduct evaluation of non-functional requirements.

4	Usage Considerations	➢ **Strengths** o Provides constraints that apply to a set of functional requirements. o Measurable expressions are provided to show performance of functional requirements as well as will provide a view of acceptance of solution. ➢ **Limitations**

| | | | <ul><li>Clarity and usefulness of non-functional requirements depends on experience of stakeholders to express needs.</li><li>Multiple users may have different requirements which might be too hard to handle.</li><li>At times such requirements may have conflicts and may require negotiation.</li><li>Strict requirements or constraint can add more time and cost which may impact solution's adoption.</li><li>Many requirements could be qualitative and hence difficult to be measured on a scale.</li></ul> |

7.31 Observation

Observation is a technique to observe a person doing a specific task and to understand how it is getting done in a specific environment.

1	Purpose	Observation is used to elicit information by viewing and understanding activities and related context. This technique provides basis for identifying needs, explore a business process, setting expectations in form of performance standards, evaluation of solution performance and supporting training.
2	Description	➢ Job shadowing involves examining a work activity as it is performed. Approach and process defines the objectives for observation. Observation of individual's work environment can help to discover tools and assets involved in performing activities which is termed as **contextual inquiry**. Two basic approaches are there – <ul><li>**Active** – Interaction happens between individuals while observing an activity. This is a good approach to smooth decision making process.</li><li>**Passive** – No interruption to work is done during the activity of the observer. Helps in understanding natural flow of events and can also be recorded if needed.</li></ul>
3	Elements	➢ **Observation Objectives** – This includes understanding the activities and elements, identifying opportunities for

		improvement, establishing performance metrics as well as assessing solutions and validating assumptions.
		➢ **Prepare for Observation** – This session involves planning the approach based on objectives, skills, experience level of participants, frequency of activities being performed, reviewing an existing documentation. Planning includes awareness of purpose of observation session, agreement on expected outcomes and making sure that session meets their expectations.
		➢ **Conduct the Observation Session** – Observation session is conducted with following activities mentioned below.
		    o Before observation session
		        ▪ purpose need to be conveyed,
		        ▪ make sure to participant that their performance is not judged,
		        ▪ inform the participant that they can stop the observation at any time
		        ▪ recommend sharing of concerns while performing the activity
		    o During the observation session
		        ▪ watch the person perform the activity and note specific tasks or steps,
		        ▪ record observation, time taken to complete the work and quality of the outcome
		        ▪ ask appropriate questions while work is being performed.
		➢ **Confirm and Present Observation Results** – Notes and data recorded are reviewed and followed up with the participants to fill any gaps. This is achieved by sharing the notes and data with participants and data is collated, aggregated, summarized to identify differences, similarities and trends.

4	Usage Considerations	➢ **Strengths**
		    o Realistic and practical insights about activities and tasks can be gained.
		    o Any informal tasks and related workarounds can be observed.
		    o Productivity can be viewed and compared against performance standards.
		    o Improvement recommendations are supported by objective and quantitative evidence.

		➢ **Limitations** 　o May be disruptive to the performance of participant. 　o Can be threatening and intrusive to the person. 　o There is a chance that participant may alter work practices. 　o Time is required to plan for and conduct observations. 　o Knowledge sharing activities cannot be observed.

7.32 Organizational Modelling

Organizational model is a way to define an organizational structure using a framework of line of authorities, communications, and allocation of resources as well as their related duties.

1	Purpose	Organizational modelling is used to describe the roles, responsibilities, reporting structures that exist within an organization and to align those structures with the organization's goals.
2	Description	➢ An organizational model defines how an organization is **structured**. ➢ The purpose of an organizational unit is to bring together a group of **people** to fulfil a common **purpose** or to serve a particular **market** by sharing common set of skills and knowledge. ➢ An organizational model is a visual representation of a unit which depicts boundaries of the group, formal relationships between members, functional role for each person and interfaces between the unit and other units.
3	Elements	➢ **Types of Organizational Models** – 3 organizational models include: 　o **Functionally oriented** – Groups staff based on shared skills and areas of expertise 　　▪ **Pros** - Encourages standardization of work and reduces duplication 　　▪ **Cons** - Develop communication and cross-functional coordination problems. 　o **Market oriented** – Intended to serve particular customer groups rather than grouping employees by common skills or expertise.

		<ul><li>**Pros** – Helps to meet the needs of its customers.</li><li>**Cons** – Develop inconsistencies in process and multiple functional areas may be performing duplication of work.</li></ul><ul><li>**Matrix Model** – Has separate managers for each functional area and for each product or market area.<ul><li>**Pros** - Employees report to line manager related to work efficiency and identifying opportunities for improvements. They report to market manager who is responsible for managing service or product across functional areas.</li><li>**Cons** – Each employee has two managers and accountability is difficult to maintain.</li></ul></li></ul><ul><li>**Roles** – An organizational unit including a number of defined roles having specific responsibilities and performing certain kinds of work.</li><li>**Interfaces** – Interfaces may be between two organizational units in form of communication with people in other roles and work packages that the unit receives from or delivers to other units.</li><li>**Organizational Chart** – Basic diagram to show organizational modelling.<ul><li>**Box** depicts an **organizational unit** which refers to people, teams, departments or a mix of all. It also shows roles within an organization and people assigned to each role.</li><li>**Line** depicts **lines of reporting** which refers to accountability and control between units. A solid line depicts direct authority, while a dotted line indicates information transfer or situational authority.</li></ul></li><li>**Influencers** – Identifying all influencers is important in planning communication and making provisions for user acceptance.</li></ul>
4	Usage Considerations	<ul><li>**Strengths**<ul><li>Very common in most organizations.</li><li>Allows team members to provide support and benefit future projects.</li></ul></li><li>**Limitations**<ul><li>Models are sometimes out of date.</li></ul></li></ul>

		o Informal lines of authority not reflected in org chart and may conflict with organizational chart.

7.33 Prioritization

Prioritization is an activity to arrange items in order of their relative importance. There could be many criteria against which the prioritization can happen.

1	Purpose	This provides a framework to facilitate stakeholder decisions and to understand relative importance of business analysis information.
2	Description	➢ It is a process used to determine the relative importance of business analysis information based on **value, risk, difficulty** of **implementation** or other criteria. ➢ Prioritization is classified into one of **four** approaches – grouping, ranking, time boxing/budgeting and negotiation. ➢ Identification of an approach includes consideration of **audience, needs**, and their opinions on **value** a requirement brings to a stakeholder's respective area.
3	Elements	➢ **Grouping** – Classifying information according to predefined categories such as high, medium or low priority. ➢ **Ranking** – Ordering information from most important to least important. This leads to sequencing of requirements in an ordered list which is termed as product backlog in agile methodology. ➢ **Time boxing / Budgeting** – Prioritizing requirements based on what can be achieved in fixed time period or within fixed amount for money. Suitable for fixed deadline projects. ➢ **Negotiation** – Gain a consensus amongst stakeholders as to which requirements will be prioritized.

4	Usage Considerations	➢ **Strengths**
		    o Facilitates consensus building and trade-offs and ensures that solution value is realized and timelines are met.
		➢ **Limitations**
		    o In many cases, stakeholder may attempt to avoid difficult choices.
		    o Solution team may be influencing the result of prioritization by thinking that it may be too difficult or complex to implement certain requirements.

		o Metrics and key performance indicators are not always available while prioritizing information.

7.34 Process Analysis

Process analysis is a step by step breakdown of phases of process used to convey the inputs, outputs and operations that take place during each phase.

1	Purpose	This technique is used to assess a process for its efficiency and effectiveness as well as ability to identify opportunities for change.

2	Description	➢ It is used for various purposes including:
		    o recommending a more efficient or effective process,
		    o determining the gaps between current and future state of process,
		    o understanding factors to be included in contract negotiation,
		    o analysis on how data and technology are used in process and analyzing the impact of pending change to process
		➢ Examples of **frameworks** and **methodologies** used to for process analysis are **six sigma** and **lean**.
		➢ **Methods** used for process improvement includes value stream mapping, statistical analysis and control, process simulation, benchmarking and process frameworks.
		➢ Some examples of **changes** made to processes includes reducing the time required to complete task, modifying interfaces between units and thus reduce bottlenecks, increasing automation in decision making process and automation of activities which are repeatable.

3	Elements	➢ **Identify Gaps and Areas to Improve** – Business analysts identify gaps between current and desired future state, identify gaps and differentiate between areas adding value and non-value added areas, identify pain points and challenges of process, understand opportunities to improve the process from multiple point of view and align the gaps to improve with the strategic direction of the organization.

		➢ **Identify Root Cause** – As part of identification of root cause, business analyst understand that there may be multiple root causes, or input leading to gaps or areas of improvements, not identifying right people to identify the root cause and current measurements in place not performing as per standards.
		➢ **Generate and Evaluate Options** – It is important to generate options and alternative solutions to solve for the gaps and improve the process. Identifying value of proposed solution relative to alternative options need strong involvement of stakeholders.
		➢ **Common Methods**
		  ○ **SIPOC** – SIPOC is a process analysis method that originates in **Six Sigma** methodology and helps to understand the Suppliers, Inputs, Process, Outputs and Customers of the process being analyzed. This helps to create discussion about problems, opportunities, gaps, root causes and options.
		  ○ **Value Stream Mapping (VSM)** – Process analysis method used in **lean** methodologies. This involves picturing the inputs and application points for processing those inputs from front end of the supply chain. Value stream map provides a one page view of the steps involved in end to end process including both value-adding and non-value adding elements.

4	Usage Considerations	➢ **Strengths**
		  ○ Ensures solution address the right issues, minimizing waste.
		  ○ Many different techniques and methodologies can be used to provide flexibility in approach.
		➢ **Limitations**
		  ○ Can be time consuming.
		  ○ At times, it becomes hard to identify a technique and follow it completely as there are lot of them.
		  ○ It may prove ineffective for knowledge intensive processes.

7.35 Process Modelling

Process modelling is an analytical representation of organization's business processes.

1	Purpose	Process modelling is a standardized graphical model used to show how work is carried out and is a foundation for process analysis.
2	Description	➢ Process models describe the **sequential** flow of **work** or activities. A **business** process model describes the sequential flow of work across defined **tasks** and **activities** in enterprise. ➢ A **system** process model defines the sequential flow of **control** among programs or units within a computer system. ➢ A **program** process flow shows sequential execution of program **statements** within a software program. ➢ **Process** model decomposes a complex process into component processes. At highest level, model shows an overview of process and its relationship. At lower levels, it can define more granular activities and identify all outcomes whereas at lowest levels, model can be used for execution. ➢ Process model defines the **current state** of a process or a potential future state. ➢ Generally a process model includes **participants** in process, business **event** that triggers the process, the **steps** or activities of process, **flows** and **decision points** that logically link those activities and results of the process. ➢ Most **basic** model includes a **trigger** event, a sequence of **activities** and a **result** whereas **comprehensive** process model can include data / materials, inputs and outputs.

3	Elements	➢ **Types of Process Models and Notations** – Many different notations are used in process modelling.
		    o Most commonly used notations include:
		        ▪ **Flowcharts and Value stream mapping** – Used in business domain.
		        ▪ **Data Flow diagrams and UML diagrams** – Technology domain.

			<ul><li>**Business Process Model and Notations (BPMN)** – Used across both business and IT domains.</li><li>**Integrated Definition notation and Input, Guide, Output, Enabler diagrams** – Used for scoping.</li><li>**SIPOC and Value Stream Analysis** – Process modelling.</li></ul><ul><li>Process models consists of **key elements** like activity, event, directional flow, decision point, link and role.</li><li>**Flowchart** – Provides a good view to non-technical audiences and is good for gaining alignment with what the process is and context for a solution. It could be simple showing sequence of activities or it can be comprehensive showing swimlanes for roles.</li><li>**Business Process Model Notation (BPMN)** – Used extensively for modelling business processes. A key feature is its ability to distinguish the activities of different participants in a process with pools and swimlanes. On crossing of a boundary, work is passed to another role within organization.</li><li>**Activity Diagram** – This UML based diagram focuses on single use case. It employs swimlanes, shows synchronization bars for parallel processing and multiple exit decision points.</li></ul>
4	Usage Considerations		<ul><li>**Strengths**<ul><li>Provides basic understanding of sequential activities.</li><li>Most stakeholders are comfortable with the concepts.</li><li>Provides view of handling large number of scenarios.</li><li>Helps to identify pain points in process structure.</li><li>Can be used for training purpose as well as baseline for continuous improvement.</li><li>Provides transparency and clarity to process owners.</li></ul></li><li>**Limitations**<ul><li>In some cases, process model documentation could reflect heavy approach of old times. Hence no time is allocated for this.</li><li>Can become more complex if not structured carefully.</li><li>At times hard to provide sign off for a single individual.</li></ul></li></ul>

| | | <ul><li>Problems in process cannot be identified always by looking at a high level model.</li><li>These models can become obsolete in agile environments.</li><li>It may become hard to maintain as processes can change without changes made to documentation.</li></ul> |

7.36 Prototyping

Prototype is an early sample model of a product built to test the actual concept or process to act as a thing to be learned from or to be replicated. This is used to gain early feedback from audience.

1	Purpose	Prototyping is used to elicit and validate stakeholder needs through an iterative process to optimize user experience, evaluate design options and provide a base for development of final solution.
2	Description	<ul><li>Prototyping provides an early model of **final result** known as prototype. It provides an early view of product and helps in early stages of design.</li><li>Prototypes can be non-working models, working representations or digital depiction of a proposed product.</li><li>**Business rules** and **data** prototypes can be used to discover desired process flow and business rules.</li><li>**Data** prototyping can be used for data cleansing and transformation.</li></ul>
3	Elements	<ul><li>**Prototyping Approach** – Two common approaches used are:<ul><li>**Throw-away** – Prototypes generated with simple tools to serve uncovering of requirements and may be updated or evolved during course of discussion and development. It does not become workable code or get maintained as a deliverable once final system is implemented.</li><li>**Evolutionary of Functional** – Prototypes created to extend initial requirements into final solution.</li></ul></li></ul>

			Usually includes a prototyping tool or language to produce a working solution from prototype.
			➢ **Prototyping Examples** – Form of prototyping can be:
			  ○ **Proof of Principle or Proof of Concept** – Model verifying design of a system.
			  ○ **Form Study Prototype** – Very good model to identify ergonomic and visual factors using a sculptural representation of product made from inexpensive materials.
			  ○ **Usability Prototype** – Product model created to test how the end user interacts with the system.
			  ○ **Visual Prototype** – Model testing the visual aspects of solution only.
			  ○ **Functional Prototype** – Model to test software functionality, qualities of system for user and workflow.
			➢ **Prototyping Methods** – Following methods are used for prototyping:
			  ○ **Storyboarding** – Visually and textually detail the sequence of activities.
			  ○ **Paper prototyping** – Uses paper and pencil to draft a process.
			  ○ **Workflow Modelling** – Shows a sequence of operations performed by humans.
			  ○ **Simulation** – Demonstrate solutions or components of solution.

4	Usage Considerations		➢ **Strengths**
			  ○ Provides a visual representation of future state.
			  ○ Allows for stakeholders to provide input and feedback early in design process.
			  ○ People may feel more comfortable using throw away prototypes.
			  ○ A narrow yet deep vertical prototype can be used for technical feasibility studies.
			➢ **Limitations**
			  ○ Highly complex process, if depicted via prototype, can make the process take considerable time, effort and facilitation skill.
			  ○ Technology feasibility is needed to be done in order to initiate prototyping in some cases.

		o In case of deeply elaborated and detailed prototype, unrealistic expectation for final solution can be developed. o Stakeholders may focus on design specifications of solution rather than the requirements that any solution must address.

7.37 Reviews

Reviews technique focuses on assessing something formally with an intention to identify and make changes if required.

1	Purpose	Reviews are used to evaluate the content of work product.
2	Description	➤ The objective of review differ according to what is getting reviewed. Removal of defects is main objective of review of a **completed** work whereas resolving a question or issue is main objective of review of a work in **process**. ➤ The 3 dimensions that are used to tailor needs of organization are – **objectives** which define purpose of review, **techniques** showing how to do it and **participants** taking part in review. ➤ Reviews can include an overview of work product and objectives, checklists and reference materials, reviewing the work product and record the findings and to verify for any rework.
3	Elements	➤ **Objectives** – Prior to conduct review, objectives are clearly communicated and may include one or more goals such as to remove defects, ensure work product is complete and correct, required specifications or standards are met, establish consensus on an approach or solution, educate reviewers about work product and to measure work product quality. ➤ **Techniques** – Reviews can be formal or informal and can use below techniques to support objectives of review. o **Inspection** – Formal technique including an overview of work product, defects logged and follow-up to ensure changes were made.

		<ul><li>**Formal Walkthrough (Team Review)** – Formal technique that uses individual review and team consolidation activities seen in inspection.</li><li>**Single Issue Review (Technical Review)** – Formal technique focusing one issue before the joint review session.</li><li>**Informal Walkthrough** – An informal technique in which work product is taken through and feedback is solicited.</li><li>**Desk Check** – Reviewers who have not been involved or not provided feedback provide the same.</li><li>**Pass Around** – Informal technique in which multiple reviewers provide verbal or written feedback.</li><li>**Adhoc** – Informal technique to seek informal review or assistance from a peer.</li></ul> ➤ **Participants** – Roles involved in a particular review depends on objectives of review, selected technique and any standards which need to be followed. Following are the roles:<ul><li>**Author** – Author of work product.</li><li>**Reviewer** – Peer or stakeholder examining work product according to review objectives.</li><li>**Facilitator** - Neutral facilitator who facilitates review session, keeps participants focused on objectives and ensures that each section of work product is reviewed.</li><li>**Scribe** – A neutral participant with strong communication skills to document defects, suggestions, issues and questions during session.</li></ul>
4	Usage Considerations	➤ **Strengths**<ul><li>Help to identify defects early in work product lifecycle.</li><li>Parties involved in review become engaged in outcome.</li><li>Some techniques can be performed by reviewer at a convenient time rather than interrupting normal work such as desk checks and pass around.</li></ul>➤ **Limitations**<ul><li>Rigorous team reviews take time and effort.</li><li>It is not guaranteed that review by one or two participants will remove all defects.</li></ul>

		○ If review comments are shared via email, then there may be many messages to process.

7.38 Risk Analysis and Management

Risk Analysis is a review of uncertain event or condition associated with a particular event or action.

1	Purpose	Risk analysis and management identifies areas of uncertainty that could negatively affect value, evaluates uncertainties and develops and manages ways of dealing with the risks.
2	Description	➢ A negative impact is identified on value of the solution when risks are not properly identified and managed. ➢ Risk analysis and management involves identifying, analyzing and evaluating risks. ➢ It is an ongoing activity. Existing risks can be monitored and new risks can be identified by consultation and communication with stakeholders.
3	Elements	➢ **Risk Identification** – Risks are identified and recorded in **risk register** that supports the analysis of those risks. Various attributes of risks that are captured in risk register are risk event which shows one or several occurrences, risk condition which talks about one specific condition, consequence, probability, impact, risk owner and mitigation plan. ➢ **Analysis** – Risk analysis involves **understanding** risk and **estimating** the level of risk. Likelihood of occurrence is expresses as a probability and measured in high, medium or low. Impact of any risk can be described in terms of cost, duration, solution scope, quality, or any factors agreed by stakeholders such as reputation, compliance or social responsibility. ➢ **Evaluation** – Risk analysis results are compared with potential value of the change or the solution to determine if the level of risk is acceptable or not.

			➢ **Treatment** – Risks can be acceptable at a certain level but it may be necessary to take measures to reduce risk. Once an approach is identified to deal with the risk, **risk response plan** is developed and assigned to owner with authority for that risk. Following approaches can be taken to address a risk:
			  o **Avoid** – Source of risk is removed or plan is adjusted to make sure that risk doesn't occur.
			  o **Transfer** – Liability of dealing with risk is shared with third party.
			  o **Mitigate** – Reduce the possibility of risk occurring.
			  o **Accept** – Decide not to do anything but to accept risk.
			  o **Increase** – Decide to take on more risk to pursue an opportunity.

4	Usage Considerations		➢ **Strengths**
			  o Can be applied successfully on strategic risks, tactical and operational risks.
			  o A successful risk response on one initiative can be useful lessons learned for other initiatives.
			  o Ongoing risk management help to evaluate changes in solution, re-evaluate risks and required planned responses.
			➢ **Limitations**
			  o Number of possible risks to most initiatives can easily become unmanageably large.
			  o High chance that significant risks are not identified.

7.39 Roles and Permissions Matrix

Roles and permissions matrix show a list of specific roles and operations assigned to those roles.

1	Purpose	It is used to ensure coverage of activities by denoting responsibility, to identify roles, to discover missing roles and to communicate results of a planned change.
2	Description	➢ Roles and permissions allocation involve identifying roles, associating them with solution activities, and then denoting authorities who can perform these activities. ➢ A role is a label for a group of individuals who share common functions. Each function is portrayed as one or more solution activities. A single activity can be associated with one or more roles by designating authorities.

3	Elements	➢ **Identifying Roles** – To identify roles, business analyst reviews organizational models, procedure manuals and system user guides as well as meet with stakeholders to uncover additional roles.
		➢ **Identifying Activities** – Business analysts use functional decomposition to break down each function into sub parts, to understand the workflow and division of work as well as uses cases to represent tasks. Initial level roles and responsibilities may be identified in a **RACI** (Responsible, Accountable, Consulted, and Informed) matrix.
		➢ **Identifying Authorities** – Identified roles are permitted to perform certain actions which is termed as authorities. Authorities for each role are identified with respect to each activity.
		➢ **Refinements** –
		    o **Delegations** – Delegation path can be identified for authorities amongst each other on a short term or permanent basis. **Example** – A sponsor may delegate decision taking to business owner in his/her absence.
		    o **Inheritances** – In case of authority assignment at an organizational hierarchy level, assignment pertain to only that user's organizational level.

4	Usage Considerations	➢ **Strengths**
		    o Provides procedural checks by restricting individuals from performing certain actions.
		    o Provides documented roles and responsibilities for activities.
		➢ **Limitations**
		    o Too much detail for specific initiative can be time consuming and too little detail can exclude necessary roles or responsibilities.

7.40 Root Cause Analysis

Root cause analysis is a method of problem solving used for identifying the root causes of faults or problems.

1	Purpose	It is used to identify and evaluate the underlying causes of a problem.

2	Description	➢ Root cause analysis is a proper approach to **examine** a problem or situation that focuses on problem's origin as proper point of correction rather than dealing with its effects only.
		➢ Root cause analysis can be used to identify root cause of an occurring problem for corrective action which is called **reactive analysis** and identifying problem area for preventive action which is termed as **proactive analysis**.
		➢ Root cause analysis uses four main activities –
		    o Problem statement definition describing issue to be addressed.
		    o Data collection gathering information about the nature, location and timing of the effect.
		    o Cause identification which investigates the patterns within a problem
		    o Action identification which defines corrective action that will prevent or minimize occurrence.

3	Elements	➢ **Fishbone Diagram** – Fishbone diagram or cause-and-effect diagram is used to identify and organize possible causes of problem. It serves as a map that depicts possible cause and related effects.

		➢ **The Five Whys** – It is a process of exploring nature and cause of a problem. It is used to reach to root cause of the problem and is a simplest tool to use when problems have a human interaction component. In fishbone diagram once all ideas are captured, five whys can help to drill down to root cause for each of them.

4	Usage Considerations	➢ **Strengths**
		   o Helps to maintain objective perspective.
		   o Enables stakeholders to specify an effective solution for corrective action.
		➢ **Limitations**
		   o Works best when training is provided to ensure the root causes are identified rather than just symptoms.
		   o May not be suitable for complex problems.

7.41 Scope Modelling

Scope modelling refers to technique that provides detailed view of limits for a business domain and related elements.

1	Purpose	Scope models define the nature of one or more limits or boundaries and place elements inside or outside those boundaries.

2	Description	➢ Scope models usually show and describe the boundaries of control, change, a solution or need.
		➢ These models show elements that could be:
		   o **In-scope** – Model identifies a boundary as seen from inside as well as elements contained by that boundary.
		   o **Out-of-scope** – Boundary from outside and elements that are not contained by that boundary.
		   o **Both** – Model identifies a boundary as seen from both sides as well as elements on both sides of boundary.

3	Elements	➢ **Objectives** – Scope models are typically uses to clarity the span of control, relevance of elements and where effort will be applied. ➢ **Scope of Change and Context** – Elements that will be altered as part of the change are considered as well as external elements that are relevant to the change. For the elements within scope of change, way are identified to

			modify those elements. On other hand, interactions are developed between change, current and proposed solution and context for those elements which are outside scope of change.
			➢ **Level of Detail** – Purpose of analysis defines the appropriate level of abstraction at which scope elements are described. Enough detailed elements provides a meaningful reduction of uncertainty and can be described by enumerating them or by grouping them into logical bound sets.
			➢ **Relationships** – Diagramming techniques used for exploring relationships of specific types, include:
			  o **Parent-child or Composition-subset** – Relates elements of same type by way of hierarchical decomposition.
			  o **Function-Responsibility** – Relate a function to its agent who is responsible to execute it.
			  o **Supplier-Consumer** – Relates elements by way of transmission of information or materials between them.
			  o **Cause-Effect** – Relates elements by logical contingency in order to identify chains of associated elements that are involves in change.
			  o **Emergent** – Several elements can interact to produce results that cannot be predicted.
			➢ **Assumptions** – Definition of need, causality of outcomes, impact of changes, applicability and feasibility of solution are couple of assumptions considered as part of scope modelling.
			➢ **Scope Modelling Results** – Results can be represented as textual descriptions of elements, diagrams showing relationships of scope elements and matrices depicting dependencies between scope elements.

4	Usage Considerations		➢ **Strengths**
			  o Help to define contractual obligations.
			  o Provides base for estimation of project effort.
			  o Helps in justifying in-scope/out of scope decisions in requirements analysis.
			  o Assess the completeness and impact of solutions.
			➢ **Limitations**

		o Can lack sufficient level of granularity that is needed for clear scope identification. o Changing a scope model may be difficult due to political reasons. o Complex boundaries cannot be addressed by traditional scope models.

7.42 Sequence Diagrams

Sequence diagrams provide a view of how objects interact with each other in form of messages in a specific order. It is also called as interaction diagram.

1	Purpose	Sequence diagrams are used to model the logic of usage scenarios by showing the information passed between objects in the system through execution of the scenario.
2	Description	➢ A sequence diagram shows how **processes** or objects interact during a scenario. ➢ Sequence diagram shows how **objects** used in the scenario interact and how user interface components interact. ➢ Objects sending messages to each other are represented as boxes that are aligned from left to right with a vertical line showing the scope and lifeline of the object. Messages that are sent from one object to another are shown as horizontal arrows. These diagrams are also called as event diagrams.

3	Elements	➢ **Lifeline** – Shows a lifespan of an object and is drawn as a dashed line that vertically descends from object box.
		➢ **Activation Box** – It shows a period during which an operation is executed. It is activated by incoming solid line arrow.
		➢ **Message** – Interaction between two objects shown as an arrow coming from sender object to recipient object. Different types of messages are shown:
		    o **Synchronous call** – Transfers control to receiving object. Sender cannot act under a return message is received.
		    o **Asynchronous call** – Allows the object to continue with its own processing after sending the signal.

			May send multiple signals but accept only one at a time.
4	Usage Considerations		➢ **Strengths** 　o Visual interaction between objects in a chronological manner. 　o Helps stakeholders to show interaction between objects in a visual manner. 　o Use cases can be refined into one or more sequence diagrams to provide more details. ➢ **Limitations** 　o Time and effort are wasted creating a complete set of sequence diagrams. 　o Have historically been used for modelling system flows.

7.43 Stakeholder List, Map or Personas

Stakeholder list, map and personas refer to jotting down list of stakeholders, mapping them to show relationships with solution and grouping them in a way it is easy to understand and empathize with.

1	Purpose	Stakeholder lists, maps and personas assist in analyzing stakeholders and their characteristics.
2	Description	➢ **Stakeholder analysis** involves identifying the stakeholders that may be affected by a proposed initiative or that share a common business need. ➢ Common types of stakeholder characteristics that are worth identifying and analysing includes level of authority within domain, attitudes toward change and business analysis work and role as well as level of decision making authority.
3	Elements	➢ **Stakeholder Lists** – Various techniques such as brainstorming and interviews are applied to generate a stakeholder list that is central to both stakeholder analysis activities.

			➤ **Stakeholder Map** – Diagrams that depict the relationship of stakeholders to solution and to one another. Common ones include:
			 ○ **Stakeholder Matrix** – Maps the level of stakeholder influence against the level of stakeholder interest. Four quadrants show:
			  ▪ **High Influence /high impact** – This group must be engaged regularly.
			  ▪ **High influence /low impact** – Stakeholder needs should be met and their level of interest keeps on increasing.
			  ▪ **Low influence / high impact** – Stakeholders are supporters and potential goodwill ambassadors for the change effort.
			  ▪ **Low influence / low impact** – Stakeholders can be kept informed using general communications.
			 ○ **Onion Diagram** – Shows the involvement of stakeholders with the solution along with those interacting with the solution and those who participate as part of larger organization or outside organization in business process.
			➤ **Responsibility (RACI) matrix** – Pre requisite for this is to have all stakeholders identified.
			 ○ **Responsible (R)** – Person performing the work on task
			 ○ **Accountable (A)** – Person held accountable for successful completion of task and is decision maker.
			 ○ **Consulted (C)** – Stakeholder who will be asked to provide an opinion about the task.
			 ○ **Informed (I)** – Stakeholder group is kept up to date of the task and is notified of its outcome.
			➤ **Personas** – Personas are helpful when there is a desire to understand the needs held by class of users. It is written in a narrative form a focuses on providing insights into goals of group. They bring users to life.

4	Usage Considerations		➤ **Strengths** ○ Identifies specific people who must be engage in elicitation activities. ○ Useful to understand changes in impacted groups over time.

		➤ **Limitations**
		    o Members working in same team may not use this technique because they perceive change as a minimal thing.
		    o Assessing information about a specific stakeholder representative can be complicated and feel risky.

7.44 State Modelling

State modelling is a technique that shows how an object operate from one state to another on triggering of an event or a condition.

1	Purpose	Describe and analyze different possible states of an entity within a system, how entity changes from one state to another and behaviour of entity in each state.
2	Description	➤ An entity is an **object** or **concept** within a system. Lifecycle of every entity has a beginning and an end. ➤ A state model describes a set of possible states of entity, sequence of states that the entity can be in, how an entity changes from one state to another, events and conditions causing the entity to change status and actions that can or must be performed in each state.
3	Elements	➤ **State** – An entity has finite number of states and it can be in more than one state at a time. Each entity state describes a name and activities that could be performed while in that state. ➤ **State Transition** – A transition may be conditional or automatic. It is describes in terms of event that causes the transition, condition which determine whether or not the entity must respond to that event, and actions that occur in association with the event. ➤ **State Diagram** – It shows the lifecycle of one entity starting from it coming into existence and going through all states till it is no longer of use. A **state** is shown as a rectangle with rounder corners. **Transition** from one state to another is shown with one directional arrow pointing from start state to

		destination state. **Beginning** and **end** of the entity's life cycle is shown with special symbols. ➢ **State Tables** – Two dimensional matrix showing states and transitions between them. Each row shows a starting state, transition and end state.

4	Usage Considerations	➢ **Strengths**
		    o Identifies business rules that apply to entity being modelled.
		    o Identify and describes the activities that apply to entity at different states of entity.
		    o Very much effective documentation and communication tool than plain text.
		➢ **Limitations**
		    o Good for complex entities understanding. Simple entities may not need to spend time and effort behind this.
		    o Building a state model appears simple at the start but achieving a consensus by the model can be difficult and time-consuming.

7.45 Survey or Questionnaire

Survey refers to a technique of defining measure of opinions from a group of people via asking questions whereas questionnaire refers to a set of questions with choice of answers devised for purpose of survey.

1	Purpose	Used to elicit information from a group of people in a structured way and in a relatively short period of time.
2	Description	➢ Survey or questionnaire presents a set of questions to stakeholders whose responses are collected and analyzed in order to formulate knowledge about subject matter of interest. Two types of questions are used in survey or questionnaire: o **Close-ended** – Respondent are asked to select from Yes/No or multiple choice question. Very easy to analyze responses as they can be tied to numerical coefficients.

		○ **Open-ended** – Respondent are asked free form question without asking to select an answer from a list of predefined responses. It can be more difficult and time consuming to analyze responses as they are unstructured.
3	Elements	➤ **Prepare** – Following things are considered while preparing for survey: ○ Define the objective ○ Define the target survey group ○ Choose appropriate survey or questionnaire type out from close-ended and open-ended. ○ Select the sample group. ○ Select the distribution and collection methods including communication mode. ○ Set the target level and timeline for response. ○ Determine if individual interviews are needed to support surveys. ○ Write the survey questions. ○ Test the survey or questionnaire using a usability test to identify errors. ➤ **Distribute the Survey or Questionnaire** – Distribution can be done via email, in-person or survey tool which considers the urgency of obtaining results, level of security required and geographic distribution of respondents. ➤ **Document the Results** – As part of documenting results, business analysts **collate** the responses, **summarize** the results, **evaluate** the details for any emerging themes, **formulate** categorizes for encoding of data and **break down** data into measurable increments.
4	Usage Considerations	➤ **Strengths** ○ Quick method and relatively inexpensive to administer. ○ Easier to collect information from a larger audience. ○ Effective, less time consuming and efficient way of eliciting requirements when stakeholders are geographically dispersed. ○ Closed ended questions will lead to use of quantitative data for use in statistical analysis whereas open ended questions will lead to identification of insights and opinions. ➤ **Limitations**

		<ul><li>Specialized skills in statistical sampling methods is required while analyzing survey of potential respondents.</li><li>Response rates may be too low.</li><li>Open ended questions may require more analysis.</li><li>Ambiguous questions may be left unanswered and may require follow up on answers provided.</li></ul>

7.46 SWOT Analysis

SWOT analysis refers to a technique for identifying and analyzing the internal and external factors that can have an impact on viability of a project.

1	Purpose	SWOT Analysis is a very good technique to evaluate organization's strengths, weaknesses, opportunities and threats to both internal and external conditions.
2	Description	<ul><li>SWOT analysis is brief, specific, realistic and supported by evidence as well as serves as an evaluation of organization against identified success factors.</li><li>A SWOT analysis can be used to:<ul><li>evaluate an organization's current **environment**</li><li>share information **learned** with stakeholders</li><li>identify the best possible **options** to meet an organization's needs</li><li>identify potential **barriers** to success and create actin plans to overcome barriers</li><li>adjust and redefine **plans** throughout a project as new needs arise</li><li>identify areas of **strength** that will assist an organization in implementing new strategies</li><li>develop criteria for evaluating project **success** based on given set of requirements</li><li>identify areas of **weakness** that could undermine project goals</li><li>develop strategies to address outstanding **threats**</li></ul></li></ul>
3	Elements	<ul><li>**SWOT** acronym is explained below:<ul><li>**Strengths (S)** - Any particular activities / processes that group does well and leads to success.</li></ul></li></ul>

			Example – Organization may be good in providing up to 97% of lending amount to customer. The strength here is funding capability. ○ **Weaknesses (W)** – Actions or functions which are poorly done or not at all done. **Example** – Servicing of loan within loan lifecycle is not properly done and customer complaints are raised for the same. ○ **Opportunities (O)** – External factors of which the assessed group may be able to take advantage of such as new technology. **Example** – Outsourcing of the loan servicing to one of the vendor may help in getting better customer satisfaction. ○ **Threats (T)** – External factors that can negatively impact the assessed group such as new competitor. **Example** – Acquisition of vendor providing loan servicing to one of the organization may lead to threat of changing strategies and operational structure.
4	Usage Considerations		➢ **Strengths** ○ It is a valuable tool to aid in understanding of organization, product and process. ○ Enables to direct the stakeholder's focus to the factors that are important to business. ➢ **Limitations** ○ Results of SWOT analysis needs more detailed analysis. ○ Unless a clear context is defined the result may be unfocused and contain factors which are not relevant.

7.47 Use Cases and Scenarios

Use cases refers to actions that are required to enable a goal and scenario refers to one single path through the use case.

1	Purpose	Describes how a person or system interacts with the solution to achieve a goal.
2	Description	➢ Use cases describe the **interactions** between **primary** actor, **solution** and **secondary** actors needed to achieve primary actor's goal. ➢ **Primary** or basic flow represents the most direct way to accomplish the goal of the use case. **Alternative** flows show the exceptions that could lead to failure to complete the goal. ➢ Use case diagrams are graphical representation of relationships between actors and one or more use-cases. ➢ A **scenario** is written as a series of steps performed by actors or by solution to achieve a goal. Use case describes several scenarios.

3	Elements	Following elements are captured in use case:
		➢ **Use Case Diagram** – An overview of actors interacting with the solution and any relationships between use cases. Relationships between actors and use cases are called associations. An association line indicates that an actor has access to the functionality represented by the use case. 2 commonly used relationships are:
		    o **Extend** – Additional behaviour insertion into a use case. This can be used to show alternative flows that has been added to existing use case.
		    o **Include** – Allows a use case to make use of functionality present in another use case. Mostly useful to show a shared functionality between several use cases.
		➢ **Use Case Description** –
		    o **Name** – Use case has a unique name.
		    o **Goal** – Brief description of a successful outcome of use case.
		    o **Actors** – An actor is any person or system external to solution that interacts with that solution.

		○ **Preconditions** – Any fact that must be true before the user case can begin. ○ **Trigger** – It is an event that strikes the flow of events for a use case. At times, temporal (time) event can initiate a use case. ○ **Flow of Events** – Series of steps performed by actor and solution during the execution of use case. This may include alternative and exception flows. ○ **Post-conditions or Guarantees** – It is any fact that must be true when the use case is complete. Separate post conditions are true for successful and unsuccessful execution of use case which is called as **guarantee**.
4	Usage Considerations	➤ **Strengths** ○ Can clarify scope and provide a high level understanding of requirements. ○ Very easy to understand due to their narrative flow. ○ Articulates functional behaviour of the system. ○ Ensure that business value of use case is articulated. ➤ **Limitations** ○ Decisions and business rules should not be recorded directly in use cases but managed separately. ○ Flexible format of use case may capture unnecessary information at times. ○ No relation is there between use case and solution design, hence extra effort will be required for same.

7.48 User Stories

User stories is a technique to capture a description of a software feature from an end user perspective including the type of user, what they want and why.

1	Purpose	User story represents a small concise statement of functionality or quality needed to deliver value to specific stakeholder.

2	Description	➤ A user story is typically a sentence or two that describes whose need is addressed by story, goal the user is trying to accomplish and any additional information that may be critical to understanding of the scope of story.
		➤ User stories can be used to **capture** stakeholder needs and prioritize them, create a basis for **estimating** and **planning** solution delivery, generating user acceptance **tests**, **metric** for measuring delivery value, unit for tracing related requirements and a unit of project management and **reporting**.
		➤ User story need to follow **INVEST** principle. It must be:
		   o I – **Independent** enough to be executed end to end.
		   o N – **Negotiable** to an extent where we can split it to granular level.
		   o V – **Valuable**. Must provide business value to stakeholders.
		   o E – **Estimable**. Team should be able to estimate it in any format they decide.
		   o S – **Small**. It should be small enough to be completed within a sprint.
		   o T – **Testable**. It should be testable from perspective of having proper acceptance criteria.

3	Elements	➤ **Title (optional)** – Title describe the activity stakeholder wants to carry out with the system.
		➤ **Statement of Value** – Format for user story has 3 components:
		   o **Who** – a user role or persona
		   o **What** – Necessary action or behaviour
		   o **Why** – Benefit of value received by user
		   o **Example** – As a <actor>, I want to <do X>, so that <X is achieved>. Acceptance criteria is written in format of 'Given.. When.. Then".

		➢ **Conversation** – Helps team to explore and understand the feature described in story and value it will deliver to stakeholder. ➢ **Acceptance criteria** – It defines the boundaries of a user story and help the team to understand what the solution needs to provide to deliver value.

4	Usage Considerations	➢ **Strengths**
		  o Easy to understand at stakeholder level.
		  o Focuses on value to stakeholders.
		  o Tied to small, implementable, testable slices of functionality leading to frequent customer feedback.
		➢ **Limitations**
		  o Team could lose sight of broader picture if stories are not traced back.
		  o Extra documentation will be required to meet the baseline for future work or stakeholder expectations.

7.49 Vendor Assessment

Vendor assessment refers to assessment of a prospective vendor to check if they are fit for business from a perspective of a product or service.

1	Purpose	A vendor assessment assesses the ability of a vendor to meet commitments regarding the delivery and consistent provision of a product /service.
2	Description	➢ Vendor assessment provides a sense of reliability about vendor and also ensures that product or service will meet organization's expectations and requirements. ➢ Assessment may be formal through submission of a Request for Information (RFI), Request for Quote (RFQ), Request for proposal (RFP) or Request for Tender (RFT). ➢ Organizational standards, complexity of initiative and solution's criticality towards delivery will influence the level of formality in which vendors are assessed.
3	Elements	➢ **Knowledge and Expertise** – Vendors can provide knowledge and expertise not available within organization. ➢ **Licensing and Pricing Models** – When a solution component is purchased from a third party vendor having

			different licensing models, cost-benefit analysis is conducted to understand the usage scenarios about the options. ➤ **Vendor Market Position** – Comparison between vendors with its competitors need to be done to decide which market players the organization wants to get involved. ➤ **Terms and Conditions** – Terms and conditions refer to the continuity and integrity of provided products/services. Providing terms for execution of customizations, regular update schedule and roadmap of features planned for delivery can be considered as part of it. ➤ **Vendor Experience, Reputation and Stability** – Vendor's experience with other customers may provide valuable information on how likely contractual and non-contractual obligations will be met. It may be needed to take steps to ensure there are no risks if a vendor continues financial difficulties, and it will be possible to maintain the solution even if vendor's situation changes radically.

4	Usage Considerations		➤ **Strengths**
			  o Opportunity to develop a productive and fair relationship with suitable and reliable vendor for long term.
			➤ **Limitations**
			  o Time and resources are consumed.
			  o Does not prevent the risk of failure as partnership evolves.
			  o Subjectivity may bias evaluation outcome.

7.50 Workshops

Workshops refers to conducting of a discussion for a period or practical work on a subject.

1	Purpose	It is an approach to bring stakeholders together in order to collaborate on achieving a predefined goal.
2	Description	➤ Workshop is a **time focused event** attended by stakeholders to gain consensus on requirements or a topic, review artefacts or generate new ideas for product/service. ➤ It is a very **productive** approach to promote trust, mutual understanding and strong communication among stakeholders as well as produce deliverables that guide future work. ➤ It generally involves a representative group or stakeholder, a defined goal, interactive and collaborative work, a defined work product and a facilitator.

3	Elements	➤ **Prepare for workshop** – Preparation for workshop includes:
		  o defining purpose and desired outcomes
		  o identify key stakeholder, facilitator and scribe
		  o create agenda
		  o determine approach for capturing outputs
		  o schedule the session and invite participants
		  o arrange room logistics and equipment
		  o send agenda in advance to attendees
		  o if possible, conduct pre-workshop interviews
		➤ **Workshop Roles** – Several roles involved are:
		  o **Sponsor** – Ultimate accountable for workshop's outcome.
		  o **Facilitator** – Facilitate the session, helps in decision making and conflict resolution and ensures that all participants have an opportunity to be heard.
		  o **Scribe** – Documents the decisions in format determined prior to workshop and any issues that are deferred during session.
		  o **Timekeeper** – Keeps track of time spent on agenda.
		  o **Participants** – Includes key stakeholders and SME's.
		➤ **Conduct the Workshop** – Facilitators generally begin with statement of its **purpose** and desired **outcomes**. Ground **rules** must be established for collaboration and can include to

		respect opinions of others, everyone need to contribute, discuss the issues and not people, discuss off topics to specific time frame and an agreement on how decisions are made. In addition, workshop's purpose and outcomes are validated from time to time against session activities. ➢ **Post Workshop Wrap Up** – Facilitator follows up on any open action item that were recorded at workshop, completes the documentation and distributes it to attendees.

4	Usage Considerations	➢ **Strengths**
		    o Agreement can be achieved in short period of time.
		    o Provides a means to gain a mutual understanding
		    o Costs are lower than those for multiple interviews.
		    o Quick feedback on issues or decisions are provided by participants
		➢ **Limitations**
		    o Stakeholder availability may make it difficult to schedule the workshop.
		    o Success of workshop is highly dependent on expertise of facilitator and knowledge of participants.
		    o Involving too many participants can slow down workshop process. Too less participants can lead to taking decisions which don't represent the needs of majority of stakeholders.

7.51 Glossary

- **Backlog:** The backlog is used to record, track, and prioritize remaining work items
- **Backlog Refinement:** Periodic review of the entire backlog should occur because changes in stakeholder needs and priorities may necessitate changes to the priority of some of the backlog items. In many environments, the backlog is reviewed at planned intervals.
- **Organizational unit (OU):** Any recognized association of people within an organization or enterprise.
- **Scope modelling:** Scope model is used to describe the scope of the analysis or scope of the solution. It allows the definition of "complete" scope, containing the boundaries of a business domain
- **Request for information (RFI):** An RFI is typically the first and most broadly cast of a series of requests intended to narrow down a list of candidates.
- **Request for quotation (RFQ):** An RFQ is generally used to obtain pricing, delivery information, terms and conditions from suppliers. In this case, requestors have a clear understanding of what they need, including requirements and specifications.
- **RFP:** An RFP, "Request for Proposal," is a document that asks vendors to propose solutions to a customer's problems or business requirements. An RFP is usually what follows an RFI; in fact, it's rare that a company will go from an RFI to an RFQ (for reasons that will become clear below). An RFP should contain much more specificity in terms of what a company's needs are by outlining the business goals for the project and identifying specific requirements that are necessary for the work being requested.
- **Subject Matter expert:** A subject-matter expert or domain expert is a person who is an authority in a particular area or topic. The term domain expert is frequently used in expert systems software development
- **RACI Matrix:** Responsible, Accountable, Consulted, and Informed matrix (RACI matrix): A tool used to identify the responsibilities of roles or team members and the stakeholders
- **Decision Analysis:** An approach to decision making that examines and models the possible consequences of different decisions and assists in making an optimal decision under conditions of uncertainty.
- **SIPOC:** A SIPOC diagram is a tool used by a team to identify all relevant elements of a process improvement project before work begins. It helps define a complex project that may not be well scoped and is typically employed at the Measure

phase of the Six Sigma DMAIC (Define, Measure, Analyze, Improve, Control) methodology.

- **Rough Order of Magnitude (ROM):** Almost always, the project manager begins by determining a rough order of magnitude (ROM) estimate, which is just what the name sounds like. This estimate gives a "ballpark," or order of magnitude, for the project.
- **Discount Rate:** In practical application, the discount rate can be a useful tool for investors to determine the potential value of certain businesses and investments who have an expected cash flow in the future.
- **Metric:** Quantifiable level of an indicator that an organization uses to measure progress.
- **Benchmarking:** Benchmarking is a process of measuring the performance of a company's products, services, or processes against those of another business considered to be the best in the industry, aka "best in class." The point of benchmarking is to identify internal opportunities for improvement.
- **Feasibility:** A feasibility study is an analysis that takes all a project's relevant factors into account—including economic, technical, legal, and scheduling considerations—to ascertain the likelihood of completing the project successfully
- **Revenue Streams:** Revenue Streams are the various sources from which a business earns money from the sale of goods or provision of services. The types of revenue that a business records on its accounts depend on the types of activities carried out by the business.
- **Customer Segment:** Groups of customers based on common characteristics
- **Customer Segmentation:** Process of dividing customers into groups based on common characteristics
- **Value proposition:** A value proposition refers to the value a company promises to deliver to customers should they choose to buy their product.
- **Vendor:** A vendor, also known as a supplier, is a person or a business entity that sells something. Large retail store chains such as Target, for example, generally have a list of vendors from which they purchase goods at wholesale prices that they then sell at retail prices to their customers.

7.52 Exercises and Drills

Q1. Complete the following crossword:

Across

1. Studies conducted to compare Organizational practices with best-in-class practices.

3. Benchmarking and Market Analysis is used to improve Organizational **3**.

5. Brainstorming is generally conducted by a **5.**

6. After the BA makes the Focus Group Plan, **6** is assigned to conduct the Focus Group.

Down

2. Researching information from customers to understand the need of a product or service.

4. The main difference between focus group and brainstorming is that the former is **4.**

Q2. Match the following

1. A limitation of bench marking apart from being time consuming	a. Request for Information (RFI)
2. A limitation of market analysis apart from being time consuming	b. Lack of innovative solution
3. A method used to gauge the capability of the competition when doing benchmark study	c. Expensive

Q3. Match the following

1. Brainstorming is used to	a. Improve upon existing ideas
2. Focus groups is used to	b. Observer
3. A participant in who is optional in focus group, but has no role in brainstorming discussions	c. Generate Ideas

Q4. Match the elements of Brainstorming with their respective activities.

1. Preparation	a. Share Ideas Record Ideas Build on each other's ideas Elicit as many ideas as possible
2. Session	b. Discuss and Evaluate Create List Rate Ideas Distribute Final List
3. Wrap-up	c. Define areas of interest Determine Time Limit Identify Participants Establish Evaluation Criteria

Q5. Match the following

1. Eliciting requirements directly from a stakeholder or a group of stakeholders.	a. Conducting a Survey
2. Eliciting information from a group of stakeholders and/or SMEs by evaluating their opinions and experiences.	b. Emailing a Questionnaire
3. Eliciting information from a group of stakeholders and/or SMEs by throwing in the same set of questions to the group.	c. Conducting One-on-One or Group Interviews

Q6. Solve the following crossword

Across

1. Eliciting requirements directly from a stakeholder or a group of stakeholders with a predefined set of questions

3. Eliciting information from Surveys or Questionnaire with predefined responses are called _ - ended.
Eg: Yes/No

Down

2. Eliciting requirements directly from a stakeholder or a group of stakeholders without predefined set of questions, but from the responses of the interviewee/s

4. Eliciting information from Surveys or Questionnaire without predefined responses are called **4** -ended.
Eg : What problem do you see in this?

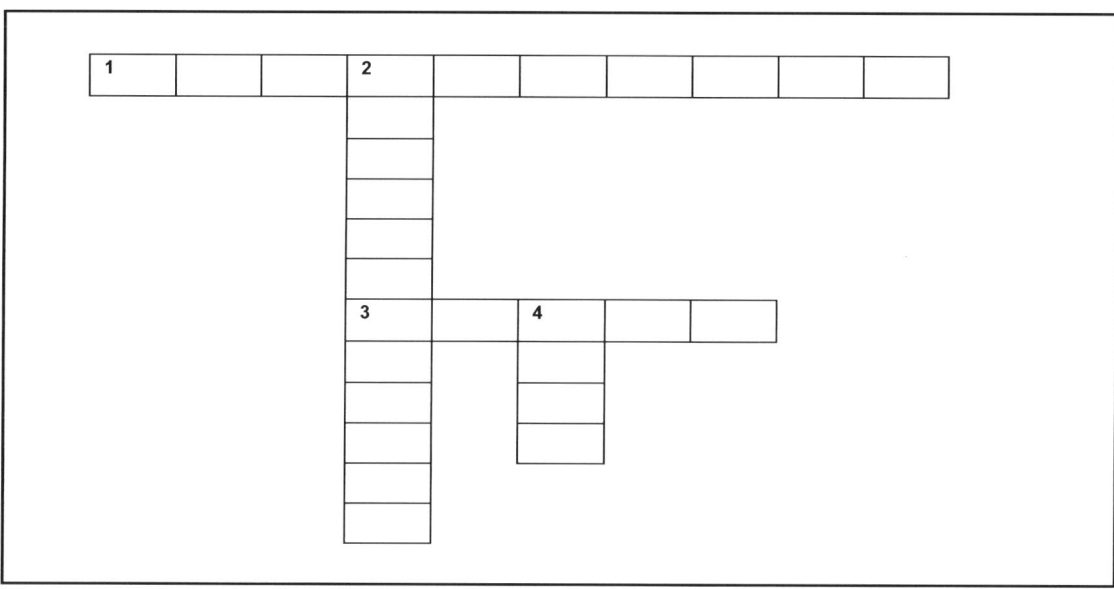

Q7. Match the following

1. Catalogue of the stakeholders affected by a change, business need, or proposed solution, and a description of their attributes and characteristics related to their involvement in the initiative.	a. Personas
2. A group or individual with a relationship to the change, the need, or the solution.	b. Stakeholder Matrix
3. The role a business analyst takes when representing the needs of a stakeholder or stakeholder group.	c. Stakeholder List
4. A fictional character that exemplifies the way a typical user interacts with a product.	d. Stakeholder
5. Diagrams that depict the relationship of stakeholders to the solution or to one-another	e. Stakeholder Proxy
6. Diagrams that shows how involved the stakeholders are with the solution	f. Stakeholder Map
7. Mapping the influence of stakeholder against their level of interest.	g. Onion Diagram

Q8. Match the following

1. Visual Chart with elements describing a firm's offering, infrastructure, finances and customers.	a. Value Proposition
2. Elements of a firm's offering	b. Business Model Canvas
3. Elements of a firm's infrastructure	c. Cost Structure, Revenue Streams
4. Elements of a firm's finances	d. Customer Segment, Channels, Customer Relationships
5. Elements of a firm's customers	e. Key activities, Key Resources, Key Partnerships

Q9. Match the following

1. Business Rules	a. Directive for controlling, influencing or regulating the actions of an enterprise and the people in it.
2. Business Policy	b. Analyzing large amounts of data to derive a pattern generally put as mathematical model or equation.
3. Business Policy is derivable from Business Rules	c. True
4. Business Rule is derivable from Business Policy	d. False
5. Data Mining	e. Testable directive for guiding behavior, shaping judgements or making decisions.

Q10. Solve the following crossword

Across

1. _ is generally categorized as predictive, diagnostic or descriptive.
3. Deriving decision making from answers received, when a user asks a question during data mining investigations are called **3** investigations.
4. Deriving decision making from patterns discovery during data mining investigations are called **4** investigations

Down

1. The final step in data mining after data preparation, analysis and modelling is **1**.
2. _is generally categorized as Behavioral or definitional.

Q11. Match the following (State Modelling)

1. Formal representation of status of an entity.	a. Recursive Transition
2. Change of entity from one state to another	b. Conditional Transition
3. Diagram representing lifecycle of one entity	c. Automatic Transition
4. Type of state transition, wherein the state change is triggered by an event or condition.	d. State Table
5. Type of state transition, wherein the state change is triggered by completion of required activities in the previous state or after specified time.	e. State Transition
6. Type of state transition, wherein the state change is triggered by completion of required activities in the previous state, and then coming back to the same state.	f. State
7. A two-dimensional matrix showing states and the transitions between them.	g. State Diagram

Q12. Match the following

1. Connection between two components or solutions.	a. Interface Analysis
2. Elicitation technique that helps to identify interfaces to determine the requirements.	b. Methods for process improvement
3. Assessing process for efficiency and efficacy	c. Process Analysis Methodologies
4. Six sigma, Lean are examples of	d. Process Analysis
5. Value stream mapping, statistical analysis and control, process simulation, benchmarking, and process frameworks.	e. Interface

Q13. Solve the following crossword

Across

1. A method derived from Six Sigma Methodology of process analysis, abbreviated.
3. Identifying Root Cause of an occurring problem for corrective action in Root Cause Analysis.

Down

2. A method of Lean Methodology of process analysis, abbreviated.
4. Identifying potential problem areas for preventive action in Root Cause Analysis.
5. Diagram used to identify and organize the possible causes of a problem, also called Ishikawa or Cause and Effect Diagram

Q14. Match the following

1. Organizing business vocabulary that contains the knowledge of domain is called	a. Elements of concept modelling
2. Concept modelling starts with _, typically containing noun concepts.	b. Concept Modelling
3. Noun concepts, Verb Concepts and Standard Connections together constitute	c. Glossary
4. Basic concepts are called as Givens or	d. Standard Connections
5. Standard wordings that provide structural connections between noun concepts is called	e. Noun Concepts
6. Categorizations, Classifications, Partitive connections, Roles are types of	f. Verb Concepts

Q15. Match the following

1. Diagrams that depict the transformation of data.	a. Level 1
2. Highest level diagram that generally represents the entire system.	b. Level2, Level 3 etc.
3. This layer of abstraction in DFD (Data Flow Diagrams) depicts process with respect to the system.	c. Context Diagram (Level 0)
4. Breaking down the major processes of Level 1 diagram into further layers of abstraction.	d. Elements of DFD
5. Externals, Data Store, Process and Data Flow constitute	e. Data Flow Diagrams

Q16. Solve the following crossword

Across

1. The notation of DFD, wherein the process is represented by a circle.

3. A variation of data model, used generally by SME's to describe database, such that performance, concurrency and security are taken care of.

Down

2. The notation of DFD, wherein the process is represented by a rectangle with rounded corners.

4. A variation of data model, that is independent of any solution or technology.

5. An abstraction of a solution independent model, which incorporates normalization rules while designing solution.

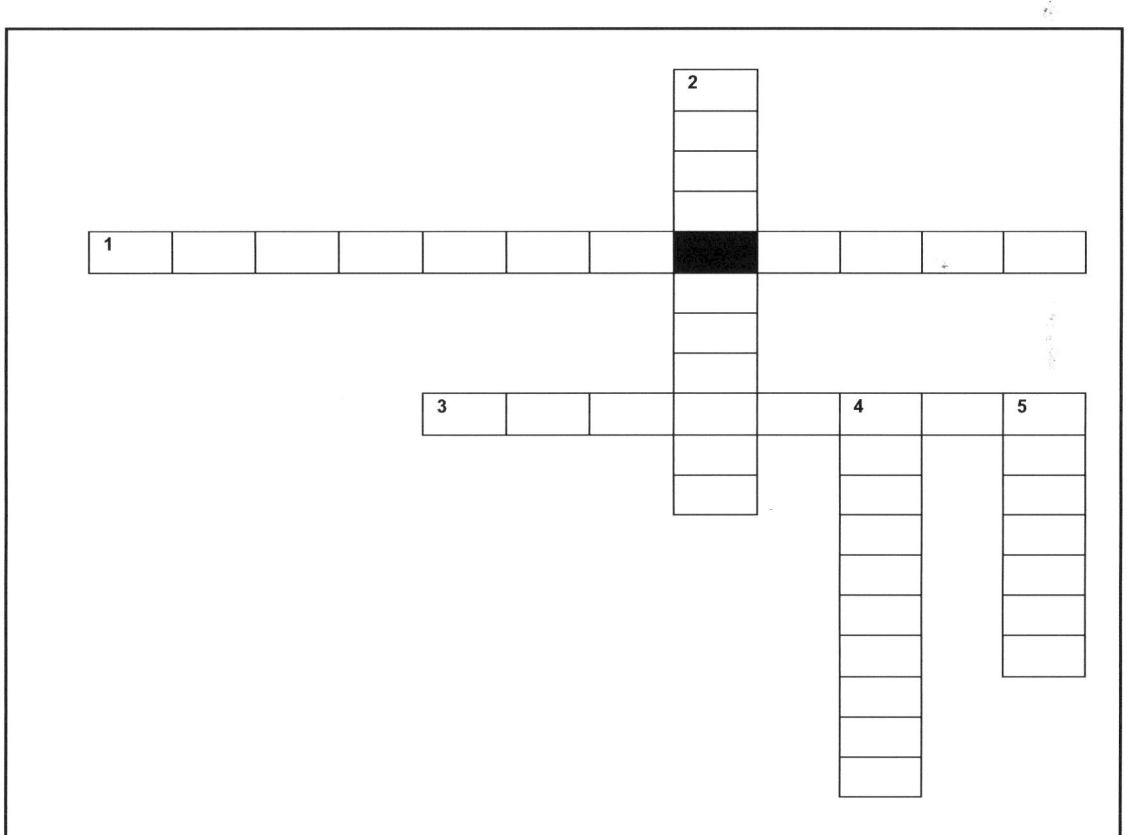

Q17. Match the following

1. Diagram that is used to depict attributes of and relationships among the Entities, classes, data objects of the business need.	a. Cardinality
2. A rectangular box, that contains attributes and has relationships with other such boxes in data modelling	b. Attribute
3. A piece of information which has name, value and description.	c. Multiplicity
4. The minimum and maximum number of occurrences to which an entity may be related.	d. Entity/Class
5. The minimum and maximum number of occurrences to which a class may be related.	e. Data Model

Q18. Match the following

1. Models that show how data and knowledge are combined to make a decision.	a. Sub-Decision
2. A model that is linked to processes, performance measures, and organizations.	b. Complex Decision Model
3. Single decision table/tree.	c. Straightforward Decision Model
4. Models that breakdown decisions into their individual components.	d. Comprehensive Decision Model
5. Business rule required to make a part of decision.	e. Decision Model

Q19. Match the following elements of Decision Modelling

1. Compact, tabular representation of a set of business rules.	a. Decision Tree
2. Representation of a set of business rules in terms of leaf nodes and branches.	b. Decision Table
3. Visual representation of information, knowledge and decision making in complex business decisions.	c. Behavioural Rule
4. Business rule that is a claim of necessity and cannot be violated.	d. Decision Requirements Diagrams
5. Business rule that is a claim of obligation and can be violated.	e. Definitional Rule

Q20. Solve the following crossword on Diagramming techniques of Decomposition

2. Diagrams that represent hierarchical partitioning of work, activities, or deliverables	1. Diagrams that represent hierarchical part-to-whole relationships between decomposition results.
	3. Diagrams that represent decomposition of a higher-level use case.
	4. Diagrams that depict results of a process or function decomposition
	5. Diagrams that show the behavior of an object inside its composite state.
6. Diagrams representing the structure of a complex decision and its potential outcomes	7. Diagrams that show how components are wired together to form larger components and/or software systems.
7. Diagrams that detail on events, conditions, activities, and effects in complex outcome.	•
8. Diagrams that represent information in categories.	

9. Acronym for diagram used to analyze the business logic for inferential and business integrity.

Q21. Match the following

1. Conducting games that help stakeholders to develop better understanding of a problem or stimulate innovative solutions to the problem	a. Product Box
2. A person who helps the participants to understand and enforce the rules of the game	b. Affinity Map
3. Steps in collaborative games.	c. Fishbowl
4. A type of collaborative game, wherein the participants develop a box which can be sold in a shop.	d. Opening, Exploration and Closing
5. A type of collaborative game, wherein the participants write features on sticky notes, and then move them closer to similar sticky notes on the wall.	e. Facilitator/Neutral Facilitator
6. A type of collaborative game, wherein the participants are split into two groups. One group speaks about the topic, and the other group listens and notes their observation.	f. Collaborative Game

Q22. Match the following

1. A file or a set of files which acts as a reference to data elements, their meanings, and allowable values.	a. Created by business analyst, hence is system agnostic
2. A type of dictionary which typically describes information in business terms and focuses on the meaning of terms and their relationship with other terms.	b. Created by Database architects and database administrators and refers to one database or one schema.
3. A type of dictionary which typically describes the physical attributes of a data element.	c. Glossary
4. Logical data dictionary	d. Logical Data dictionary
5. Physical data dictionary	e. Physical Data dictionary
6. List of terms in business domain with their definitions and common synonyms.	f. Data dictionary/ Metadata Repository

Q23. Solve the following crossword on categories of NFRs

Across

1. Degree to which a solution or component performs its designated functions.

9. Protecting solution or component from accidental or malicious access.

12. Degree to which the solution is operable and accessible when required for use.

13. Requirements dealing with local languages, laws, currencies etc.

Down

1. Ease with which a solution or component can be transferred from one environment to another

2. Ability of a solution or component to perform its required functions under stated conditions.

3. Ease with which a solution or component can be modified to correct faults.

4. Degree to which a solution or component operates effectively with other components in its environment.

5. The ability of a solution or component to incorporate new functionality.

6. Degree to which the solution functions meet user needs.

7. Regulatory, financial or legal constraints which can vary based on the context or jurisdiction.

8. Constraints on the solution that are necessary to meet certain standards or industry conventions.

9. Constraints of the Organization being served by the solution that are formally agreed to by both the provider and the user of the solution, acronym.

10. Ease with which a user can learn to use the solution.

11. Degree with which a solution can grow or evolve to handle increased amounts of work.

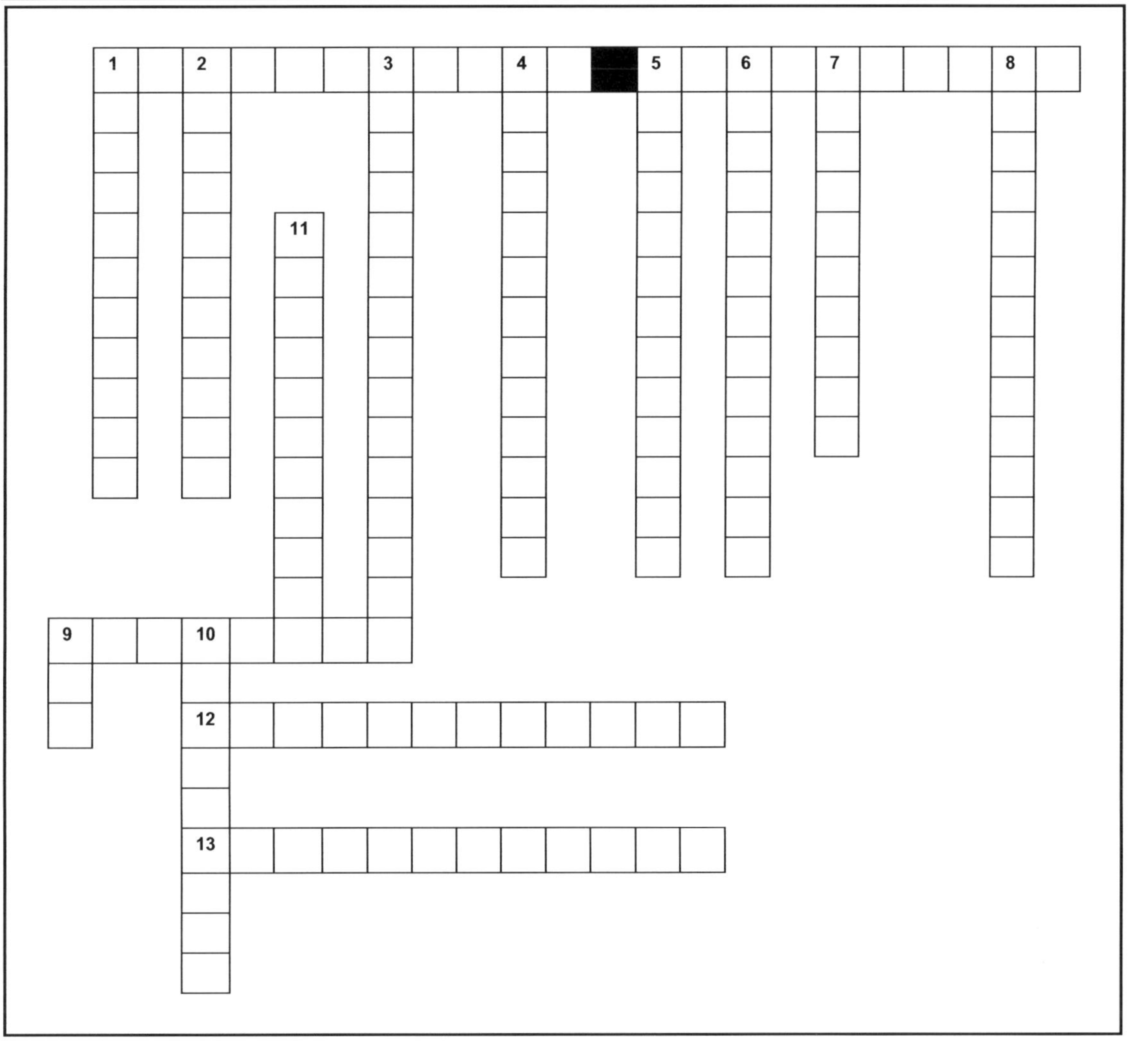

Q24. Match the following

1. Examining a work activity first hand as it is being performed	a. Elements of Observation.
2. An approach of observation, wherein the observer asks any questions as they arise while the activity is being done.	b. Passive/unnoticeable
3. An approach of observation, wherein the observer asks any questions after the activity has done.	c. Active/Noticeable
4. Define objectives, Preparation, Conduct Observation, Confirm and Present Observation results.	d. Observation or Job Shadowing

Q25. Match the following

1. A visual representation of OU, which describes the roles, responsibilities, and reporting structures that exist within the current state organization.	a. Organizational Chart
2. Type of Organizational model, wherein staff is grouped based on shared skills or areas of expertise.	b. Organizational Model
3. Type of Organizational model, wherein the OU is created to serve customer groups, geographical areas, projects or processes.	c. Functionally Oriented
4. Type of Organizational model, wherein the OU is a combination of functional and market oriented.	d. Market- Oriented
5. OU, Roles/People, Line of Reporting are depicted as a part of Modelling	e. Matrix

Answers to Exercises & Drills

Ans 1: Benchmarking, 2-Market Analysis, 3- Operations, 4- Structured, 5-Facilitator, 6-Moderator

Ans 2: 1-b, 2-c, 3-a

Ans 3: 1-c, 2-a, 3-b

Ans 4: 1-c, 2-a, 3-b

Ans 5: 1-c,2-a,3-b

Ans 6: 1-Structured, 2-Unstructured, 3 -Close, 4- Open

Ans 7: 1-c,2-d,3-e,4-a, 5-f,6-g,7-b

Ans 8: 1-b,2-a,3-e,4-c,5-d

Ans 9: 1-e,2-a,3-d,4-c,5-b

Ans 10: 1 Across -Data Mining, 1 Down- Deployment, 2- Business Rules, 3- Supervised,4- Unsupervised

Ans 11: 1-f,2-e,3-g,4-b,5-c,6-a,7-d

Ans 12: 1-e,2-a,3-d,4-c,5-b

Ans 13: 1-SIPOC,2-VSM,3- Reactive,4- Proactive, Fishbone

Ans 14: 1-b,2-c,3-a,4-e,5-f,6-d

Ans 15: 1-e,2-c,3-a,4-b,5-d

Ans 16: 1-Yourdon-Code, 2-Gane-Sarson, 3 -Physical,4-Conceptual,5-Logical

Ans 17: 1-e,2-d,3-b,4-a,5-c

Ans 18: 1-e,2-d,3-c,4-b, 5-a

Ans 19: 1-b,2-a,3-d,4-e, 5-c

Ans 20: 1-Nested,2 -Tree,3- Use Case,4-Flow,5-State Composite, 6-Decision Trees,7 Across-Cause Effect,

7 Down- Component,8- Mind Maps,9 -DMN

Ans 21: 1-f,2-e,3-d,4-a,5-b,6-c

Ans 22: 1-f,2-d,3-e,4-a,5-b,6-c

Ans 23: 1 Across-Performance Efficiency, 1 Down- Portability, 2 -Reliability, 3-Maintainability,

4-Compatibility, 5-Extensibility, 6-Functionality, 7-Compliance, 8- Certification, 9 across-Security,

9 down- SLA, 10- Usability, 11- Scalability, 12- Availability, 13- Localization

Ans 24: 1-d, 2-c, 3-b, 4 -a

Ans 25: 1-b, 2-c, 3-d, 4-e, 5-a

Chapter 9: Perspectives

Perspectives provide the context to the business analysis activities for a project. It means that the tasks and techniques become more specific as per the perspectives. The perspectives included in the BABOK® Guide are:

- Agile,
- Business Intelligence,
- Information Technology,
- Business Architecture, and
- Business Process Management.

BABOK guide describes each perspective with a common structure. The structure comprises of the following elements:

- Change Scope
- Business Analysis scope
- Methodologies, approaches and Techniques
- Underlying competencies
- Impact on Knowledge areas

8.1 Agile Perspective

1	Overview	Describes the business analysis activities in the Agile context
2	Change Scope	➤ A business analyst engages with the business sponsor to define the features in line with the business objectives. This is further broken down into a list of tasks with priority order in consultation with stakeholders ➤ The scope is constantly evolving in Agile projects. The backlog list is reviewed and re-prioritized continually. ➤ Change is expected at any point of time and rapid response to change is desired. Short iterative delivery based on prioritized backlog list allows to incorporate changes in the upcoming iterations with minimal impact. ➤ In case of major change, the entire project may be re-assessed and even may be adjourned, if needed

- **Breadth of change:** Initiatives using agile approaches can be undertaken within a single department or can span across multiple teams, departments, and divisions of an organization.
- Agile mindset is a cultural transformation of an organization as opposed to adopting a new practice or methodology
- **Depth of change:** Agile project or initiative can be part of a larger program in an organization like organizational transformation and change, Business process re-engineering or business process change
- **Value and Solutions delivered:** Agile initiatives deliver the value and the solution just like any other initiative; however, the approach is different than the other projects. Agile approach is iterative and highly collaborative. This approach is about short iterative delivery and rapid customer feedback. The solution evolves over a period.
- **Delivery Approach:** Agile approaches focus on people interactions, transparent communications, and ongoing delivery of valuable change to stakeholders. However, there could be specific characteristics to each Agile approach specific to the initiative. The teams may also adopt a hybrid approach.
- **Major Assumptions:** The major assumptions are:
    - Changes at any point in time in the project is acceptable
    - A business problem can be decomposed into needs to find the suitable solution
    - Agile initiatives have customers and SMEs, fully believing in the agile approach
    - The changes in the team is not welcome
    - The teams could be co-located for more efficient results. However distributed teams with appropriate communication channel can be also work as efficiently
    - The team members play multiple roles within the team if needed.
    - The team works with the mindset of continually improving the delivery through regular inspection
    - Agile teams are empowered and self-organizing

2	Business Analysis scope	➤ **Change Sponsor:** The sponsor of an agile initiative must have a buy-in for the agile philosophy like adaptive planning, uniform duration iterations and his/her own involvement ➤ **Change targets and agents:** A change agent (a stakeholder) is similar as any other initiative. It does not change because of being agile. The stakeholders are: 　○ Agile Team leader 　○ **Customer representative or product owner** 　○ **Team members** ➤ **Business Analyst position:** A business analyst may be working in the agile team (with or without the designation): 　○ a business analyst working on the team, 　○ the customer representative or product owner, or 　○ distributing these activities throughout the team ➤ **Business Analysis outcomes:** Open communication and collaboration is one of the principal outcomes of successful business analysis in an agile project.
3	Approaches and Techniques	○ **Approaches:** Agile itself does not represent any methodology but its an umbrella term. **Some of the** agile approaches include Crystal clear, Disciplined agile delivery, Dynamic Systems Development Method (DSDM), Evolutionary Project Management (Evo) and more… ○ **Techniques:** The commonly used techniques within agile approaches are: Behavior driven development (BDD), Kano Analysis, Lightweight Documentation, MoSCoW prioritization and more…
4	Underlying competencies	➤ In adopting the agile mindset and philosophy, the business analyst develops competencies in: 　○ Communication and collaboration 　○ Patience and tolerance 　○ Flexibility and adaptability 　○ Ability to handle change 　○ Ability to recognize business value 　○ Continuous improvement

| 5 | Impact on knowledge areas | <ul><li>**Business planning and monitoring:** In agile approaches, adaptive planning approach is used rather than predictive planning approach. An initial plan is developed, which is modified to account for change prior to the start of the net iteration.</li><li>**Elicitation and collaboration:** This is a progressive event in agile approaches. The most common pattern is an initial elicitation activity that establishes the high-level vision and scope of the solution, and an initial milestone-based plan for the delivery of the product.</li><li>**Requirement lifecycle management:** Scope of work gets more detailed and specific over a period. As that happens, the prioritization of the requirements is taken into consideration for development.</li><li>**Strategy Analysis:** Agile team members use strategy analysis to help understand and define product vision, and develop and adjust the development roadmap, in addition to conducting ongoing assessments of related risks.</li><li>**Requirements analysis and design definition:** In agile projects, Analysis and design are performed on a just-in-time basis. Analysis is performed before and during the iteration for estimation and construction respectively.</li><li>**Solution evaluation:** Throughout an agile project, the stakeholders and agile team continually assess and evaluate the development solution as it is incrementally built and refined.</li></ul> |

8.2 Business Intelligence Perspective

1	Overview	Business intelligence focuses on the transformation of data into value-added information. The Business Intelligence Perspective highlights the unique characteristics of business analysis when practiced in the context of transforming, integrating, and enhancing data.

2	Change Scope	➤ **Breadth of change:** Business intelligence initiative involves creating a uniform and consistent view of data by establishing *"Single point of truth"* for data coming from diverse sources. To achieve that. a business intelligence initiative may also involve the ***development of infrastructure services in the organization***, such as data governance and metadata management.
		➤ Agile mindset is a cultural transformation of an organization as opposed to adopting a new practice or methodology
		➤ **Depth of change:** Business intelligence initiatives focus on decision making at various levels in the organization (Executive, management and process levels) and the information needed to make the decision. The initiatives also focus on investigating the business implications at all the other levels.
		➤ **Value and Solutions delivered:** The ***value of a business intelligence initiative*** is in its ability to provide timely, accurate, high value, and actionable information to those people and systems who can use it effectively in making business decisions. Increased revenue and reduced costs are the primary indicators of improvements in company performance.
		➤ **Delivery Approach:** The infrastructure services that provide data management, analytics, and presentation capabilities, facilitate a phased or incremental development strategy in respect of:
		    ○ the inclusion, coordination and control of different data sources, and
		    ○ the analysis and development of business information and insights.
		➤ **Major Assumptions: The major assumptions are:**

			o existing business processes and transactional systems can provide source data that is definable and predictable, o the cross-functional data infrastructure that is needed to support a business intelligence solution has not been precluded by the organization on technical, financial, political/cultural, or other grounds, and o the organization recognizes that process re-engineering and change management might be needed in order to effectively realize the value from a business intelligence solution.

2	Business Analysis scope		➤ **Change Sponsor** is typically the highest level role from the organizational unit affected by the change.
			➤ **Change targets and agents:** The targets of a business intelligence initiative are the business decisions made by people or processes at multiple levels in the organization that can be improved by better reporting, monitoring, or predictive modelling of performance-related data.
			
			➤ **Business Analyst position:** A business analyst will participate as:
			   o Liaison between the stakeholders and solution providers
			   o Enterprise data modelling
			   o Decision Modelling
			   o Specialized presentation design (Dashboards)
			   o Ad hoc query design
			
			➤ **Business Analysis outcomes:** The major outcomes of the business analysis activities are:
			   o Business process coverage
			   o Decision Models
			   o Source logical data model and data dictionary
			   o Source data quality assessment
			   o Target logical data model and data dictionary
			   o Transformation rules
			   o Business analytics requirements
			   o Solution Architecture

| 3 | Approaches and Methodologies | <ul><li>**Methodologies:** The business analysts work within or alongside the methodologies applicable to other disciplines or perspectives.</li><li>**Approaches:** there are a few less formal and potentially overlapping approaches that map to business and technical contexts.</li></ul>**Types of Analytics:** There are three types of data analytics that represent incremental solutions<ul><li>Descriptive Analytics</li><li>Predictive Analytics</li><li>Prescriptive Analytics</li></ul>**Supply and Demand Driven**
The objectives and priorities of a business intelligence initiative can be based on the technical goals of improving existing information delivery systems (supply-driven) or on the business goals of providing the appropriate information to improve decision-making processes (demand-driven).
Supply-driven: assumes the view of "for a given cost, what value can we deliver?"
Demand-driven: assumes the view of "for a given value, what cost do we incur?".

Structured and Unstructured Data
Business intelligence initiatives consider two types of data – structured and unstructured. |
| 4 | Underlying competencies | <ul><li>In addition to the communication and analytical competencies, the business intelligence systems outcomes may further be enhanced by:<ul><li>Business data and functional usage</li><li>The analysis of complex data structures and their translation into standardized format</li><li>Business processes affected including KPIs and metrics</li><li>Decision modelling</li><li>Data analysis techniques</li><li>Logical and physical data models</li><li>ETL best practices</li><li>Business intelligence reporting tools</li></ul></li></ul> |

| 5 | Impact on knowledge areas | <ul><li>**Business planning and monitoring**<ul><li>A business intelligence initiative may require establishing an underlying data infrastructure to support the solution, or it might be an enhancement based on the infrastructure of an existing solution.</li><li>Scope Modelling is frequently used to differentiate between these alternatives and plan the relevant business analysis activities accordingly.</li></ul></li><li>**Elicitation and collaboration:** The cross-functional nature of business intelligence typically requires business analysts to employ specialized documentation tools and techniques to elicit types of requirements from stakeholders, both business and technical.
For example,<ul><li>Interviews with individual stakeholders identify the information and analytic insight required to support their decision making.</li><li>Data models and data dictionaries provide definitions of the structure and business rules of existing systems data.</li></ul></li><li>**Requirement lifecycle management:** This initiative typically requires implementation of infrastructure services. This creates structural dependencies within the solution, affecting the prioritization. It is often possible to achieve efficiencies by implementing related requirements at the same time.</li><li>**Strategy Analysis:** Business analysts can use high-level conceptual data models to map the current state of corporate information, to identify information silos, and to assess their related problems and opportunities. Business analysts can define change strategy options based on business needs and priorities, impact on the business operations, and the usability of existing infrastructure components.</li><li>**Requirements analysis and design definition:** Models of an existing system's data and reverse-engineered modelling is used in this initiative. Reverse-engineered modelling is used Where existing systems documentation is non-existent or out of date. A future state data model demonstrates how</li></ul> |

			the source information is generically structured in the proposed solution.
			➤ **Solution evaluation**
			   o A common enterprise limitation with the introduction of a business intelligence solution is the under-utilization of the information resource and analytic functionality that the solution provides.
			   o Business analysts explore and evaluate opportunities for additional value that are enabled by a business intelligence solution.

		➤	

8.3 Information Technology Perspective

1	Overview	The information technology perspective focusses on changes in information technology systems. The initiative could be small bug fixes or enhancements or as large as re-engineering the entire IT infrastructure.

2	Change Scope	Changes in IT systems could be initiated for multiple reasons like for creating a new organizational capability, achieve an organizational objective by enhancing an existing capability, facilitate an operational improvement, maintain an existing information technology system, repair a broken information technology system.
		➤ **Breadth of change:** Information technology initiative may focus on a single system or on multiple systems. These systems may be:
		   o A commercial off-the-shelf (COTS) system developed by an organization and implemented here
		   o A customized software
		➤ Business analysts working in IT carefully consider the context for any information technology change.
		➤ **Depth of change:** Due to the level of detail required in these types of initiatives, business analysts elicit and analyse how the organization works as a whole and how the IT system will support those operations.
		➤ **Value and Solutions delivered:** The *value of a business intelligence initiative* is in its ability to provide timely, accurate, high value, and actionable information to those people and systems who can use it effectively in making

			business decisions. Increased revenue and reduced costs are the primary indicators of improvements in company performance.
			➢ **Delivery Approach:** The infrastructure services that provide data management, analytics, and presentation capabilities, facilitate a phased or incremental development strategy in respect of:
			   o the inclusion, coordination and control of different data sources, and
			   o the analysis and development of business information and insights.
			
			➢ **Major Assumptions:** The major assumptions are:
			   o
			   o existing business processes and transactional systems can provide source data that is definable and predictable,
			   o the cross-functional data infrastructure that is needed to support a business intelligence solution has not been precluded by the organization on technical, financial, political/cultural, or other grounds, and
			   o the organization recognizes that process re-engineering and change management might be needed in order to effectively realize the value from a business intelligence solution.

2	Business Analysis scope		➢ **Change Sponsor** is typically the highest level role from the organizational unit affected by the change.
			➢ **Change targets and agents:** The targets of a business intelligence initiative are the business decisions made by people or processes at multiple levels in the organization that can be improved by better reporting, monitoring, or predictive modelling of performance-related data.
			
			➢ **Business Analyst position:** A business analyst will participate as:
			   o Liaison between the stakeholders and solution providers
			   o Enterprise data modelling
			   o Decision Modelling
			   o Specialized presentation design (Dashboards)

			○ Ad hoc query design ➢ **Business Analysis outcomes:** The major outcomes of the business analysis activities are: ○ Business process coverage ○ Decision Models ○ Source logical data model and data dictionary ○ Source data quality assessment ○ Target logical data model and data dictionary ○ Transformation rules ○ Business analytics requirements ○ Solution Architecture
3	Approaches and Methodologies		➢ **Methodologies:** The business analysts work within or alongside the methodologies applicable to other disciplines or perspectives. ➢ **Approaches:** there are a few less formal and potentially overlapping approaches that map to business and technical contexts. **Types of Analytics:** There are three types of data analytics that represent incremental solutions ○ Descriptive Analytics ○ Predictive Analytics ○ Prescriptive Analytics **Supply and Demand Driven** The objectives and priorities of a business intelligence initiative can be based on the technical goals of improving existing information delivery systems (supply-driven) or on the business goals of providing the appropriate information to improve decision-making processes (demand-driven). *Supply-driven: assumes the view of "for a given cost, what value can we deliver?"* *Demand-driven: assumes the view of "for a given value, what cost do we incur?".* **Structured and Unstructured Data** Business intelligence initiatives consider two types of data – structured and unstructured.

4	Underlying competencies	<ul><li>In addition to the communication and analytical competencies, the business intelligence systems outcomes may further be enhanced by:<ul><li>Business data and functional usage</li><li>The analysis of complex data structures and their translation into standardized format</li><li>Business processes affected including KPIs and metrics</li><li>Decision modelling</li><li>Data analysis techniques</li><li>Logical and physical data models</li><li>ETL best practices</li><li>Business intelligence reporting tools</li></ul></li></ul>
5	Impact on knowledge areas	<ul><li>**Business planning and monitoring**<ul><li>A business intelligence initiative may require establishing an underlying data infrastructure to support the solution, or it might be an enhancement based on the infrastructure of an existing solution.</li><li>Scope Modelling is frequently used to differentiate between these alternatives and plan the relevant business analysis activities accordingly.</li></ul></li><li>**Elicitation and collaboration:** The cross-functional nature of business intelligence typically requires business analysts to employ specialized documentation tools and techniques to elicit types of requirements from stakeholders, both business and technical. For example,<ul><li>Interviews with individual stakeholders identify the information and analytic insight required to support their decision making.</li><li>Data models and data dictionaries provide definitions of the structure and business rules of existing systems data.</li></ul></li><li>**Requirement lifecycle management:** This initiative typically requires implementation of infrastructure services. This creates structural dependencies within the solution, affecting the prioritization. It is often possible to achieve efficiencies by implementing related requirements at the</li></ul>

			same time.
			➤ **Strategy Analysis:** Business analysts can use high-level conceptual data models to map the current state of corporate information, to identify information silos, and to assess their related problems and opportunities. Business analysts can define change strategy options based on business needs and priorities, impact on the business operations, and the usability of existing infrastructure components.
			➤ **Requirements analysis and design definition:** Models of an existing system's data and reverse-engineered modelling is used in this initiative. Reverse-engineered modelling is used Where existing systems documentation is non-existent or out of date. A future state data model demonstrates how the source information is generically structured in the proposed solution.

			➤ **Solution evaluation**
			  ○ A common enterprise limitation with the introduction of a business intelligence solution is the under-utilization of the information resource and analytic functionality that the solution provides.
			  ○ Business analysts explore and evaluate opportunities for additional value that are enabled by a business intelligence solution.

		➤	

8.4 Business Architecture Perspective

1	Overview	Business architecture models the enterprise in order to show how strategic concerns of key stakeholders are met and to support ongoing business transformation efforts. Business analysis activities focus on the business architecture context. Business architecture follows certain fundamental architecture principles: • Scope • Separation of concerns • Scenario driven

		• Knowledge based

2	Change Scope	➤ **Breadth of change:** In the business architecture context, the business analysis activities may be carried out:
		    o Across the enterprise as a whole
		    o Across a unit (Line of business)
		    o Across a single functional unit (department)
		
		➤ **Depth of change:** The business architecture initiatives don't work at *operational or process level*, rather focused on the executive level of the enterprise. It provides the context to other initiatives.
		
		➤ **Value and Solutions delivered:**
		    o The insights provided by business architecture help keep systems and operations functioning in a coherent and useful manner and add clarity to business decisions.
		    o The architecture itself can be used as a tool to help identify needed changes.
		    o The function of business architecture is to facilitate coordinated and synchronized action across the organization by aligning action with the organization's vision, goals, and strategy.
		    o Business architecture provides a blueprint that management can use to plan and execute strategies from both information technology (IT) and non-IT perspectives.
		
		➤ **Delivery Approach:** Business architecture creates a planning framework that provides clarity and insight into the organization and assists decision makers in identifying required changes.
		    o The business architecture may define current state, future state or transition state(s) for each change
		    o Business architects play an important role in communicating and innovating for the strategy of the organization.
		
		➤ **Major Assumptions:** The major assumptions are:
		    o a view of the entire organization that is under analysis,

			o full support from the senior leadership o participation of business owners and subject matter experts (SMEs), o an organizational strategy to be in place, and o a business imperative to be addressed.

2	Business Analysis scope		➤ **Change Sponsor:** the sponsor of a business architecture initiative is a senior executive or business owner within the organization. However, the sponsor may also be a line of-business owner.
			➤ **Change targets and agents**
			    o Change targets are: Business capabilities, business value streams, initiative plans, investment decisions, and portfolio decisions.
			    o The change agents could be - management at all levels of the organization, product or service owners, operational units, solution architects, project managers, and business analysts working in other contexts
			
			➤ **Business Analyst position:** A business analyst will participate to:
			    o understand the entire enterprise context and provide balanced in
			    o provide a holistic, understandable view of all the specialties within the organization.
			➤ **Business Analysis outcomes:** The general outcomes of the business analysis activities are:
			    o the alignment of the organization to its strategy
			    o the planning of change in the execution of strategy, and
			    o ensuring that as change is implemented, it continues to align to the strategy.

3	Reference models and Techniques		➤ **Reference Models:** Reference models are predefined architectural templates that provide one or more viewpoints for an industry or function that is commonly found across multiple sectors (for example, IT or finance). o Examples are - *Business Motivation Model (BMM)*, *Control Objectives for IT (COBIT)*, *Information Technology Infrastructure Library (ITIL®)*

		➤ **Techniques:** Commonly used techniques in the business architecture context are – *Business Motivation Model* (BMM), *Business Process Architecture*, *Customer Journey Map*

4	Underlying competencies	➤ Some of the competencies needed by business analysts working in business architecture context are:
		   ○ a high tolerance for ambiguity and uncertainty,
		   ○ the ability to put things into a broader context,
		   ○ the ability to transform requirements and context into a concept or design of a solution.
		   ○ the ability to suppress unnecessary detail to provide higher level views,
		   ○ the ability to think in long time frames over multiple years,
		   ○ the ability to deliver tactical outcomes (short term), which simultaneously provide immediate value and contribute to achieving the business strategy (long term), & More…
		➤ These are in addition to the underlying competencies described in BABOK v3

5	Impact on knowledge areas	➤ **Business planning and monitoring**
		   ○ The business analyst needs to understand the following from organizational perspective:
		      ▪ strategy and direction,
		      ▪ operating model and value proposition,
		      ▪ current business and operational capabilities,
		      ▪ stakeholders and their points of engagement,
		      ▪ plans for growth, governance, and planning processes,
		      ▪ culture and environment, and
		      ▪ capacity for change.
		➤ **Elicitation and collaboration:** The business analysts have to deal with lots of ambiguity and uncertainty in these initiatives. So, they consider changes in organizational direction based on external and internal forces and changes in marketplace environment.
		   ○ In these initiatives, Business analysts elicit inputs such as strategy, value, existing architectures, and performance metrics.

- Ensuring stakeholders understand and support the organization's strategy is an essential function within the discipline of business architecture. Business architects may impose scope and constraints on a project or initiative as a means to ensure the activity aligns to the organization's strategy, which may be viewed unfavourably.

➤ **Requirement lifecycle management:** It is essential that business analysts working in the discipline of business architecture have executive support and agreement of the work to be undertaken. An architecture review board comprised of senior executives with decision-making powers can review and assess changes to the business architecture.
  - Business analysts also identify possible emerging changes in both internal and external situations (including market conditions), and decide on how to incorporate these changes into the business architecture of the organization.

➤ **Strategy Analysis:** Business architecture can play a significant role in strategy analysis. It provides architectural views into the current state of the organization and helps to define both the future state and the transition states required to achieve the future state. Business architects develop roadmaps based on the organization's change strategy.

➤ **Requirements analysis and design definition**
  - Business analysts working in the discipline of business architecture employ expertise, judgment, and experience when deciding what is (and what is not) important to model. Models are intended to provide context and information that result in better requirements analysis and design.
  - Design is done in conjunction with understanding needs and requirements. Business architecture provides the context to analyze the strategic alignment of proposed changes and the effects those changes have upon each other.

➤ **Solution evaluation:** Business analysts working in the discipline of business architecture analyze the results of measurements and factor these results into subsequent planning.

		➢

8.5 Business Process Management Perspective

1	Overview	The Business Process Management Perspective highlights the unique characteristics of business analysis when practiced in the context of *developing or improving business processes*.

2	Change Scope	Business analysts focus on bringing changes to process (or processes) to achieve the business objectives, expected through the change.
		BPM lifecycle comprises of the following activities:
		• Designing
		• Modelling
		• Execution and Monitoring
		• Optimising
		➢ **Breadth of change:** Individual initiatives may improve specific processes and sub-processes. These processes could result after decomposing more complex and large processes.
		➢ **Depth of change:** BPM Frameworks are used to analyse and to have in-depth understanding of the organizational processes.
		
		➢ **Value and Solutions delivered:**
		   o The goal of BPM is to improve operational performance (effectiveness, efficiency, adaptability, and quality) and to reduce costs and risks.
		   o Business analysts frequently consider transparency into processes and operations as a common core value of BPM initiatives.
		   o Some of the drivers for BPM initiatives are:
		      ▪ Cost reduction initiatives
		      ▪ Increase in quality
		      ▪ Increase in productivity
		      ▪ Compliance initiatives etc.
		➢ **Delivery Approach:** The delivery approach for BPM initiatives across organizations ranges from a set of tactical

			methods focused on improving individual processes to a management discipline that touches all the processes in an organization. Organizations conduct periodic assessments of key processes and engage in ongoing continuous improvement to achieve and sustain process excellence. There are several BPM implementations mechanisms are:<ul><li>Business process re-engineering</li><li>Evolutionary forms of change</li><li>Substantial discovery</li><li>Process benchmarking</li><li>Specialized BPMS applications</li></ul> ➢ **Major Assumptions:** The major assumptions are:<ul><li>Processes are generally supported by information technology systems, but the development of those systems is not covered by most BPM methods.</li><li>BPM initiatives have senior management support.</li><li>BPM systems require a tight integration with organizational strategy, but most methods do not tackle the development of strategy which is outside the scope of this perspective.</li><li>BPM initiatives are cross-functional and end-to-end in the organization.</li></ul>
2	Business Analysis scope		➢ **Change Sponsor:** The sponsor of business process initiatives are executives (top level executives) with focus on strategic objectives. These strategic objectives then help in connecting to the business processes. ➢ **Change targets:** The possible change targets for business process management initiatives are:<ul><li>Customer</li><li>Regulator</li><li>Process Owner</li><li>Process Participants</li><li>Project Manager</li><li>Implementation Team</li></ul> ➢ **Business Analyst position:** A business analyst in a BPM initiative may assume the roles of:

		o **Process Architect:** A process architect is responsible for modelling, analysing, optimizing, deploying and monitoring business processes. o **Process Analyst/Designer:** They perform analysis and assessment of as-is processes, evaluate alternate process design options, and make recommendations for change based on various frameworks. o **Process Modeller:** A process modeller captures and understands the "AS-IS" and "TO-BE" processes. (SEE THE DIAGRAM 11.5.1 from BABOK v3) ➤ **Business Analysis outcomes:** The general outcomes of the business analysis activities in this initiative are: o **Business process models:** Business process models start at the highest level as an end-to-end model of the whole process and can become as specific as modelling specific work flow. Business process models serve as both an output and a starting point for the analysis of the process. o **Business Rules:** Business rules guide business processes and are intended to assert business structure or control the behaviour of business. o **Process performance measure:** Process performance measures are parameters that are used to identify process improvement opportunities. o **Business Decisions:** Business decisions are a specific kind of task or activity in a business process that determine which of a set of options will be acted upon by the process. o **Process performance Assessment:** The success of any BPM initiative rests on the intention and capability to continuously measure and monitor the performance of targeted business processes.
3	Frameworks, Methodologies & Techniques	➤ **Frameworks:** Commonly used frameworks for BPM initiatives are: *ACCORD, Enhanced Telecommunications Operations Map (eTOM), Governments Strategic Reference Model (GSRM) etc.* ➤ **Methodologies:** Commonly used methodologies for BPM initiatives are: *Adaptive Case Management (ACM), Business*

		Process Re-engineering (BPR), Continuous Improvement (CI), Lean etc. ➤ **Techniques:** Commonly used techniques are – *Cost Analysis, Critical to Quality, (CTQ), Cycle-time Analysis, Define Measure, Analyze Design, Verify (DMADV) etc.*

4	Underlying competencies	➤ Some of the competencies needed by business analysts working in BPM context are:
		   o Strong negotiation skills,
		   o Ability to resolve conflicts,
		   o Ability to work as a neutral & independent facilitator;
		   o the ability to communicate well
		➤ These are in addition to the underlying competencies described in BABOK v3

5	Impact on knowledge areas	➤ **Business planning and monitoring**
		   o Progressive elaboration is common in the planning of BPM initiatives since the amount of information available for full planning may be limited in the initial stages.
		   o A common cause for the failure of BPM initiatives is the failure to plan for ongoing monitoring of the effect of changes to the process.
		
		➤ **Elicitation and collaboration:**
		   o During elicitation, the business analyst focuses on cause and effect of both changing existing processes and keeping the processes as they are through the elicitation and collaboration effort.
		   o As an existing process is changed, the effect of any process improvements identified on the organization, people, and technology are considered.
		   o Process changes can have significant impacts across the organization, so managing stakeholders and their expectations is particularly critical.
		➤ **Requirement lifecycle management:** The impact of BPM activities on requirements life cycle management is significant as it can drive out business requirements resulting in new design, coding, implementation, and post-implementation changes.

- **Strategy Analysis:** In a BPM context, strategy analysis involves understanding the role the process plays in an enterprise value chain.
  It involves describing the current state, future state & the change strategy.
- **Requirements analysis and design definition**
    - Requirements analysis and design definition will focus on defining the to-be process model.
    - The requirements architecture is likely to include the process model, associated business rules and decisions, information requirements, and the organizational structure.
- **Solution evaluation:** As processes are evaluated for different scenarios, they can be refined and the results are monitored.
  Solution evaluation tasks provide insight into the understanding of the impact of process improvements and the value delivered by business process change.

8.6 Glossary

- **Blueprint** - Business architectural descriptions and views are called blueprints. Business architecture provides a blueprint to management for planning and executing strategies
- **Business Process Management drivers** - Business needs are referred to as BPM drivers. Examples include increase in quality, cost reduction, increase in productivity, compliance initiatives, faster processes, etc.
- **Process transformation** - The main aim of BPM initiatives is process transformation, which is nothing but identifying, prioritizing and optimizing the business processes to deliver value to stakeholders
- **BPM Lifecycle** - Includes the following activities: Designing, Modelling, Execution & Monitoring, and Optimizing
- **Business Intelligence** - BI(Business Intelligence) is a set of processes, architectures, and technologies that convert raw data into meaningful information that drives profitable business actions.
- **Business Architecture** - Business Architecture reveals how an organization is structured and can clearly demonstrate how elements such as capabilities, processes, organization and information fit together.

8.7 Exercises and Drills

Q1. Match the following agile approaches with their description:

1. Extreme programming	A. Focuses on client valued functionality perspective to develop working software. A feature list is identified following a scoping exercise and the work is undertaken by feature teams
2. Kanban	B. Method for managing the creation of products with an emphasis on continual delivery while not overburdening the development team. Does not require fixed iterations. A key feature is to limit the work in progress items
3. Scrum	C. A decision process framework which incorporates ideas from a variety of other agile approaches. It's a people-first hybrid agile approach to software delivery
4. Feature driven development	D. An agile software development framework that aims to produce higher quality software and higher quality of life for the development team. Takes beneficial software engineering techniques to the extreme
5. Disciplined agile delivery	E. Work is performed in a series of fixed length iterations called sprint. At the end of each sprint the shippable product is demonstrated to customer for their feedback

Q2. Categorize the following under right headings:

Adaptive planning, Plan drive, Predictive planning, change driven, continuous improvement, Linear development, Product evolves with customer feedback, scope redefinition, Just enough documentation

Agile	Waterfall

Q3. Complete the following crossword:

Across

1. Type of data analytics that uses historical data to understand and analyse past business performance

Down

2. Type of analytics that applies statistical analysis methods to historical data to identify patterns and then make predictions about future events

3. Type of data analytics that is used to identify decisions to be made and to initiate appropriate actions to improve business performance

Q4. Match the following BPM methodologies with their description:

1. Business Process Re-engineering	A. A method used when processes are not fixed and have a lot of human interaction
2. Lean	B. Rethinking and redesigning of business processes to generate improvements in critical performance measures. In other words, it is about recreating core business processes with the aim of improving cost, quality, service, and speed
3. Six sigma	C. A continuous improvement methodology that focuses on elimination of waste in a process
4. Adaptive case management	D. A continuous improvement methodology that focuses on elimination of variations in the outcome of a process

Q5. Match the following BPM techniques with their description:

1. Value stream analysis	A. A focused, rapid effort to improve delivery of value in a specific activity/ sub-process
2. Kaizen event	B. Also known as House of Quality. It is a matrix relating customer desires and product characteristics to organizational capabilities
3. Voice of customer (VoC)	C. A set of questions that is used for information gathering
4. 5 Ws and a H	D. Used to assess the value added by each functional area of a business as part of an end-to-end process
5. Theory of Constraints Thinking Process	E. A set of logical cause-and-effect models used to diagnose conflicts, identify root causes of those problems and define future states of a system

Answers to Exercises & Drills

Answer 1: 1- D, 2- B, 3 – E, 4 – A, 5 – C

Answer 2:

Agile	Waterfall
Adaptive planning	Predictive planning
Change driven	Linear development
Continuous improvement	Plan driven
Product evolves with customer feedback Scope redefinition Just enough documentation	

Answer 3:

    1- Prescriptive

    2- Descriptive

    3- Predictive

Answer 4: 1 – B, 2 – C, 3 – D, 4 – A

Answer 5: 1 – D, 2 – A, 3 – B, 4 – C, 5 – E

Printed in Great Britain
by Amazon